Shareholders' Liability

Shareholders' Liability

The Comparative Law Yearbook of International Business

Special Issue, 2017

PUBLISHED UNDER THE AUSPICES
OF THE CENTER FOR INTERNATIONAL LEGAL STUDIES

General Editor

Dennis Campbell

Director, Center for International Legal Studies
Salzburg, Austria

A C.I.P. Catalogue record for this book is available from the Library of Congress

ISBN 978-90-411-8411-5

e-Book: ISBN 978-90-411-8412-2

web-PDF: ISBN 978-90-411-8416-0

Published by Kluwer Law International
P.O. Box 316, 2400 AH Alphen aan den Rijn, The Netherlands
sales@kluwerlaw.com
www.wklawbusiness.com

Sold and distributed in North, Central and South America
by Wolters Kluwer Legal & Regulatory U.S.
7201 McKinney Circle, Frederick, MD 21704, USA
customer.service@wolterskluwer.com

Sold and distributed in all other countries
by Turpin Distribution Services Ltd.
Stratton Business Park, Pegasus Drive
Biggleswade, Bedfordshire SG18 8TQ
United Kingdom
kluwerlaw@turpin-distribution.com

Printed on acid-free paper

© 2017 Kluwer Law International

All rights reserved. No part of this publication may be reproduced, stored in a retrieval system, or transmitted in any form or by any means, electronic, mechanical, photocopying, recording or otherwise, without prior written permission of the publishers.

Permission to use this content must be obtained from the copyright owner. Please apply to: Permissions Department, Wolters Kluwer Legal, 76 Ninth Avenue, Seventh Floor, New York, NY 10011-5201, United States of America. Email: permissions@kluwerlaw.com. Website: www.wklawbusiness.com

Printed in the United Kingdom

MIX
FSC® C103993

The Center for International Legal Studies

The Center for International Legal Studies is a non-profit research and publications institute established and operating under Austrian law, with its international headquarters in Salzburg, Austria.

The Center has operated since 1976 in Salzburg, and it has close cooperation with the faculties of law of the University of Salzburg, Boston University and Suffolk University in the United States, Lazarski University in Poland, Eötvös Loránd University in Hungary, and numerous other universities and educational institutions in Europe.

The Comparative Law Yearbook of International Business prints matter it deems worthy of publication. Views expressed in material appearing herein are those of the authors and do not necessarily reflect the policies or opinions of the Comparative Law Yearbook of International Business, its editors, or the Center for International Legal Studies.

Manuscripts proposed for publication may be sent by email to:

The Editor
Comparative Law Yearbook of International Business
office@cils.org

Table of Contents

Liability of Shareholders in Modern Company Law   1
   Tamás Fézer

Argentina
   Maximiliano A. Batista and Tomás A. Dellepiane   19

Belgium
   Vincent Jodard, Mattias Verbeeck, and Sarah Arens   45

Brazil
   Adriana Camargo Rodrigues   67

Croatia
   Dionis Jurić, Antonija Zubović, and Edita Čulinović Herc   93

Germany
   Annette Kespohl   127

Indonesia
   Iswahjudi A. Karim, Karen Mills, and Margaret Rose   141

Mexico
   Vanessa Romero   161

Portugal
   Luis Soares de Sousa and Diogo Horta Osório   189

United States
   Michael J. Katz   211

Index   245

Editor's Note

Shareholder liability was once discussed only in terms of liability for the debts of the corporation in which the shareholders hold interest. That is now a shifting scene, influenced in the main by the emergence of shareholder activism and derivative litigation, with its attendant increase of risk for officers and directors, and "fee shifting" provisions in corporate bylaws, allowing corporations to seek legal fees from unsuccessful shareholder plaintiffs.

In this edition of the *Comparative Law Yearbook for International Business*, practitioners from 10 jurisdictions examine recent developments in shareholder liability. The introductory chapter "Liability of Shareholders in Modern Company Law", sets the stage for reports from Argentina, Belgium, Brazil, Croatia, Germany, Indonesia, Mexico, Portugal, and the United States.

Dennis Campbell, General Editor
Center for International Legal Studies
Salzburg, Austria, Europe

Liability of Shareholders in Modern Company Law

Tamás Fézer
University of Debrecen
Debrecen, Hungary

Introduction

Company laws have long been searching for the perfect system of safeguards in order to ensure the credibility and solvency of companies, and to protect the best interests of the creditors.[1] This understandable attempt invoked shifts of paradigms multiple times over the past few decades. As the economic environment and market rules have a huge impact on the evolution of company laws worldwide, the new challenges of the 21st century, especially the aftermath of the most recent financial crisis, raise new questions in the area of company law.

Companies are the creations of national laws, as international business law, and even the supranational law of the European Union (EU), have not been able to establish a framework system for companies.[2] This phenomenon results in very diverse concepts for company laws, even in countries that are geographically close to each other. Not only universal unification or harmonization but regional approximation of laws suffer from firm motivation of the states as they all believe that company laws must reflect national specialties as part of the culturally diverse field of private law.

Another obvious opposition of the states these days is the fact that company law may boost the economy and the willingness of foreign investors to start businesses in the given country. In case of a desired approximation, even on a regional level, the competitiveness of some countries may also be in danger, and investors would not consider company law as a relevant factor when making their decision on where to position the company. The other angle of such diversity is that national

---

1 The author's research for this article was supported by the János Bolyai Research Scholarship of the Hungarian Academy of Sciences.
2 Court of Justice of the European Union, *The Queen* vs. *H. M. Treasury and Commissioners of Inland Revenue, ex parte Daily Mail and General Trust Plc.* Case Number 81/87, Paragraph 20.

laws aim to provide safeguards to the creditors in different ways. These safeguards may be categorized based on what aspect of company law they select as the ground for ensuring warranties.

It can be the core capital, the internal structure and the relationship between the various company bodies, or the liability of the key figures acting on behalf of the company. None of these ideas have proved to be a perfect solution to all possible claims of the creditors, however, weaknesses and strengths may be identified in the various concepts, and the position the state takes on this important question most likely describes the general approach to company law in the given country. We tend to believe that every decision in the area of company law has impact on the decisions of the investors, therefore, it results in changes in the attitude of the investors that impact the economy and the market in that state.

However, if we really want to be honest, the nature and content of company law is just one of the many factors investors consider when making a decision on where and how to run their businesses. Tax laws, procedural rules, access to justice and alternative dispute resolution methods are equally important, and the obvious factor of consumers' buying power, wealth, political stability and other natural attributes of the market all play significant roles in this respect.

For decades, company laws followed a somewhat simple approach to provide safeguards to creditors against the insolvency and fraud of companies. This approach believed that, if a business association type (typically partnerships) involves background liability of the members for the debts of the business association, the core capital has no function in providing safeguards to creditors, therefore, minimum requirements for the core capital were either non-existent or served only one purpose: to get the members engaged in the business activity and make them invest something at the formation stage.

In case the law established for a business association type allowed members/shareholders to limit their liability for the debts of the company, the law commonly imposed a minimum core capital obligation to the founders in exchange for their limited liability. This theory worked — and in some places it still holds — as a form of pre-check at the stage of establishing a company, and allowed company registration courts or authorities to decide whether the company complies with the legal requirements and can get allowed to step onto the market and start conducting business activity.

Soon, however, this core capital centered concept proved to be somewhat inefficient during the operation of companies as the core capital requirements at the formation stage could not ensure that those acting on behalf of the company took all necessary and reasonable steps to prevent the insolvency of the company, as their liability was not an issue since they "purchased" their immunity when they complied with the minimum core capital requirements.

The end of the 20th century and then the financial crisis in 2008 urged legislators and courts to evolve new concepts in order to guarantee the protection of creditors and to ensure the transparent operation of the business associations. Wrongful trading rules, however, were established for the managers and those considered to be the key personnel of companies at the early stage of the shift of concepts. Still, legislators and courts had to face the fact that the decision-making bodies of the companies that consist of the shareholders/partners may play an equally important role in pushing the company to insolvency through bad, malicious or unreasonably risky decisions.

The various models on the relationship between the decision-making body and the management of a company also raised concerns that shareholders/members may also be liable for the debts of the company toward the creditors in certain situations. The liability of shareholders is obviously more eminent in private companies and close corporations than in public ones as shareholders have a more obvious control over the company's operations.

In addition, in the special situation of company groups (e.g., holdings) and dominant, majority shareholders, the liability of shareholders get to another dimension. This study analyzes the theoretical considerations behind the concept of shareholders' liability in general, and describes selected models and cases in Europe and in the United States in order to identify the new trends and cases when the liability of shareholders toward the company or its creditors and third parties may be relevant.

Checks and Balances

Most company structure models accept that one body of the company, the supreme body, cannot be seized from its general function: to serve as a decision-making body. It also results that the various models leave the decision-making power of the supreme body intact and that their primary focus is on how to ensure that the management is properly supervised for the best interest of the company and the shareholders. The supreme body, however, has a right to transfer some of its powers to either the management or the supervisory board.

Most jurisdictions leave only a few fundamental decisions in the hand of the supreme body: to decide on the financial report of the company and to decide on what to do with the profit. This is why, in many public companies, the general meeting of the shareholders is only called once a year and only to discuss these two strategical decisions. The rest of their competences are delegated to the management. In the German structure model, the supervisory board gets decision-making powers over the management of the company in order to promptly sanction any irregular or potentially harmful act of the management.[3] In this case, the shareholders do not have to evaluate the concerns of the supervisory board; they only have to pick the right, trustworthy members to the supervisory board.

The classic structure concept on the clear separation of duties is that decision-making must remain in the hands of the shareholders. It grants the final decision to the supreme body, and the supervisory board only monitors the activity of the management and reports the irregular or potentially harmful acts to the supreme body that will eventually rule on the question.[4]

Finally, the third structure model merges the functions of management and supervision into one special body, the board of directors, that involves executive and non-executive directors as well providing typically majority voting rights to the non-executives in questions of the management.[5] We should see that the shareholders take very different positions depending on which structure model the company follows.

In case of the strong supervisory board and the board of director concepts, the shareholders have limited options to get close to the operation of the company; therefore, their potential to cause damage to third parties or to the company itself is minimal. In case of the clear separation of powers model, the shareholders can and do keep a close eye on the operation of the company, and they may be involved in the process that ultimately pushes the company to the edge of insolvency.

Even in this model, the question of liability may become very complicated. Corporate torts also presume some fault on the side of the tortfeasors, in our case, the shareholders. Fault, however, is a very fragmented category as the method on how to measure someone's negligence or intention strongly depends on the following factors: the level of his knowledge, access to information, state of mind, professionalism, and so on. We cannot state that shareholders are professionals

---

3 Hopt, *The German Law of and Experience with the Supervisory Board*, Law Working Paper, Number 305/2016, at p. 3.
4 Hopt, *The German Law of and Experience with the Supervisory Board*, Law Working Paper Number 305/2016, at p. 2.
5 Hopt, *The German Law of and Experience with the Supervisory Board*, Law Working Paper, Number 305/2016, at p. 3.

in every case and that they understand the way of business in the sector in which the company is acting.

Therefore, general rules are difficult to establish based on the simple fact of whether the shareholder supported the wrong and harmful decision or not. Company laws typically suggest that shareholders are persons that also need protection against the management, and minority shareholders may enjoy extra rights against the decisions of the majority.[6]

This approach suggests that shareholders take different positions when we examine their level of knowledge, their access to information, and their professionalism and competency related to business matters. This is why in a limited-liability company, the starting point is that shareholders will not be held liable for the debts of the company and for the unsatisfied claims of the creditors. Still, it is not difficult to feel the anomaly between the function of the supreme body and its members, the shareholders, and this somewhat lenient interpretation of fault.

The supreme body of the company has authority over the acting organs and persons of the company by electing them, supervising them, authorizing them and showing guidance to them through some strategical decisions (e.g., amending the instrument of constitution, the articles, deciding on raising or reducing capital). It means that these decisions of the supreme body also function as beacons to the management, and the acts of the management can only be judged through these instructions.

If these instructions are proved to be wrong and harmful, managers may have a successful defense against a tort claim, and the creditors can easily be left without satisfaction.[7] The structure of the company may seem to be a question of internal matters of the company and, still, it has a significant impact on whether the liability of shareholders may become an issue or not.

What Interest Does Concept of Limited Liability Protect?

Limited liability became the essential characteristic for most companies, and it successfully resulted that shareholders may invest in multiple firms, creating a diverse stock portfolio, while it also led to the fact that more investors could participate in the market.[8] The doctrine of limited

---

[6] Directive 2007/36/EC of the European Parliament and of the Council of 11 July 2007 on the exercise of certain rights of shareholders in listed companies.
[7] Mendelson, "A Control-Based Approach to Shareholder Liability for Corporate Torts", *Columbia Law Review*, Volume 102, at p. 1231.
[8] Kahan, "Shareholder Liability for Corporate Torts: A Historical Perspective", *Georgetown Law Journal*, Volume 97, at p. 1086.

liability, however, eroded especially because corporate torts (e.g., environmental torts, accounting frauds) claimed for a concept that allowed creditors to pierce that thick corporate veil. It must be said that the concept of limited liability only protects the shareholders' assets and the assets of the company. In addition, the doctrine of limited liability only counts if the tort or wrongdoing was committed by the company. In case the shareholder acts in a tortious capacity, outside the general scope of the limited liability doctrine, he may be held liable personally.

The important question is to identify these cases when the shareholders did not act under scope of this principle, rather, they stepped out of the veil of the company and committed a tortious act. Limited liability should only protect shareholders against the claims of creditors and other third parties (e.g., injured parties of a tort claim) if the claim arose from an activity that can be recognized as the general risk of conducting business activities.

A company becoming insolvent does not necessarily mean that it is a case when the shareholders must bear individual responsibility for the unsatisfied debts. An extra factor based on the circumstances that justify the claim against the shareholders is needed, and this link must be obvious and certain.

Cases in various jurisdictions analyzed situations when the shareholders used their limited liability to maliciously satisfy their personal needs not in relation to the business activity of the company using the company's assets,[9] cases when the shareholders kept the management in tight leash and practically forced their will to them that eventually led to insolvency,[10] and cases when the sole member of the company was found personally liable for the debts as the sole purpose of setting up a company was to create a scheme, a front to his malicious activity.[11]

A shareholder also was found liable for the company's debts and the doctrine on the corporate veil was pierced by the court when the shareholder made an economically destructive withdrawal. Such liability, however, can only arise if the shareholder intentionally inflicted damage on the company by withdrawing assets which would have been necessary to settle the company's debts, and that led to the insolvency of the company.[12] All these cases have one thing in common: shareholders abused their limited liability, and this is why they were found liable.

---

9 *Kinney Shoe Corp.* vs. *Polan*, 939 F.2d 209 (4th Cir. 1991).
10 *Re Hydrodan (Corby) Ltd.* (1994) 2 B.C.L.C. 180.
11 *Flash* vs. *Conn*, 109 U.S. 371.
12 Federal Court of Justice, 23 April 2012 (II Z.R. 252/10).

The concept of limited liability of shareholders traces to the original approach on companies that these entities are separate from their founders, therefore, they have their own assets and their own liability for the decisions private individuals make on their behalf. Case law attached to limited liability, however, changed a lot almost everywhere in the world. The famous case of the United Kingdom, *Salomon vs. A. Salomon & Co. Ltd.*, set grounds for the theory on the company being a separate legal entity back in 1896.[13] The case analyzed whether the shareholder owning the vast majority of the shares in a company can be held liable for the act of the company.

According to the facts, Salomon transferred to his own company his business of making boots and shoes. The company consisted of Salomon and his family. The company bought the business from Salomon, and issues shares and a debenture secured by a floating charge on the assets. The business soon became insolvent, and the creditors argued that Salomon and the company were one and the same. They claimed that his debenture was void as no one can be his own creditor. The court sustained the concept of limited liability and that the company was a legal entity separate from its founder and rejected the claim.

Another case from the common law world, however, took a different position even if the claim related to a contractual obligation. In the *Gilford Motor Company Ltd* vs. *Horne* case, Horne left the Gilford Motor Company in order to start his own business in the form of a limited liability company.[14] When he left, he agreed that he would not solicit any of his former employer's customers. Horne claimed that he took that obligation as a private individual and that his newly formed company is a separate legal entity that is individually liable for its own actions, and he as the shareholder of the company cannot represent the company and its will. The court ruled for Gilford Motor and observed that the company and Horne were one and the same, and that Horne committed a fraudulent activity when he tried to go behind his contractual obligation by forming a company.

It is really difficult to see a pattern here. Both cases were about contractual obligations; still, the court, in the *Salomon* case, enforced the concepts of limited liability and separate legal entity while, in the *Gilford Motor Company* case, the judge went behind the company veil concept and allowed the plaintiff to get protection against the fraudulent activity of the shareholder. If one takes an in-depth analysis of the two

---

13 *Salomon vs. A Salomon & Co Ltd* (1896) U.K.H.L. 1, (1897) A.C. 22.
14 *Gilford Motor Company Ltd.* vs. *Horne* (1933) Ch. 935.

cases, one can see a notable difference in the facts. In *Salomon*, it is difficult to prove the intention of Salomon that forming a limited liability company served a fraudulent purpose. Since Salomon's family got involved in the business and that required Salomon to transfer his successful business to the family-run company, the insolvency does not seem to be an intentional fraud of Salomon.

In the *Gilford* case, however, Horne clearly set up the company to escape from the contractual obligation he took, and therefore the exception under the limited-liability rule seemed adequate. The Gilford argument also was applicable in the *Kelner* vs. *Baxter* case. Baxter and two others agreed on behalf of a company yet to be formed to purchase trade stock for its business.[15]

Later, they formed the company, and accepted and used the trade stock but never paid for the stock. The court ruled that, since the company was not even formed when Baxter and his associates took the obligation, they had to bear responsibility for paying the stock. The company could not be held liable as it could not ratify a pre-incorporation contract with retrospective effect to a date before the company existed. The *Kelner* case proved that courts can easily penetrate through the company's protective veil in cases when the shareholders acted with clear fraudulent intention.

On the other hand, when the shareholder is the one that requires that his assets and the company's assets should be treated as one and the same, the courts are not willing to accept this argument. Another interesting case from the United Kingdom, *Macaura* vs. *Northern Assurance Co. Ltd.*, proves this angle of the dispute.[16] Macaura was a landowner who sold timber from his estate to a company of which he was the sole owner. He insured the timber that was laying on his land under his own name as the insured person as shown by the policies issued by the insurance company. A few weeks later, the timber was destroyed in a fire. Macaura claimed the insurance money based on the insurance policy. The insurance company claimed that the timber belonged to the company and not to Macaura and, as a consequence of it, the destroyed timber was not properly insured, and the insurance company was not obliged to pay the insurance money. The court noted that the timber belonged to the company at the time of the fire and that Macaura was not identical to his private limited-liability company, therefore, he had no insurable interest over the timber.

---

15 *Kelner* vs. *Baxter* (1866) L.R. 2 C.P. 174.
16 *Macaura* vs. *Northern Assurance Co. Ltd.* (1925) A.C. 619.

This brief analysis of some historical cases in the laws of the United Kingdom proves that courts are willing to break the concept on the shareholders' limited liability in cases when a clear fraudulent activity or intent of the shareholders can be proved. The concept of limited liability, however, stands in all other cases when the creditors or claimants simply wish to use the shareholders' assets for satisfaction. One may conclude that the concept of limited liability of the shareholders separates the assets of the company from the assets of the shareholders, and the shareholders are not held liable for the contractual obligations of the company and for its debt under normal circumstances. Simply, until the shareholders play by the rules and respect the purpose of the limited liability principle, they are protected from the company's creditors and, in general, from third-party claims.

Piercing Company's Protective Veil

The concept of limited liability was originally created to protect shareholders from the inevitable risks of business activities and against the claims of those that suffer harms and damage as a consequence of the risky business activities. The doctrine also wanted to encourage investors to invest in businesses risking only the money they invested and not their own assets. If the doctrine is used to hide a malicious activity behind the thick veil of the company, shareholders cannot enjoy the protection of limited liability.

The concept of limited liability might have overcome the norm of unlimited liability by the 19th century, when legislators in Europe and the United States started to come up with excuses under the rule in order to make shareholders accountable for certain unlawful behaviors. One of the still existing exceptions is the problem when the shareholder transfers property to the company at an over evaluation of its true market value. Some authors refer to this problem as the problem of "watered stocks".[17] Watered stocks are harmful to the other shareholders and the company, and to the creditors too. The company makes a bad deal in such situations, while the creditors get a false picture of the solvency and the capital of the company.

This concept leads us back to the importance of the minimum core capital. Since the core capital was the price for the limited liability and an instrument to build trust toward the creditors, any fraudulent activity

---

17 Cook, "Watered Stock" — Commissions — "Blue Sky Laws" — Stock Without Par Value", *Michigan Law Review*, Volume 19, at p. 584.

related to the core capital may undermine its importance and function. In Europe, most national laws insisted on having an accountant or other professional to evaluate the monetary value of any in-kind performance a shareholder wanted to contribute to the core capital. This rule, however, disappeared from many legal systems as it, especially in case of private companies, formed an unnecessary burden and expense at the time of company formation. It led to a more lenient policy that allowed shareholders to evaluate the monetary value of the in-kind performance with mutual consent, and created liability on their side in case an over evaluation was carried out in bad faith.[18]

Other historically relevant situations also can be identified in which the legislator felt the need for an exception to the limited liability principle. In the United States, for example, some states (e.g., New York and Illinois), as well as Canada, adopted the concept of shareholder joint and several liability for unpaid worker wages.[19] This view emerged from the fear that limited liability will serve as a tool for the rich to consolidate their wealth, to the detriment of the workers.[20] In addition, certain exceptions were created to hold the shareholders liable for the full extent of their investment for company debts.

It is an important principle when national laws levied the rules on when to pay the full amount of the shareholder's contribution. In private companies, it is especially common that the legislator gives grounds for delayed payments, and the shareholder only has to provide a certain amount of his contributions at the time of formation; the rest may be paid at a later period of operation.[21] This rule got significant importance

---

18 In Hungary, Annex 1 II/1(bb) of the Company Registration Act 2006 allows shareholders to evaluate the value of the in-kind performance without having an auditor to perform this action.
19 Tucker, "Shareholder and Director Liability for Unpaid Workers' Wages in Canada: From Condition of Granting Limited Liability to Exceptional Remedy", *Law & History Review*, Volume 26, at p. 66.
20 Tucker, "Shareholder and Director Liability for Unpaid Workers' Wages in Canada: From Condition of Granting Limited Liability to Exceptional Remedy", *Law & History Review*, Volume 26, at p. 68.
21 In Hungary, Article 3:162(1) of the Civil Code 2013: "Where according to the memorandum of association a member is required to provide less than half of their respective cash contribution before the application for registration is submitted, or if the memorandum of association provides for a time limit of over one year from the time of registration of the company for making available the part of the cash contribution that was not paid before the application for registration is submitted, the company may not be allowed to pay any dividend insofar as the unpaid profit calculated relative to the members core deposits according to the provisions on the payment of dividends reaches the initial capital together with the cash contributions which the members have already paid up."

in the years of the most recent financial crisis. In order to support businesses and to make the company formation process easier, mostly legislators in the European continent levied the rules on shareholder contribution.

If, however, the company's debts cannot be satisfied from the company's assets, creditors may turn against the shareholders who still have not performed their full contributions as undertaken in the instrument of constitution of the company, and force them to pay the rest. It is an interesting observation how this rule made some plaintiffs try their cases in situations of corporate torts against the creditors. Courts, however, systematically deny that such rules could give grounds to individual liability of the shareholders for torts committed by the company.[22] It is clear that this rule was created only to help contractual creditors and not claims arisen from a tort.

It appears to be the norm that shareholders may only be individually or jointly and severally liable toward third parties if these third parties are contractual creditors, and their claim arises from the fact that the company's assets were insufficient to satisfy their claims. To summarize, all fraudulent activities of the shareholders should somehow be connected to the intent to empty the company's assets.

Controlling Shareholders

In both public and private companies, shareholders act through majority decisions. A majority decision typically requires the consent of more than one shareholder, therefore, liability cannot be imposed on one of them simply by stating that they governed the company into insolvency. In a company, the owners are the shareholders, while the control over the daily operation is the duty of the management.

Company managers or directors bear liability for the actions they take to represent the company toward the company itself. In most jurisdictions, they are rarely liable directly towards the creditors of the company or third parties who suffer harm or damage as a result of some tortious activity.

Usually, in tort cases, the directors are liable directly or jointly and severally with the company toward the third parties if they acted with intent.[23] In contractual obligations, the legislator lists those cases when

---

22 In Germany, BGH VersR 1972, 274 M,D,R, 1972, at p. 316.
23 Hungarian Civil Code 2013, Article 6:540(3).

the directors owe a direct liability toward the company's creditors.[24] In the latter cases, the so-called wrongful trading principles may serve as grounds for the director's liability toward the creditors of the company in case the company's assets are not enough to satisfy their claims. Shareholders, on the other hand, do not have individual and direct liability toward the creditors even in these cases as they only marked some strategical points for the daily operation through their decisions in the supreme body.

This concept immediately changes when a shareholder gets the majority of the shares, or he *de facto* or *de jure* exercises control over the operation of the directors. Controlling shareholders dominate the company through their majority voting rights or through their control rights over the management/directors, and it leads to two special forms in the shareholders' liability.

In the first scenario, the controlling shareholder has majority votes, therefore, the decisions of the supreme body are heavily influenced by him, and they are dependent on his approval. As most national laws require simple majority in the supreme body for most decisions, a majority shareholder may easily decide over many important questions on his own. This dominant position makes him a sole shaper of the company's strategies, and he may also be the one who can appoint or fire directors at will without the obligation to obtain consent from other shareholders.

In the second scenario, the controlling shareholder has either *de facto* or *de jure* dominance over the managers of the company, so the directors act for the order of the controlling shareholder. In such cases, the controlling shareholder's liability may be similar to the director's liability as the nature of their actions is comparable to the activities of

---

24 In Hungary, Article 33/A(1) of the Bankruptcy Act 1991: "Any creditor or the liquidator — in the debtors name — may bring action during the liquidation proceedings for the court to establish that the former executives of the economic operator failed to properly represent the interests of creditors in the span of three years prior to the opening of liquidation proceedings in the wake of any situation carrying potential danger of insolvency, in consequence of which the economic operators assets have diminished, or that they prevented to provide full satisfaction for the creditors' claims, or failed to carry out the cleaning up of environmental damages. Any person with powers to influence the decision-making mechanisms of the economic operator shall also be considered an executive of the economic operator. If damage is caused by several persons together their liability shall be joint and several. A situation is considered to carry potential danger of insolvency as of the day when the executives of the economic operator were or should have been able to foresee that the economic operator will not be able to satisfy its liabilities when due."

the managers. Directors of the company must be loyal to the company, and it imposes the fiduciary duty of managers to serve the best interest of the company. Typically, the company's interests come first, and not the shareholders'.

In practice, except for the specific cases of insolvency, the company's interests may be very similar to the shareholders' interests. The shareholders, as a group, form the company, so the director's fiduciary duty can be interpreted as a duty toward the shareholders. National laws list various duties under the general scope of the fiduciary duty of the director, like the duty to fully disclose the conflict of interest and to obtain the shareholders' approval in case there is a transaction between the company and the director. It also means that the breach of this duty may result in a void transaction, and the breaching director will be liable for the profit he/she made under the transaction and for any loss the company might have suffered from the transaction.

Some legal systems also entitle the company to recover damages from the third party as well.[25] Another angle of the directors' fiduciary duty is that they bear individual liability for the consequences of their decisions toward the company. It requires directors to act using reasonable skill and care that presumes some professionalism at their end. While shareholders may be treated as lay investors, directors cannot use the defense of being a bystander as their duty toward the company involves a professional standard of care. Legal systems provide various solutions to the problem on how to treat the liability of the controlling shareholder.

English company law steps up with the concept of the shadow director. The shadow director is "a person in accordance with whose directions or instructions the directors of the company are accustomed to act".[26] This definition suggests that the act of the shadow director must amount to directions and instructions and must be intentionally influential on the activities of the *de jure* directors.

While the definition of the shadow director is not that exact in Germany and Estonia, these civil law legal systems admit that in such cases the controlling shareholder's liability must be similar to the *de jure* director's.[27] While a shadow director is not necessarily a controlling shareholder, in practice, he most likely holds a controlling block in the company. Once a controlling shareholder meets the requirements

---

25 Company Act 2006, Section 260(3).
26 Company Act 2006, Section 251(1).
27 German Stock Corporation Act 1965, Article 117(2); Estonian Commercial Code 1995, Article 167(1).

of a shadow director, English, German and Estonian company laws burden him with the same liability as for the *de jure* directors.

The real conflict in this situation is that the supreme body of the company has a right to decide on actions against both the *de jure* directors and the shadow director. As it seems obvious that a controlling shareholder would never vote against himself, and the supreme body may fail to take actions, English law created the category of derivative action when an individual shareholder can sue in the name of the company. Civil law legal systems (e.g., Germany and Estonia), however, take procedural boundaries more seriously, therefore, derivate actions are not available solutions there.

Therefore, most civil law legal systems order that a controlling shareholder cannot vote in such cases, and the majority shall be counted among the other shareholders.[28] The controlling shareholder is not a bystander in these cases, therefore, his biased vote will not count. While this special form of shareholders' liability puts an increased level of vigilance on the controlling shareholder, one must emphasize that even in these cases, the general conditions of liability also must be met.

It is important to stress, as in the fault-based liability regimes, that the malicious, fraudulent intent of the shadow director must be proved in order to impose liability on him. It may, however, be an interesting scenario if the national law imposes strict, no-fault-based liability on the directors for the damage they cause to the company. Hungarian law is a great example of this setting.

The new Hungarian Civil Code says very little about the liability of directors as it refers to the rules of liability for damages for loss caused by non-performance of an obligation.[29] These latter rules impose strict liability on the breaching party, therefore, fault is irrelevant when deciding over the liability. As the new Code is quite young, judicial practice has not had a chance to further interpret how these rules on liability for non-performance of a contractual obligation should be applied in cases when a company director breaches his fiduciary duties, however, unless the breaching party successfully proves that unforeseeable circumstances beyond his control served as an impediment and that caused the breach, he is held liable for the damages in a no-fault system.

As a derivative of the rules, we may say that, in Hungary, a controlling shareholder who acts as a shadow director may be liable for any loss the company suffers as a consequence of improper management

---

28 Hungarian Civil Code 2013, Article 3:18.
29 Hungarian Civil Code 2013, Article 3:24.

activities, disregarding his fault. It also implies that the *de jure* directors may be jointly and severally liable together with the shadow director for such damages. We do not believe that the *de jure* directors can easily defend themselves by referring to the fact that their actions were instructed and controlled by the shadow director (controlling shareholder), as their loyalty and fiduciary duty is toward the company and not one of its shareholders.

European Union Approach to Shareholder Liability

In 2007, the European Union's Council and the European Parliament adopted a Directive on the exercise of certain rights of shareholders in listed companies (the "Shareholder Rights Directive").[30] The Directive lists a series of rights granted to shareholders in listed companies, mainly in relation to their voting rights and rights to information. The Directive does not, however, cover the issues of liability of shareholders, while other bits of EU legislation contain small traces of the problem.

The EU Directive on single-member private limited liability companies[31] sets an obligation that the fact that all shares of the company are held by a single person along with the identity of the sole member must either be recorded in the file or entered in the company register in the Member States.[32] This provision ensures that creditors will get proper information about the company being controlled by a single shareholder, therefore, it is much easier to enforce the rules enacted for the cases of shareholder liability against the only member of the company, even if these cases of liability are listed in the national laws of the Member States.

None of the so-called company law directives contain clear liability rules against the shareholders; we may only find such situations established in the national laws. The company law related norms of the EU have not moved to the direction when shareholders must act with due diligence and must prevent the company from getting insolvent. EU law does not impose clear fiduciary duties on the shareholders; it still

---

30 Directive 2007/36/EC of the European Parliament and of the Council of 11 July 2007 on the exercise of certain rights of shareholders in listed companies.
31 Directive 2009/102/EC of the European Parliament and of the Council of 16 September 2009 on the area of company law on single-member private limited liability companies.
32 Directive 2009/102/EC of the European Parliament and of the Council of 16 September 2009 on the area of company law on single-member private limited liability companies, Article 3.

focuses on the management-shareholder relationship where shareholders must be armed against the autonomous activities of the directors, therefore, rights to provide sufficient information about the company's operation to the shareholders are the main concern.

In April 2014, the European Commission presented a proposal for the revision of the Shareholder Rights Directive to tackle corporate governance shortcomings related to the behavior of companies and their boards, shareholders, intermediaries and proxy advisors. The proposal aims to strengthen shareholder engagement in listed companies in order to make them more focused on the operation of the firm instead of being just simple investors. The proposal states that, too often, shareholders support managers' excessive short-term risk takings and do not monitor closely the companies they invested in. The proposal specifically mentions the lack of shareholder oversight on related-party transactions as a source of the problem.

According to the proposal, related-party transactions cover transactions between a company and its management, directors, controlling entities or shareholders. These transactions typically create the opportunity to obtain value belonging to the company to the detriment of shareholders, especially minority shareholders, therefore, they impose a huge risk on the solvency of the company. The proposed rules would require listed companies with related-party transactions representing more than five per cent of the companies' assets or transactions, which can have a significant impact on profits or turnover, to submit these transactions to the approval of shareholders and may not unconditionally conclude them without their approval.

The proposal, however, aims to provide more rights to the shareholders, and plans to establish new obligations on the directors before engaging the company in certain transactions. Failing to comply with the proposed rules would result in liability for the directors, while the proposal does not cover the scenario when the shareholders abuse these new rights and let a problematic and harmful transaction pass. One can see that EU law does not cover the problem of shareholders' liability, so these questions are settled by national laws in very diverse ways.

Conclusion

The concept of limited liability of the shareholders in a limited liability company started to erode from the moment the principle was established in order to cure the negative effects of the limited-liability doctrine in company law. At first, the legislator only focused on clearly fraudulent and malicious behaviors of the shareholders in order to penetrate the protective corporate veil and allow creditors and third parties to carry out a lawsuit against the shareholders in a limited liability company. These days, company law has to fulfill various interests.

On one hand, it has to ensure that is flexible enough to boost the economy and urge the formation of companies in a country by both nationals and foreign investors. On the other hand, company laws must be secure and certain enough in order to offer safeguards and protection to the creditors, minority shareholders, employees and in some cases the members of society.

Corporate governance became an issue worldwide only in the last couple of decades. This phenomenon does not only focus on the directors/ managers of the companies but on the shareholders in the company, burdening them with a more vigilant overseeing obligation over the management and the activities of the company. The European Union has not moved in the direction of creating clear cases of shareholder's liability and to the direction of burdening shareholders with controlling obligations. Therefore, there is no general standard for the shareholders on what grounds they may be found liable for the company's debts or in case of corporate torts.

Certain situations may find the shareholders in a position when they have to face an increased level of duty of care and act as directors burdened with clear fiduciary duties. These situations are typically linked to the problems of controlling shareholders who often act as shadow directors, or shareholders in a dominant position overseeing and controlling a group of companies.

While we do not suggest that shareholders must bear a general liability for the misconduct of the company towards third parties, the new trends in corporate governance certainly claim for an increased and more precise list of the duties of the shareholders. The investor/ shareholder position comes at many advantages in a limited liability company. Still, it should have its obligation side as well in order to establish a responsible behavior of companies toward the members of society and actors of the economy as well.

Argentina

Maximiliano A. Batista and Tomás A. Dellepiane
Pérez Alati, Grondona, Benites, Arntsen & Martínez de Hoz
Buenos Aires, Argentina

Introduction

In General

Limited liability is a fundamental principle of corporate law. The effects of limiting the liability of an investor are very important for the development of the economy and the conduct of business (and the bearing of risk). Many legal systems not only provide limited liability for shareholders of an entity, but also recognize that legal entities have a different legal personality and existence *vis-à-vis* their shareholders.

Under Argentine law, the general rule is that legal entities have a separate and different legal personality and existence from those individuals or corporations that own a stake in them or otherwise control them. In this regard, Article 143 of Argentina's Civil and Commercial Code provides that "the legal person is a wholly separate person from its members. Its members are not liable for the obligations of the legal person, except for the cases expressly provided by this law, or special laws"; and Article 148 establishes that: "Legal persons are: a) companies; associations; foundations . . .".

Corporations in Argentina

The corporation (*sociedad anónima* or SA) is the most widely used form of business organization in Argentina; it is used by small, medium, and large foreign or local investments. The rights and obligations of shareholders in Argentine corporations, as well as their potential liability, are governed, mainly, by the General Companies Law.

Corporations can be incorporated as a sole-owner corporation (*sociedad anónima unipersonal* or SAU), incorporated by only one shareholder, or as a regular stock corporation that must be incorporated by two or more shareholders. Shareholders may be individuals or legal entities and, except for specific cases provided by the law and regulations, there are no nationality or residence requirements to own or hold shares in a corporation. Foreign entities and/or foreign individuals may own up to the total (100 per cent) of the authorized capital stock of the company. If a foreign legal entity wishes to hold shares in an Argentine corporation, it must register with the Public Registry of Commerce under Article 123 of the General Companies Law in order to be able to fully exercise its rights as a shareholder.

Except for specific cases provided by the law and regulations that may request a larger amount (e.g., banks or insurance companies), the minimum capital required for corporations is AR$100,000. Capital stock must be represented by registered non-endorsable shares or shares in book-entry form which shall be paid with the company's shareholders' contributions. According to the General Companies Law, the capital stock shall be totally subscribed at the time of incorporation.

The company's shareholders' contributions must be denominated in Argentine currency. Each share must have the same face value and grant equal rights within the same class (different classes of shares may be created). As a general rule, ordinary shares are entitled to one vote each; however, shareholders may create different classes of shares through the bylaws, with up to five votes per share.

If preferential shares are issued with preference regarding equity, such shares may have no voting rights (except for some specific shareholders' resolutions); however, their holders must always have the right to participate in the shareholders' meetings and speak at them. They will be entitled to vote as ordinary shareholders as long as the payments to them are in arrears, or if the listing of the shares has been suspended or withdrawn for any reason (the latter provision applying only for corporations that make public offering of their shares).

In principle, shares are freely transferable; bylaws may impose transfer restrictions, but they may not prohibit transfers. Any transfer of shares and of any lien on them must be notified in writing to the board of directors of the corporation. Transfers of shares and any lien on them are valid *vis-à-vis* third parties as from the registration thereof in the corporation's stock ledger.

The shareholders' meeting as the governance body of corporations is in charge of discussing and approving every relevant corporate resolution, such as approval of annual financial statements, amendments of by-laws, capital increases, appointment of the members of the board of directors, mergers, and spin-offs. The vote of the majority of the shareholders with shares entitled to vote in a shareholders' meeting is required to pass a corporate resolution. The quorum and majorities vary depending on the agenda (ordinary or extraordinary meetings) and if it is the first or second call to the meeting.

To be validly held, ordinary shareholders' meetings require, at first call, the attendance of shareholders representing a majority of the shares entitled to vote. At the second call, the quorum is met with the attendance of any number of shares entitled to vote. In both cases, resolutions may be adopted by an absolute majority of the present votes that can be issued on the respective decision, unless the by-laws require a higher number. On the other hand, at extraordinary shareholders' meetings a quorum of sixty per cent of shares entitled to vote is required at the first call, and a quorum of thirty per cent of shares entitled to vote at the second call, unless the by-laws require a lower or higher number.

At extraordinary shareholders' meetings, either on first or second call, the resolutions must be taken by an absolute majority (e.g., more than fifty per cent) of the present votes that can be issued on the respective decision, except if the by-laws require a larger number. The required majorities cannot be reduced through the by-laws. For certain special cases (transformation, extension, anticipated dissolution, relocation of the corporate domicile to another country, material change of the corporate purpose, merger, or spin-off) either on first or second call, the resolutions must be adopted by the favorable vote of the majority of the outstanding shares entitled to vote, with no application of plural vote, if any.

The management and administration of a corporation is vested in the board of directors (administration body), which must be composed of a minimum of one director and a maximum number to be determined in the bylaws. Most corporations in Argentina are closely held companies in which it is common to find the shareholders sitting on the board of directors. In certain cases, the General Companies Law requires the corporation to have a board of directors composed of at least three members.

While the members of the board of directors may be foreigners, the majority of the board members must be Argentine residents (Argentine citizenship is not required). Alternate directors also may be appointed in order to replace regular directors in case of death, illness, or absence and must be appointed in case the corporation has not appointed a syndic or surveillance committee. Directors are appointed for the term provided in the by-laws, which may not exceed three fiscal years, and may be re-elected. In principle, the legal representation of the corporation is vested in its chairman; however, the bylaws also may grant the legal representation of the company to one or more directors.

As a general rule, the members of the board of directors are not personally liable for the acts performed on behalf of the corporation in the ordinary course of business. Such acts are exclusively considered to be performed by the corporation as a separate legal entity. The liabilities of directors arise from the breach of certain standards of conduct. As a general standard of conduct, Article 59 of the General Companies Law provides that directors ". . . must act with loyalty and with the diligence of a good businessman". The standard provided by the General Companies Law is imprecise and ambiguous, and there have been several attempts to define and determine the extent of such standard by legal scholars and case law.

The members of the board of directors are elected by the shareholders, who may or may not approve the performance of each member of the board in the annual shareholders' meeting. Furthermore, shareholders are entitled to revoke at any time the appointment of any member of the board through a shareholders' meeting.

According to Article 276 of the General Companies Law, any shareholder may, on behalf of the corporation, commence civil liability actions against a member of the board of directors for failure to perform his duties, for any violation of the law or the by-laws, or for any damage suffered by the corporation caused through negligence, abuse of powers, or serious fault, provided that such an action has not been commenced by the corporation within three months after a decision to that extent was made by the shareholders. If the corporation initiates such action, the decision to file it entails the removal of the directors in question. Shareholders also have individual courses of action against directors.

The Capital Markets Law states in its Article 76 that, for companies with publicly traded shares, the liability action provided in Article 276 of the General Companies Law may be exercised by the shareholders either to claim damages for the benefit of the company, in order to recover the whole damage suffered by it, or to claim the proportional damage suffered indirectly by the claimant. In the latter case, any compensation for damages must be given directly to the claimant. The defendant director sued for the whole damage suffered by the corporation may opt to accept the claim only for the indirect damage suffered by the claimants.

Shareholders of Argentine corporations do not have a personal right to access the corporate books and records, under Article 55 of the General Companies Law. The rationale is that they are entitled to elect the syndics of the corporation, who are in charge of controlling the board of directors and are generally elected at the same time as the directors. To be a syndic it is required to be a lawyer of a certified public accountant or a company only having such professionals as members[1] and not to be related to the directors.[2]

---

1 General Companies Law, Article 285.
2 General Companies Law, Article 286.

Article 294 of the General Companies Law states a minimum percentage that the shareholder must hold in order to be authorized to request information of the corporation. Article 294 provides that syndics must provide information related to their function to the requesting shareholder(s), when such shareholder(s) represent(s) at least two per cent of the capital of the company. The only case in which shareholders have the right to access the corporate books and records is in the case of small corporations, in which it is not required to elect syndics.[3]

Shareholders' Liability

In General

According to the General Companies Law, shareholders of a corporation are not liable *vis-à-vis* the entity or third parties for the obligations assumed by the corporation. This principle of limitation of liability is one of the corporation's most salient features.

Once a business is properly incorporated as a corporation, it has a legal existence separate from its owners (i.e., the shareholders or controlling entities), and they are not liable for the obligations of the business beyond the amounts they have contributed, and the company's actions or omissions are not directly attributable to them.

The assets that belong to a corporation do not belong to any of the members; nor are any or all of its members obligated to cover the debts of the corporation provided they have not expressly committed themselves as guarantors of the corporation. Notwithstanding this general rule, liability is not absolutely limited. The above-mentioned principle is subject to certain exceptions. Such exceptions are:

(1) Liability for acts prior to the registration of the corporation with the Public Registry of Commerce;
(2) Liability arising from resolutions adopted in null or invalid shareholder meetings;
(3) Liability of a controlling shareholder for damages caused to the controlled company;
(4) The theory of the "piercing of the corporate veil" that is reflected in Article 54, Paragraph 3 of the General Companies Law;
(5) Abuse of privileged information;

---

[3] General Companies Law, Article 284.

(6) Shareholders with a conflict of interest with the corporation, who do not abstain from voting the decision in conflict in the shareholders' meeting; and
(7) Extension of bankruptcy liquidation proceedings under the Argentine Bankruptcy Law, as amended.

Liability for Acts before Registration of Corporation with Public Registry of Commerce

There are several stages in the formation of a corporation. In principle, the corporation is created with the signing of the articles of incorporation, which state when the rights and obligations of the shareholders start, under Article 36 of the General Companies Law. However, the same provision states that shareholders are liable for all those acts carried out on behalf of the corporation if they were in charge of its representation and administration.[4]

The shareholder who does not pay in time the capital it subscribed must be liable for interest and damages; if it did not have a stated time to do so, the deadline must be the date of registration of the corporation with the Public Registry of Commerce.[5] The shares that have not been fully paid in due time may be publicly auctioned through an auctioneer or, if they were publicly traded, through a stockbroker. The corporation may opt for the cancellation of the shares with loss of the partial payment already made but, to do so, the corporation must summon the shareholder to pay in the remaining amount within a thirty-day period.[6]

The incorporators (*promotores*) are unlimitedly, jointly, and severally liable for the obligations undertaken to incorporate the corporation, including expenses and bank commissions. Once the corporation is registered, it will assume all liabilities legitimately undertaken by the incorporators and refund them any expenses necessary for the incorporation. Underwriters of the shares issued by the corporation may not be liable for these obligations (unless they also are incorporators).[7] Directors, incorporators, and the corporation are unlimitedly, jointly, and severally liable for all the obligations necessary to incorporate it, as long as the corporation is not registered.

Directors, incorporators, and any persons doing acts on behalf of the corporation (other than those necessary to incorporate it) are

---

[4] General Companies Law, Article 36.
[5] General Companies Law, Article 37.
[6] General Companies Law, Article 193.
[7] General Companies Law, Article 182.

unlimitedly, jointly, and severally liable for such acts.[8] The registration of the corporation at the Public Registry of Commerce releases the incorporators and directors from any liability arising from corporate obligations toward third parties necessary for the incorporation. Within three months after the registration, the board of directors may decide that the corporation also assumes the liabilities for the other acts not necessary for its incorporation, but this decision must be ratified by an ordinary shareholders' meeting.

However, this decision does not release the incorporators, directors, or third parties from their liability; it only adds one person, the corporation, to those who are liable for such acts.[9] A similar provision is included for insurance companies in Article 8 of Law Number 20,091, but in this case the unlimited joint and several liability is wider because it includes shareholders, directors, and syndics, until the registration of the corporation at the Public Registry of Commerce.

Resolutions Adopted in Null or Invalid Shareholder Meetings

Article 254 of the General Companies Law provides that:

> "The shareholders who voted in favor of any resolution [subsequently] declared null void, must be unlimitedly and jointly responsible for any consequences resulting therefrom, without prejudice to any other responsibility which directors, syndics and members of the surveillance committee may have. A subsequent shareholder meeting may revoke the challenged decision . . . . Liability for any effects already caused or which are a direct consequence of such decision shall subsist."

Article 251 of the General Companies Law provides that:

> "Any decision of the shareholders' meeting adopted in violation of the law or the by-laws can be contested in order to void it by those shareholders who have not voted in favor of such decision and by the absent shareholders who prove their entitlement to vote as of the time of the contested decision. The shareholders who voted favorably to the contested decision, can still annul it, if their vote is void for a defect in their expression of will."

---

[8] General Companies Law, Article 183.
[9] General Companies Law, Article 184.

As explained above, the vote of the majority of the shareholders with shares entitled to vote in a shareholders' meeting is required to pass a corporate resolution. The flip side of this system is the liability that shareholders may have if they vote in favor of a resolution that is later declared null and void.

Under Article 254 of the General Companies Law, several events must occur for the shareholders that voted in favor of the invalid resolutions to be held liable. First, the relevant claimant (i.e., other shareholders or third parties, as the case may be) would need to file a claim in a court law seeking the declaration that a certain shareholders' meeting resolution is null and void. Second, and upon the issuance of a court ruling voiding a shareholders' meeting resolution, the relevant claimant should file a second court claim, seeking that the relevant shareholder be held liable for the damages caused by the resolution declared null and void.

Only if the aforementioned two judicial proceedings have ended with final rulings voiding the shareholders' meeting resolution and upholding the respective shareholder liability, could the latter be held jointly, severally, and unlimitedly liable for the damages caused by such resolution, together with the other shareholders that have voted accordingly.

Furthermore, the mere fact of a shareholder having voted in favor of a judicially declared null and void resolution would be insufficient for purposes of holding such shareholder liable for the damages, if any, caused by the referred ruling. Most legal scholars agree that, in addition to meeting the requirements mentioned hereinbefore, a shareholder can be held liable only if it is proved that such shareholder has not acted in compliance with the standards of conduct required by the General Companies Law.

Such standards of conduct include, mainly, acting with "loyalty", i.e., shareholders must reasonably acknowledge that their votes are casted in favor of corporate resolutions that are not contrary to the articles of incorporation, bylaws, applicable laws, or contracts then in force and acting with the diligence of a "good businessman", i.e., shareholders are expected to act in accordance with certain technical and moral qualities, together with minimum knowledge and skills in order to understand the company's ongoing business and matters subject to a shareholders' meeting review.

Finally, a shareholder that voted in favor of a shareholders' resolution that was declared null afterwards can only be held liable for damages caused by such resolution, if such damages can be effectively proved in court. As general rule, the burden of proof is on the party asserting the shareholders' liability.

Liability of Controlling Shareholder for Damages Caused to Controlled Company

Article 54, first paragraph, of the General Companies Law provides that a controlling shareholder or whoever exercises control upon the company, even if not a shareholder, is liable for damages caused to a controlled company by willful misconduct or negligence.

Furthermore, a controlling shareholder that uses resources or assets of the company for its own, or a third party's, advantage and benefit is obliged to return to the controlled company the resulting profits, but the losses are for its exclusive account (Article 54, second paragraph).

The definition and scope of control in Argentine law can be found in Article 33 of the General Companies Law and in Article 2 of the Capital Markets Law. In both cases, a controlled company is defined as one corporation in which another corporation, whether directly or through another controlled company, holds a participating interest that allows the controlling company to form the corporate will in the ordinary shareholders' meeting and/or exercises a dominant influence as a consequence of stock or participating interests, or due to another special relationship between the companies.

Piercing Corporate Veil

In General

There is a general consensus that the limited liability and the piercing of the corporate veil is one of the most confusing areas of corporate law. The piercing of the corporate veil, or disregard of the legal entity doctrine, was initially characterized by Argentine legal scholars under the concept of "abuse of the legal personality".

The first recorded case applying this principle referred to government entities. In *Gómez, Gerardo* vs. *Comisión Administradora de Emisoras Comerciales y LS 82 TV Canal 7*,[10] the National Supreme Court rejected a defense of lack of standing to be sued opposed by a government-owned agency controlling several radio and television stations when the plaintiff demanded payment of a claim he had against the Ministry of Public Works because, according to the court's reasoning, both entities ultimately belonged to the same person, the National Government.

---

10 *Gómez, Gerardo* vs. *Comisión Administradora de Emisoras Comerciales y LS 82 TV Canal 7*, 28 February 1969, *Fallos* 273:111.

Some years later, the National Supreme Court, in *Compañía Swift de La Plata S.A.*,[11] applied the same principle in a case of a local company in bankruptcy proceedings by declaring its foreign controlling shareholder was liable for the debts of its bankrupted subsidiary. The principle of disregard of the legal entity (and its attached limited liability) in certain cases was later incorporated into Argentine statutory law pursuant to an amendment to the General Companies Law by Law Number 22,903 in 1983. It has been classified into two different types of disregard: direct and indirect.

Direct disregard is the one in which the piercing of the corporate veil benefits third parties who are creditors of the corporation. Courts used this type of disregard mostly in bankruptcy cases. In fact, *Compañía Swift de La Plata* was a bankruptcy law case. The court decision extended the bankrupt company's liability to its controlling company. Indirect disregard is the one in which the piercing of the corporate veil benefits third parties who are creditors of the company's shareholders. This type of disregard was used mostly in family and inheritance cases, in which the legal entity was used to violate inheritance rights and to hide marital assets in divorce procedures.

The piercing of the corporate veil or disregard of the legal entity theory is stated in the last paragraph of Article 54 of the General Companies Law, as amended by Law Number 22,903, which provides that:

> "The company's actions which conceal the pursuance of extra-corporate (*ultra vires*) goals, constitute a mere vehicle to violate the law, public policy or good faith, or frustrate third party rights, must be attributed directly to the shareholders or to the controlling entity which made them possible, which shall have unlimited joint and several liability for the damages caused."[12]

Article 54 creates a legal remedy by which the recognition of the separate legal existence of a corporation may be denied in a particular situation. The remedy further allows the direct attribution of the abusive or fraudulent actions or omissions to those who committed them using the company as a shell or as a mere instrument, and thus penalizes the shareholders or controlling entities having engaged in said conduct with the "dismantling" of the corporate "instrumentality". The relevant test for disregarding a legal entity is not the existence of common control or of a common management or other corporate relations or business ties,

---

11 *Compañía Swift de La Plata S.A.*, 4 September 1973, *Fallos* 286:257.
12 An almost identical provision was recently incorporated in the Civil and Commercial Code.

but rather the misuse or abuse of the corporate form or instrumentality to achieve reprehensible purposes that are defined in the law.

Based on this particular provision, Argentine courts may pierce the corporate veil of a legal entity and, eventually, hold some or all of its shareholders or controlling entities liable for the damages inflicted in the following situations and/or circumstances:

(1) Company actions that pursue extra-corporate (*ultra vires*) goals;
(2) Company actions or omissions that evidence the use of a separate legal entity as a mere vehicle to violate the law, public policy, or good faith; and
(3) Company actions or omissions that evidence the use of the company as a mere vehicle to frustrate third parties' rights.

Argentine courts are very reluctant to resort to this remedy and tend to pierce corporate veils only in very extreme cases.[13] Under the General Companies Law, a corporation will, in principle, shield its shareholders from being personally liable for the corporation's debts. Legal scholars almost unanimously agree that the piercing of the corporate veil must be applied restrictively, in exceptional situations, and that mere allegations that the company committed fraudulent actions or frustrated third parties' rights is not sufficient to use this remedy.

When the conditions to apply the piercing of the corporate veil are met, as a general rule, the party seeking to do so must bear the burden of proof. However, this rule is not absolute. The party that is in a better position to produce evidence must bear such burden (theory of dynamic burden of the proof) when, for instance, direct proof is impossible or extremely difficult. Almost every time, either the corporation, or its managers, are in a better position to produce evidence due to the fact that they have the agreements with third parties, the financial statements, and corporate books in their possession.

Company Actions Pursuant to Extra-Corporate Goals

The first category of actions made by the company that Article 56 defines is actions pursuing extra-corporate goals. The scope of the term "extra-corporate goals" has derived in multiple discussions since it is

---

[13] National Commercial Court of First Instance, Number 24, Secretary 48, 19 July 2007, *Ropall Indarmet S.A.* vs. *Jean Gallay S.A.*, states that, "[b]eing an exceptional resource, that must be limited to concrete cases, when through the legal entity it has been sought and achieved goals contrary to the law, and it is configure an abuse of the legal capacity of that entity, that can lead to the result of equate the company with the partners".

not defined by the General Companies Law or in any other part of the Argentine legal framework.

When the corporation, through its specific actions, operates as a mere formal instrument for the shareholders' or controlling persons' interests, distinct from those that are natural to the corporation, having the corporation committing acts, incurring omissions, or adopting measures incompatible with its resources and functional autonomy, such actions must be deemed as extra-corporate.

Unlawfulness is not required for any given corporate act to be considered extra-corporate or *ultra vires*. It has been stated that an inquiry of the corporate goals of each particular legal entity should be made. Once these formal goals are identified, all those falling outside must be deemed extra-corporate or *ultra vires*. The disregard of the legal entity is generally considered to apply only in relation to the specific situation or action that might be at stake.

Company Actions That Constitute Mere Vehicle to Violate Law, Public Policy, or Good Faith, or to Frustrate Third-Party Rights

The actions of companies that constitute a mere vehicle to violate the law, public policy, or good faith or to frustrate third parties' rights, whether solely or combined, allow the disregard of the legal entity and constitute an exception to the principle of corporate separateness.

The violation of the law may include actions or omissions whereby the conduct of the corporation produces in itself a violation of the law and situations in which the application of any relevant laws is being circumvented through fraud. The violation of the law must be ascertained in the broad meaning of the term "law". This ground is sometimes confused with the frustration of third parties' rights; however, it is generally understood that, when the situation involves a violation of rights arising under the law (and not based on contract), said breach is to be considered a violation of the law.

The principle of good faith is a fundamental principle of Argentine law, which mandates an honest, loyal, faithful, and diligent reciprocal behavior. A disregard of the corporate entity may take place when upholding corporate separateness would lead to a situation that is offensive to the good faith. Violation of good faith as a ground for disregarding the legal entity means that neither fraud nor violations of the law are required.

The inclusion of the violation of the good faith within Article 54 of the General Companies Law involves the incorporation of an "open regulation" which enables the application of the disregard theory to situations that are unknown. As a general rule, Argentine courts are prudent in applying this remedy and a restrictive analysis is made before disregarding the corporate veil.

The decision issued in the *Ceretti* case[14] is probably the most relevant regarding the violation of good faith in connection with Article 54 of the General Companies Law. In this case, the court first addressed the existence of control. It had no major difficulties in establishing the existence of direct ownership or internal control. The court held that:

> ". . . in the instant case a dominant influence has been verified due to the special ties that exist between the corporations, which appear visibly in the designation of the representatives (attorneys in-fact) of the controlled entity, which, at the same time, are President and Vice-president of [the controlling entity]. This is an external control, which escapes the inter-corporate shareholdings, that are unknown in the case of [the controlled entity]."

The reporting Judge further stated that: "a situation of control having been established . . . it remains to decide whether there has been an abusive use of the corporate instrumentality".[15] The court found that the plaintiff had proved two situations that represented a clear violation of the good faith by means of an undue utilization of the corporate entity:

(1) The confusion between the management of the companies in such a manner that third parties could not clearly distinguish the controlling entity from the controlled one;[16] and
(2) The insufficient capitalization of the controlled entity, which was deemed to be a ghost or shell company, with no assets backing the transactions with its creditors.

Consequently, the court decided to directly attribute the actions of the controlled entity to the controlling entity as well as to assign an unlimited joint and several liability to the latter for the damages caused by the former.

Frustration of Third-Party Rights

In General. It is generally agreed that the last situation contemplated by Article 54 of the General Companies Law, frustration of third parties'

---

14 National Commercial Court of Appeals, 24 August 1987, *Ceretti, César Roberto* vs. *Ditto S.A. et al.*, JA 1990-I-137.
15 The first conclusion that can be drawn from this decision is that the existence of common control or common management was not *per se* sufficient.
16 The President and Vice-President of the controlling entity were, at the same time, representatives (attorneys in-fact) of the controlled company with full powers in its management and direction.

rights, requires fraud. The scope of this concept is extremely wide and is largely associated with the frustration of third parties' rights arising under private agreements.

As noted, the theory of the piercing of the corporate veil, as adopted by the General Companies Law, is a remedy that must be used restrictively and exceptionally. Commercial Courts in Argentina uniformly show that the disregard of the corporate personality must be applied in a prudent manner, with restrictive criteria and only in exceptional cases, and only if the evidence produced on trial supports such decision. Broadness in disregarding a legal entity is not the rule; the rule is of restrictive application. In other words, the disregard of the legal entity must be limited to very specific cases, and must be understood as a remedy of last resort.

Indirect Disregard. In this case, the shareholder's liability toward a third party is assumed. The issue is whether the corporation must be liable for its shareholder's debts. In *Aguinda Salazar, María y otros* vs. *Chevron Corporation s/ medidas precautorias*,[17] litigation in Ecuador resulted in a judgment against the United States company Chevron Corporation, which was extended by the Ecuadoran court to the defendant's subsidiaries in Argentina, even though these companies had not participated in its parent company's activities in Ecuador that resulted in the latter's liability.

The Ecuadoran court based its judgment on the theory of the piercing of the corporate veil. The Argentine National Supreme Court reversed a lower court's decision and ruled that the Ecuadoran judgment was not admissible in Argentina, because it had been rendered in violation of the due process, since the Argentine companies had not been a party to the litigation against Chevron Corporation in Ecuador. It further stated that piercing the corporate veil is an exceptional remedy under Argentine law and it cannot apply without a proper trial with a right of defense, which had not happened in the Ecuadoran case.

Abuse of Privileged Information

The Capital Markets Law includes the abuse of privileged information as a separate source of liability for shareholders.[18] Shareholders may not

---

17 *Aguinda Salazar, María y otros* vs. *Chevron Corporation s/ medidas precautorias*, 4 June 2013, *Fallos* 336:503.
18 Capital Markets Law, Article 117.a.

use any reserved or privileged information to obtain, for themselves or for third parties, advantages of any kind, either from the purchase or sale of negotiable securities or any other transaction related to the public offering regime.

The positive difference in pricing obtained by those who have misused privileged information within six months, regarding any negotiable security to which the issuer is related, must belong to the issuer (disgorgement), that will be able to recover it.[19] The action of recovery shall expire on the third anniversary of the day of the violation of the law.[20] If the issuer does not move to recover this amount within 60 days of being summoned to do so, the claim may be submitted by any shareholder.[21] The action of recovery under the Capital Markets Law may be added to the liability action of Article 276 of the General Companies Law, without need of a shareholders' meeting decision.[22]

Furthermore, the perpetrator may be subject to penalties imposed by the National Securities Commission,[23] which may be a warning; a fine ranging from AR$5,000 to AR$20-million, which could be increased to twenty per cent of the illegal benefit or the inflicted damages, if they were higher; prohibition to be director, administrator, controllers, and external auditors of authorized markets or any other entity under supervision of the National Securities Commission; and suspension of up to two years to publicly offer securities or to participate in public offers, or prohibition to do so.[24] The penalties must be graduated according to the gravity of the violation of the law, the volume of operations, the benefit obtained, or the damage inflicted.[25]

Shareholders with Conflict of Interest with Corporation

Article 248 of the General Companies Law provides that:

> "The shareholder who in a particular transaction, for its own account or for account of third parties, has an interest that is contrary to the interest of the company, shall abstain from voting on any matter relating thereto. In case a shareholder violates this

---

[19] Capital Markets Law, Article 117.a.
[20] Capital Markets Law, Article 118.
[21] Capital Markets Law, Article 117.a.
[22] Capital Markets Law, Article 118.
[23] Capital Markets Law, Article 117.a.
[24] Capital Markets Law, Article 132.
[25] Capital Markets Law, Article 133.

prohibition, such shareholder will be held liable for damages effectively caused by such action, if the decision would not have been approved without its vote."

It is generally agreed that the interest of the company is the legitimate aspiration of the entity to fulfil its corporate purpose, i.e., the reason why the entity was incorporated. Any shareholder who has a conflicting interest with the interest of the company in a specific transaction must abstain from voting thereon. Although the vote is a fundamental political right of the shareholders, in case of conflict of interest, the social interest (corporate interest) prevails over the individual interest of the shareholder. If a shareholder violates the prohibition, the shareholder will be held liable for damages effectively caused by such action, if the decision would not have been approved without its vote.

Competent Jurisdiction

The competent courts for any lawsuit arising from these provisions on shareholder liabilities and, in general, all matters regarding corporate law are the local commercial courts. If there is a federal issue, the competent courts are the federal courts and, in the jurisdictions where there is a specialized civil and commercial federal court, this court.

There is an exception to this rule in Article 46 of the Capital Markets Law, which provides that all stock exchanges must have a permanent arbitral tribunal, to which the entities whose shares are bonds traded in it must be subject. The competent jurisdiction of the arbitral tribunal is very wide; it covers all actions derived from the General Companies Law, specifically including lawsuits challenging the validity of corporate resolutions and liability lawsuits against its shareholders. In all cases, the shareholders and investors shall have the right to opt for the competent judicial courts and, in case the applicable law orders the aggregation of several claims being heard by a judicial court and an arbitral tribunal, the cases must be consolidated before the judicial court.

Labor Law

The extension of a company's liabilities to its shareholders also is enshrined in the Labor Contract Law. Article 31 of the Labor Contract Law provides that:

> ". . . if one or more businesses, even with a separate legal personality each, are under the direction, control or administration

of others, or are in such way interrelated so that they constitute a permanent economic group, they must be jointly and severally liable for purposes of their obligations towards their employees and the social security administration, inasmuch as there have been fraudulent maneuvers or reckless behavior."

The interpretation of this statute by the labor courts has been far from uniform. The main difference lies on the weight given to the requirements of "fraudulent maneuvers or reckless behavior". Over the last twenty years, Argentine labor courts have issued rulings pursuant to which the corporate veil of certain companies was pierced and consequently liability was extended to their members of the board and shareholders for debts owed to the companies' employees.[26]

The main issue brought to the courts' attention was payments to the employees that were not duly registered (or not registered at all). Some courts decided that the practice of not registering part of the salary paid to the employee is forbidden by Article 140 of the Labor Contract Law and Article 10 of Law Number 24,013 and, therefore, is a typical labor fraud, which has as its main purpose the evasion of social security contributions.[27]

Other courts decided that the possibility of extending the corporation's liability to its shareholders under Article 54 of the General Companies Law was a corporate law remedy and, therefore, it did not apply to relations under labor law, especially because penalties for fraud to the social security system specifically existed in Law Number 24,013.[28] Although the National Supreme Court is, in principle, not competent for hearing cases based in non-federal law, such as labor law and corporate law, it is nonetheless authorized to do so when the judgment of the lower court is deemed arbitrary.

Eventually, the issue was taken by the National Supreme Court in a case regarding the extension of liability to a corporate director, *Carballo, Atiliano* vs. *Kanmar S.A.*[29] The National Supreme Court adopted the arguments used by the Attorney General in his prior opinion

---

26 National Labor Court of Appeals, Panel III, 19 February 1998, *Duquelsy, Silvia* vs. *Fuar S.A. y otros*.
27 National Labor Court of Appeals, Panel X, 31 August 1998, *Gauna María S.* vs. *Nerone Jorge Dante y ot. s/ despido*; ídem, Sala X, 31 July 2000, *Palomeque, Aldo R.* vs. *Benemeth S.A. y otros*, La Ley 2001-B, 539.
28 National Labor Court of Appeals, Panel I, 6 November 2000, *Tegler Moreno, Augusto* vs. *Truper S.A. y otro s/despido*.
29 *Carballo, Atiliano* vs. *Kanmar S.A.*, 31 October 2002, *Fallos* 325:2817.

of 12 September 2001, who briefly alleged that the extension of the company's liability for irregular payments to one of its directors is an exception rather than the rule and can only be supported by strong evidence, and that the difference between the company and its directors is particularly important in the case of corporations, because they are an essential tool for economic development.

A few months later, the National Supreme Court ruled in a similar way in *Palomeque, Aldo* vs. *Benemeth S.A. y otro*.[30] In this case, the co-defendants were shareholders as well as directors and Article 54 of the General Companies Law had been specifically applied by the lower court. Again, following the arguments of the Attorney General's prior opinion, the National Supreme Court stated that:

(1) It had not been proven that the corporation itself was fictitious or fraudulent, constituted with the aim of violating the law;
(2) It had not been proven that there was an employment agreement between the plaintiff and the corporation's shareholders; and
(3) The difference between the company and its shareholders is particularly important in the case of corporations because they are an essential tool for economic development.

Subsequently, lower courts generally followed *Palomeque* and stated that failure to pay social security contributions or register salary payments was not an automatic evidence of the corporation being fictitious or fraudulent with the purpose of violating the law and, therefore, the extension of the liability to its shareholders could not be based only on that evidence.[31] The lower courts further elaborated that if there was no evidence of specific works for the shareholders, rather than for the corporation, Article 2 of the General Companies Law determines that legal entities are different from their partners and that

---

30 *Palomeque, Aldo* vs. *Benemeth S.A. y otro*, 3 April 2003, *Fallos*, 326:1062.
31 National Labor Court of Appeals, Panel I, 27 October 2005, *Rey Castro, José* vs. *San Sebastián S.A. y otros s/ despido*; ídem, Panel IV, 17/11/2004, *Vicente, Sergio* vs. *Satelital Trust S.A. y otros s/ despido*; ídem, Panel V, 29 December 2003, Cardozo, Melchora c/ Lahisi Consultores S.A. s/ despido; ídem, Panel VI, 29 November 2013, *Aguiar, Gerardo David* vs. *J.M.P. S.A. y otros s/ despido*, DT 2014 (JUNIO), 1572; ídem, Panel VIII, 30 May 2003, *Pares, Lorena* vs. *Selecto S.A. y otro s/ despido*; ídem, Panel VIII, 30 November 2004, *Ayala, Carlos Antonio y otros* vs. *Boeing S.A. y otros s/ despido*; ídem, Panel VIII, 23 November 2005, *Núñez, Gustavo* vs. *Lumicolor S.A.*; ídem, Panel VIII, 28 December 2005, *Páez, Mariano Justo* vs. *Leet S.A.*; ídem, Panel VIII, 31 March 2006, *Barbosa, María del Carmen* vs. *Socorro Médico Privado S.A. y otro s/ despido*.

the latter are not liable for the corporation's actions, and that a failure to duly register an employment does not amount to a corporation violating the law.[32]

However, in one case, the lower court refused to follow *Palomeque* and extended the liability to the corporation's shareholders.[33] Since in Argentina there is no *stare decisis* (obligation of the lower courts to follow the Supreme Court's precedents), the lower court was allowed to do so as long as it indicates and explains its differences, even though such decision was likely to be reversed on appeal. In another case, the lower court tried to distinguish *Palomeque* by not applying Article 54 of the General Companies Law; in this case, the lower court ruled that it is sufficient to prove the violation of the labor law, viz., the irregular registration of the employee on purpose.[34]

The National Supreme Court also rendered another landmark decision in a similar case, *Tazzoli, Jorge Alberto* vs. *Fibracentro S.A. y otros s/ despido*.[35] The case was similar to *Carballo* and *Palomeque* regarding its main issue, which was a deficient registration of the employment agreement. The Supreme Court reasoned that Law Number 24,013 contemplated specific penalties for such violations of the law and that the application of the extension of the corporation's liability to its directors and shareholders was not supported by the law.

An intermediate position was taken by a lower court in a case in which the failure to duly register the employee triggered a special compensation to be paid by the employer in case of termination of the employment relation. The court extended the liability to the shareholders only with respect to the special compensation, but not with respect to the normal one.[36] The courts also have analyzed the case of the incorporation of different companies by the same individual shareholders and the transfer of employees from one company to the other and similar maneuvers to avoid the liability of the most solvent companies; it decided

---

32 National Labor Court of Appeals, Room Panel IV, 2 February 2004, *Acosta, Florentino* vs. *Vadra, Carlos y otros s/ despido*.
33 National Labor Court of Appeals, Panel III, 28 November 2003, *Romazan, Iryna* vs. *P.E.M.A.S.A. S.R.L. y otros s/ despido*.
34 National Labor Court of Appeals, Panel VII, 12 June 2003, *Cabral Ruiz, Elizabeth* vs. *Edusoft S.A. y otro s/ despido*; *idem*, 19 December 2007, *Chichizola, Jorge Omar* vs. *Comercial Gaboc S.R.L. y otros s/ despido*.
35 *Tazzoli, Jorge Alberto* vs. *Fibracentro S.A. y otros s/ despido*, 4 July 2003, *Fallos* 326:2156.
36 National Labor Court of Appeals Panel VI, 30 June 2006, *Rey Quintana, Daniel Eduardo* vs. *Mercolab Argentina S.A. y otros s/ despido*.

in this case that the shareholders were liable jointly and severally with the various corporations, because the complex corporate structure was deemed part of the maneuver.[37]

An employee may not extend the corporation's liability to its shareholders in a labor claim without substantial evidence of the shareholder's direct involvement.[38] A similar position appeared in more recent case law, in which the court extended the liability to a shareholder regarding whom the plaintiff had proven was actively involved in the corporation's affairs.[39]

Violations of the employment agreement by themselves do not amount to the incorporation of a corporation with fraudulent aims or the violation of the law; therefore, the extension of the corporations' liability to its shareholders must be rejected.[40] A claimant employee must obtain a final judgment against the corporate employer to be able to collect money from the employer's shareholder, by application of Article 54 of the General Companies Law, because the shareholder could only be liable to the extent of the damages suffered.[41]

Additionally, in the case of companies that have ceased to operate without being formally liquidated and wound up, labor courts have held the shareholders of such companies liable for debts to the employees.[42] The argument used by the court in these cases was that the omission to formally liquidate a company was equivalent to tactically disappearing from a specific place, which should not allow its shareholders to benefit from the type of company chosen nor from the limitation of liability for obligations of the company. This interpretation and utilization of this remedy was only used by the labor courts.

---

[37] National Labor Court of Appeals, Panel II, 16 May 2006, *Cosentino, Francisco* vs. *Eurovial S.A*; idem, Panel III, 11/11/2005, *Belloni, Mariano y otros* vs. *Global Food Argentina S.A.*

[38] National Labor Court of Appeals, Panel II, 15 February 2007, *Mops, Hernán Alejandro* vs. *Collectivemind Argentina S.A.*

[39] National Labor Court of Appeals, Panel II, 20 March 2013, *Dolgay Hundewadt, María Valeria* vs. *Vadelux S.A.*

[40] National Labor Court of Appeals, Panel II, 12 March 2003, *Durban, Fernando* vs. *Andrea Peinados S.A.*

[41] National Labor Court of Appeals, Panel I, 28 February 2006, *Bosc, Ernesto Fernando and others* vs. *Editorial Sarmiento S.A.*

[42] National Labor Court of Appeals, Panel V, 10 June 1988, *Pacheco de Pugliese* vs. *Abreviar Editores.*

Bankruptcy Law

As explained above, the shareholders of a corporation are not liable for the debts of the relevant corporation since corporations are different legal entities from their shareholders and/or controlling entities. However, the Bankruptcy Law in certain special situations allows disregard of the corporate separateness and the extension of the bankruptcy liquidation proceedings (*quiebra*) to related companies, thus holding these related companies liable for the debts of the company undergoing bankruptcy liquidation proceedings.

Although the first cases in which Argentine courts applied the disregard theory dealt with insolvency issues (e.g., *Compañía Swift de La Plata*), the circumstances in which bankruptcy is extended to shareholders or controlling entities are not necessarily limited to situations involving a disregard of the legal entity.

Despite having similarities, both remedies, the extension of bankruptcy and the piercing of the corporate veil, have different consequences. While the first pursues the declaration of bankruptcy of a person or entity that is different from the principal debtor, the second seeks to directly attribute the actions or omissions of the entity to those who made them possible, and impose on such persons unlimited joint and several liability for the damages caused.

The Bankruptcy Law contemplates two distinct types of insolvency proceedings. The first is a reorganization proceeding (*concurso preventivo*) that aims to rehabilitate the debtor. This procedure is analogous to a "Chapter 11" reorganization under the United States Bankruptcy Code. The other is a liquidation proceeding (*quiebra*) that contemplates a liquidation of the debtor's business and is equivalent to a "Chapter 7" liquidation under the United States Bankruptcy Code.

The rules that specifically govern the extension of the bankruptcy proceedings to related companies in the Bankruptcy Law only apply to the liquidation proceedings (*quiebra*) and not to the reorganization proceedings. Consequently, under Argentine law, only the bankruptcy liquidation proceedings (*quiebra*) could be extended to related companies. In that respect, Article 161 of the Bankruptcy Law provides that courts have the authority to extend bankruptcy liquidation proceedings to:

(1) A person (individual or entity) that has used the assets of the debtor as its own, thereby defrauding creditors — This situation refers to an abuse by a person that is not the principal debtor. The requirements for this type of bankruptcy extension are a person

that is not the principal debtor who uses or disposes of the principal debtor's assets (whether directly or indirectly) as if such person were the owner, the actions are made under the appearance that the disposition of assets is made by the principal debtor, and there is fraud.

(2) A parent (or otherwise controlling) company of the debtor that has improperly deviated the interest of the controlled company for the parent's company's own benefit or for the benefit of the parent's economic group — This situation refers to the abuse by the controlling entity. The requirements for this cause of bankruptcy extension are a controlling person (whether an individual or a legal entity) that engages in undue deviation of the corporate interest for the benefit of the controlling entity or of the economic group of which it forms part, and the debtor is subject to a unified direction.

(3) A person whose assets are commingled with the assets of the debtor — Article 161 of the Bankruptcy Law provides for extension of liquidation proceedings when there is commingling of assets. This is a situation in which assets are so intertwined that it is impossible to distinguish who owns what. The requirements for this cause of bankruptcy extension are the existence of commingling of assets as an objective fact and impossibility of precisely establishing the ownership of most of the assets and debts. In these cases, the doctrine of *venire contra factum* (similar to estoppel) becomes applicable since the person who creates a situation of confusion in the ownership of assets implicitly waives the benefits of corporate separateness.

Bankruptcy law first adopted this doctrine in 1973 based on the holding in the *Compañía Swift de La Plata* case. The legal regulation of bankruptcy extension has a very specific purpose which is to extend the liability of the debtor in bankruptcy to its shareholders or controlling parents, increasing the available assets and providing creditors with an alternative cover for their credits. The extension of bankruptcy also has a punishment purpose on grounds that the law cannot admit the incorrect use of its technical instrumentalities. However, under Article 161 of the Bankruptcy Law, a court will only extend the bankruptcy proceedings to a shareholder of a company undergoing bankruptcy proceedings if the following requirements are met:

(1) The shareholder must be a controlling shareholder, who could be the one that has the necessary participation in such company to direct the acts of such company (i.e., to form the corporate will)

or each of the shareholders that acting jointly have the participation described (e.g., as a result of a shareholders' agreement); and

(2) The controlling shareholder improperly diverted the interest of the debtor for the parent's own benefit or for the benefit of the parent's economic group.

Both requirements must be met for a court to be able to extend the bankruptcy proceedings to a controlling shareholder. The mere fact of being the controlling shareholder does not imply that the bankruptcy proceedings will be automatically extended to such controlling shareholder. Such control must have been improperly used to divert the interest of the controlled company for its own benefit or for the benefit of another controlled company or company of the same economic group.

The only persons entitled to request the extension of the bankruptcy proceedings are the receiver (*síndico*) in such bankruptcy liquidation proceedings (*quiebra*) and the creditors of the company undergoing liquidation proceedings (*quiebra*). Courts have denied to the shareholders of a company the right to request the extension of the bankruptcy liquidation proceedings.[43] The request for the extension of the bankruptcy liquidation proceedings to a related company must be made within a six-month period as from the date in which the receiver presented its information memorandum. The judge of the bankruptcy proceedings is the judge competent to decide whether the liquidation proceedings are to be extended to a related company, pursuant to an ordinary trial.

Article 172 of the Bankruptcy Law clearly states that the extension of the bankruptcy of a company may not apply to other companies of the same economic group, even if there is a situation of corporate control, but the requirements of Article 161 are not met. Courts are generally very strict in applying the requisites required by the law to extend the liquidation procedures to controlling shareholders.

Shareholders, directors, and syndics also have unlimited joint and several liability with an insurance company after the Public Registry of Commerce registers the resolution of the National Superintendency of Insurance revoking the company's authorization to operate.[44] This is a provision more likely to apply in a bankruptcy-like context. Insurance companies never go into bankruptcy proceedings; they may be declared

---

43 National Commercial Court of Appeals, Panel E, 27 November 1987.
44 Insurance Companies Law, Article 8.

in mandatory liquidation (*liquidación forzosa*) by the National Superintendency of Insurance, in which case the authorization is revoked and the liquidation is conducted by the regulator itself.[45] The procedure is usually similar to a bankruptcy proceeding.

Tax Law

Tax law was apparently the first field of law in Argentina in which the possibility of disregarding the separation between a company and its shareholders was upheld by the courts.

In 1973, shortly before rendering its judgment in *Compañía Swift de La Plata*, the National Supreme Court issued its decision in *Parke Davis y Cía. de Argentina S.A.I. y C.*,[46] in which it applied an existing provision of the Tax Procedure Law (still in force) that establishes the so-called "economic reality principle", which is similar to the United States tax law principle of "substance over form". Under Article 2[47] of the Tax Procedure Law:

> ". . . to determine the true nature of the taxable event, [the tax administration] shall review the economic actions, situations and relations that taxpayers do, pursue or establish. When taxpayers submit these actions, situations or relations to legal forms or structures other than those private law manifestly offers or authorizes to adequately implement the true and effective economic intention of the taxpayers, [the tax administration] shall disregard the inadequate legal forms and structures and shall consider the real economic situation as under the forms or structures that would apply under private law, regardless of those chosen by the taxpayers, or would be allowed to apply as being the most adequate to the taxpayers' true intentions."

Article 1 of the Tax Procedure Law reads accordingly:

> "In interpreting the provisions of this law or of the laws subject to its regulation, it must be taken into consideration their purposes

---

45 Insurance Companies Law Number, Article 51.
46 *Parke Davis y Cía. de Argentina S.A.I. y C.*, 31 July 1973, *Fallos* 286:97.
47 This is the current number of the Article. The number it had at the time of the challenged tax periods was 12.

and their economic significance. Only when it is not possible from their text or spirit to determine the meaning or extension of the rules, concepts or terms of the above mentioned provisions, it must be allowed to resort to the rules, concepts and terms of private law."

Likewise, the National Supreme Court, in re *Tejedor S.A.*,[48] held that: "[i]n tax matters, it is compulsory to respect the real nature of the facts, circumstances and economic relationships that taxpayers do, pursue or establish in order to preserve the purpose and significance of tax regulations".

In the *Parke Davis* case, the National Supreme Court upheld a court of appeals decision that disallowed the deductions for royalties paid by the Argentine company to its foreign controlling shareholder, because such payments would violate the reality that they were in fact dividends, since they were paid to its controlling shareholder. The National Supreme Court expressly stated that this conclusion was only for tax purposes and did not affect the separation between the two companies for private law purposes. A decade later, in *Kellogg Co. Arg. S.A.C.I. y F.*,[49] the National Supreme Court again disregarded the different legal personality of two Argentine related companies, but in this case in favor of the taxpayer and over the tax administration's objections.

The enactment of specific provisions to curb tax avoidance has reduced the impact of these Supreme Court decisions. Article 14 of the Tax Crimes Law provides that for tax crimes committed with the aid or for the benefit of a legal entity, the prison term must be imposed on its directors, managers, syndics, members of the supervision committee, administrators, attorneys-in-fact, or representatives, who have participated in the punishable act. Shareholders are not mentioned among them. While shareholders could hold one of such positions (and in closely held corporations they often do), it is not as shareholders, but as corporate officers, that they could be criminally responsible for tax crimes.

---

48 *Tejedor S.A.*, 24 November 1992, *Fallos* 315:2798.
49 *Kellogg Co. Arg. S.A.C.I. y F.*, 26 February 1985, *Fallos* 307:118.

Belgium

Vincent Jodard, Mattias Verbeeck, and Sarah Arens
Van Bael & Bellis
Brussels, Belgium

Introduction

The successive financial and sovereign debt crisis together with the rise of a new e-economy has revealed the need for most companies to reinvent themselves. Belgium is no exception. Recent events such as the decision of the Caterpillar Belgium's shareholders to close the factory in Gosselies or the massive restructuring in the bank (ING and Optima) and insurance (AXA) sectors have shown that shareholders play a central role in this process in today's globalized economy.

The delicate state of the economy has caused shareholders to be increasingly present in the life of companies with the aim to reach their investment goals. While shareholders' rights have been continuously strengthened under European Union (EU) and Belgian corporate law over the years, their obligations and, in particular, the sources of their liability *vis-à-vis* the company, *vis-à-vis* other shareholders, or *vis-à-vis* third parties (e.g., creditors) have followed the same path.

Traditionally and for the vast majority of companies in Belgium, shareholders tend to restrain their liabilities by opting to found or invest into a company with a "limited liability" form. By doing so, investments and risks are, in principle, fostered. However, shareholders might, under certain circumstances, still incur substantial liabilities at every stage of the lifetime of a company, from the foundation towards the exit.

The aim of this article is to present an overview of a selection of important sources of liabilities of shareholders of Belgian (listed or non-listed) limited-liability companies through the various stages of their existence (foundation through exit). Our attention will be focused on limited-liability companies as they constitute the majority of companies in Belgium.

Liability at Early Stages of Company

In General

In the majority of cases, shareholders found or invest into a company as opposed to a simple partnership, to benefit from what the Anglo-Saxon countries commonly call the corporate veil: a company has a separate legal personality, distinct from those that control it. As a legal consequence, a shareholder could, in principle, not be held liable for the companies' debts and its liability is restricted to its contribution in the share capital of the company.

Belgium mainly knows three types of limited-liability companies, namely, the private limited-liability company or SPRL (*besloten vennootschap met beperkte aansprakelijkheid / société privée à responsabilité limitée*), the cooperative limited-liability company or SCRL (*coöperatieve vennootschap met beperkte aansprakelijkheid / société cooperative à responsabilité limitée*), and the limited-liability company or SA (*naamloze vennootschap / société anonyme*).

Despite the apparent absence of liability for the shareholders who would have opted for one of the three recognized forms of limited-liability companies, there are circumstances where the "corporate veil" could be pierced and the shareholders could incur certain liabilities. Certain of the most important sources of liability are discussed in the next sections, depending on the stage of existence of the company.

Liability of Founders

In General

Company founders incur a joint and several liability with the company, for irregularities committed at incorporation or insufficient initial share capital, irrespective of whether they were aware of the irregularities committed or the amount of their participation.

This ground for liability only concerns the "founders", i.e., the parties present at the execution of the deed of incorporation of the company with a view to subscribe to the share capital.[1] The other shareholders present for the deed of incorporation of an SA are not considered as "founders" within the meaning of the Companies' Code, if the "other" founders represent at least one-third of the share capital. This liability regime is subject to a prescription period of five years.[2]

Irregularities Committed at Incorporation

The subscriber may not be a minor, an incapable person, or a person deprived of legal capacity and its consent may not be vitiated. Should

---

1 Companies Code, Articles 225, 401, and 450.
2 Companies Code, Article 2262 *bis*, Paragraph 1, Indent 2.

the subscription be considered invalid, the founders may be held liable *vis-à-vis* all interested parties for the entire amount of the share capital that has not been validly subscribed and for the possible difference between the minimal required amount and the actual subscribed amount.[3] Moreover, the invalidity of the subscription may result in a situation where the minimum requirement of two shareholders is no longer met. This may, in turn, lead to the nullity of the SPRL or the SA.[4]

The minimal amount of the share capital must have been fully and validly paid up;[5] if not, the founders may be held liable *vis-à-vis* all interested parties up to the required minimum.[6] Nor may the company (SPRL or SCRL) have subscribed to its own shares or depositary receipts.[7]

The founders may be held liable if the required statements in the deed of incorporation are missing or false if the nullity of the company has been ordered or if the value of the contribution in kind is clearly exaggerated or fictitious.[8] In addition, if the sole founder of an SPRL is a legal entity, it will be held jointly liable for the company's debts until a second person becomes shareholder of the company.[9]

Insufficient Initial Share Capital

If the company goes bankrupt within three years following its incorporation, the founders may be held liable if, at the time of incorporation, the share capital was manifestly insufficient to enable the company to pursue its normal and reasonably foreseeable activity during at least two years.[10]

---

[3] Companies Code, Article 229, Indent 1; Article 456, Indent 1; and Article 405, Indent 1.
[4] Companies Code, Article 227, Indent 4 and Article 454, Indent 4.
[5] The amount is €18,550 for an SPRL and SCRL, of which one-fourth or €6,200 must be paid up in the case of an SPRL (Companies Code, Article 223) and at least one-fifth or €6,200 must be paid up in case of an SCRL (Companies Code, Articles 397 and 398). The minimum amount of the SA's share capital is one-fourth or €61,500, which must be fully and unconditionally paid up (Companies Code, Article 448).
[6] Companies Code, Article 229, Indent 2; Article 405, Indent 2; and Article 456, Indent 2.
[7] Companies Code, Article 217 or Article 354.
[8] Companies Code, Article 229, Indent 4; Article 405, Indent 3; and Article 456, Indent 3.
[9] Companies Code, Article 213, Paragraph 2.
[10] Companies Code, Article 229, Indent 5; Article 405, Indent 5; and Article 456, Indent 4. In the case of an SCRL, the capital that will be taken into account is the fixed capital, as described by the articles of association (Companies Code, Article 390, Paragraph 1).

In order to assess whether this was the case, one must refer to the financial plan, which must be drawn up prior to the incorporation of the company.[11] The financial plan must indeed mention the minimum resources that are required to ensure a normal activity of the company during at least two years. This financial plan is not publicly available. It is kept by the notary public and may only be communicated at the request of Belgian Commercial Courts in case a bankruptcy occurs within the first three years of incorporation.

The financial plan will be a key element in the court's assessment of whether the share capital and other financial resources were manifestly insufficient. If the Court holds that at the time of incorporation such resources were manifestly insufficient, it may hold all founders liable, irrespective of their fault or the amount of their contribution in the company.

The founders will be ordered to personally provide the difference between the capital provided and the capital that was actually required. Founders may, however, avoid any liability if they can prove that the bankruptcy was caused by events that could not be anticipated at the time the financial plan was drawn up, such as an economic low, the loss of an important client, or bad management.

Liability During Lifetime of Company

Sole Shareholder Liability

The sole shareholder of an SA bares a specific liability in case the shares in the SA are consolidated in its hands for more than one year. The sole shareholder will be jointly liable with the company for all obligations having arisen after the consolidation of the shares, if, after one year, no new shareholder has entered the company, the company has not been converted into an SPRL, or the company has not been wound up.[12]

Acquisition of Shares of Non-Listed Companies

The most common way in which a purchaser may acquire shares in a Belgian company is pursuant to an agreement entered into with the seller (and current shareholder of the company). In accordance with general

---

11 Companies Code, Articles 215, 391, and 440.
12 Companies Code, Article 646.

Belgian contract law, a sale of shares is in principle concluded, and the shares are deemed to be transferred, as from the moment when the transferor and the transferee have reached an agreement on the object of the sale (e.g., the number of shares) and the purchase price.

The Companies Code further requires that a share transfer must be registered by the transferor and the transferee (or their proxyholders) in the share register of the company.[13] Failure to register does, however, not affect the validity of the transfer but could allow the company and third parties to contest the transfer since the transferee and/or transferor would then need to prove that the shares have been transferred in another way. In the specific case of dematerialized shares, transfer of shares operates by transfer from account to account, eventually through a settlement organization if the transferor and the transferee are registered to a different account holder.

Bar a few exceptions, liability of the shareholders relating to their capacity as owners of the shares also is transferred as of the moment of the transfer. To avoid or restrict certain sources of liabilities, the purchaser may request from the seller specific guarantees or exclusion of liabilities in respect of certain events, contractually agreed upon between the parties and for which the seller will continue to bear certain liabilities although the shares in the company would have been transferred. These limitations are subject to negotiations and are commonly linked to the due diligence or included in a separate disclosure document.

Acquisition of Shares of Listed Companies: Takeover Bid

Takeover Bid

Shareholders of listed companies face additional obligations in case they want to launch a public takeover bid on all shares. This contrasts with the acquisition of shares in non-listed companies where, in general, no specific requirements apply. In addition, they will in certain circumstances be obliged to launch a takeover bid on all outstanding shares which may have far-reaching consequences.

The Belgian regulatory framework on takeover bids is largely based on Directive 2004/25/EC of 21 April 2004 on takeover bids. The Directive has been transposed in Belgian law by the Law of 1 April 2007 on public takeovers (the "Takeover Law"), the Royal Decree of 27 April 2007 on public takeovers (the "Takeover Decree"), and the Royal Decree of 27 April 2007 on squeeze-out bids.

---

13 Companies Code, Article 504.

The Belgian takeover regulation also is, in part, inspired by a number of widely publicized cases where it was argued that the rights of certain shareholders had been infringed upon. The most famous case in that regard is undoubtedly the takeover bid by the De Benedetti Group on the Société Générale de Belgique. While a comprehensive review of the Belgian takeover legislation falls outside the scope of this article, these are the main requirements with which a takeover bid must comply:

(1) It must relate to all voting securities of the target that are not yet owned by the bidder;
(2) The bidder must have the necessary funding to pay in full the bid price, either in the form of an unconditional and irrevocable bank credit facility or in a bank account; in the case of an exchange offer, the securities to be offered in exchange must be available to the bidder, or it must have the power to issue or acquire such securities from another person;
(3) If the bid relates to different categories of securities, the differences between the bid prices offered for each of these categories of securities must only result from the inherent differences between these categories;
(4) The bidder must commit itself to pursue the bid until its term; and
(5) A bid can only be subject to any type of conditions approved by the Belgian Financial Services and Markets Authority (FSMA).[14]

The bidder is free to determine the price for the bid. In the case of a bid by a controlling shareholder, the consideration offered must, however, be reviewed by an independent expert to be appointed by the target's independent directors. The independent expert must decide whether the consideration is fair when compared to a bid in a competitive market.[15]

Mandatory Takeover Bid

An even more far-reaching obligation the shareholder of a listed company may run into is the mandatary takeover bid. A shareholder is under an obligation to launch a takeover bid if it holds, as a result of an acquisition or an acquisition by persons acting in concert with it, directly or indirectly more than 30 per cent of the voting securities in a Belgian listed company.[16]

---

14 Takeover Decree, Article 3.
15 Takeover Decree, Article 23.
16 Takeover Law, Article 5; Takeover Decree, Article 50(1).

These obligations aim to prevent the situation in which a shareholder buys just enough shares to gain control over a listed company and leaves the other shareholders with shares that are worth way less and practically impossible to sell. The consideration of the mandatory bid must be at least equal to the higher of:
(1) The highest price paid for the securities by the bidder during the twelve months preceding the announcement of the bid; and
(2) The weighted average market price of the securities during the thirty calendar days before the event triggering the obligation to launch the mandatory bid.[17]

A mandatory bid is not required when the 30 per cent threshold is exceeded in a number of limited exceptions provided by the Takeover Decree (for example, in the event of an acquisition as a result of a voluntary takeover bid or in the case of transfers between affiliated companies).[18]

Acquisition of Shares Not Fully Paid Up

In General

As mentioned above, shares subscribed by shareholders at the time of incorporation must be paid up in accordance with the minimum requirements laid down by the Companies Code. The minimum amount that should be paid up depends on the company form.

Irregularities Committed at Incorporation

Should a shareholder ultimately not fully pay up its shares, the company holds a claim against such shareholder, for the amount not fully paid up. Such claim exists from the moment the shareholder commits to subscribe to the share capital of the company.

Often, the articles of association contain the terms and conditions regarding the paying up of the shares. If this is not the case, the board of directors may lay down the procedure to be followed. It is only when the board of directors requests that the shares be fully paid up that such claim becomes enforceable.

---

17 Takeover Decree, Article 53.
18 Takeover Decree, Article 52.

As creditors of a company must be able to rely on the fulfilment of the paying up obligations, they may, under the provisions of the Companies Code,[19] request the shareholders to pay up the shares in accordance with the terms and conditions of the articles of association. This right of the company's creditors aims at avoiding a deadlock situation since the enforceability often depends on a decision of the board of directors, where, in many cases, the defaulting shareholder holds a seat.

The articles of association of an SA sometimes include the right for the board of directors to sell the shares of a shareholder that is not complying with the obligation to pay up its shares. This right to sell is connected with a revocation right of the board which can revoke the ownership right of the shareholder if it does not pay up its shares.

Transfer of Shares

It is, however, possible that a shareholder transfers its shares before they have been fully paid up. The question then arises as to who, the transferor or the transferee, will be obligated to pay up the shares. This issue has been addressed in the Companies Code, but only with regard to the SA.[20] However, it is seen in case law and supported by the majority of the legal doctrine that this provision also is applicable to the SPRL.

Pursuant to Article 507 of the Companies Code, the transfer of shares which have not been fully paid up does not exclude the joint liability of the seller of the shares for the debts existing prior to the publication of the transfer and up to the total amount that has not been paid up. The transferor holds a claim against the transferee and all subsequent transferees in this respect.

Apart from such liability towards third parties, two other situations may be distinguished. First, in relation to the liability between the transferor and the transferee, the obligation to pay up the shares is considered to have been transferred to the transferee, along with the legal title. Unless parties agreed otherwise, the transferee shall be liable to pay up the shares, without recourse against the transferor. Second, regarding the liability of the transferor *vis-à-vis* the company, it is accepted that the transferor may no longer be held liable for the payment of shares requested after the registration of the transfer in the share register. However, in case the payment was already due prior to the transfer, the company holds a claim against the transferor.

---

19 Companies Code, Article 199, Indent 3.
20 Companies Code, Article 507.

Distribution of Dividends

In General

Three types of dividends may be distinguished: the regular dividend, the advance dividend, and the interim dividend. Overall, no dividend may be distributed when the net assets, as reflected in the annual accounts, are or will be, following such distribution, lower than the amount of the paid-up capital, plus any reserves of which the distribution is prohibited by law or the articles of association.[21]

At the occasion of the annual shareholders' meeting, the shareholders may decide to distribute a dividend and determine the amount thereof. Once the distribution of the dividend has been voted and agreed, each shareholder will hold a right to claim the dividend distribution.

This is final and irrevocable, but payment only becomes due at the date of the dividend payment determined by the shareholders' meeting or the board of directors. In addition, the board of directors — and the shareholders' meeting according to certain legal authors — may distribute an advance dividend in the course of the financial year. This advance on the definitive dividend is only available for the SA and is subject to all legal requirements laid down in the Companies Code:[22]

(1) The articles of association must authorize the board of directors to distribute this advance dividend;
(2) The distribution may only be sampled from the profit of the current financial year;
(3) The board of directors must draw up a statement of assets and liabilities that will be verified by the statutory auditor;
(4) The decision to distribute the dividend must be taken within two months following the statement of assets and liabilities; and
(5) The decision may not be taken any earlier than six months after the closing of the previous financial year and after the approval of the annual accounts in relation to that financial year.

Finally, in the course of the financial year and on the occasion of a special general meeting, the shareholders may decide to distribute a third type of dividend, the interim dividend. While there is no legal basis for this practice, its lawfulness has been confirmed by the Belgian Supreme Court in 2003.[23]

---

[21] Companies Code, Articles 320, 429, and 617.
[22] Companies Code, Article 618.
[23] Supreme Court, 23 January 2003, *R.D.C.*, 2003, at p. 836.

Liability

The shareholders may be sanctioned if the dividend distribution has been decided in breach of the applicable legal provisions, with the exception of the nullity of the shareholders' decision. The illegal dividend must be returned by the shareholders who received the dividend, if the company proves that they were aware of the irregularity of the distribution or if they could not be unaware considering the circumstances.[24]

It should be noted that in this case the company's directors are more severely sanctioned than the shareholders. The shareholders' behavior must be linked to bad faith and the breach of the legal requirements merely requires the reimbursement of the dividend. The company's directors may incur civil and criminal liability by implementing the shareholders' decision to distribute the illegal dividend or when they decide to distribute an advance dividend in case the legal requirements have not been met.[25] The heavy sanctions applicable to the directors may be explained by the fact that they propose the dividend distribution to the shareholders.

In addition, a shareholders' decision may constitute an abuse of majority shareholder power in case of the systematic retention of profits, if this is unnecessary and cannot be justified by the corporate's interest of the company. For example, if the majority shareholders decide not to distribute the dividend but use the profits to grant themselves remuneration for their other functions, the non-distribution of dividend may be considered abusive. Besides the annulment of the decision, a shareholder may introduce various types of claims against the abusing shareholder.[26]

Liability in Shareholder Disputes

Abuse of Power under General Tort Law

Shareholders' disputes mostly concern disputes between majority and minority shareholders. This comes from the fact that most decisions taken by the shareholders' meeting are taken with the majority of the

---

[24] Companies Code, Article 619.
[25] Companies Code, Article 648.
[26] Including the *action en retrait* (Companies Code, Articles 340 and 642), the *action en exclusion* (Companies Code, Articles 334 and 636), and the *action sociale minoritaire* (Companies Code, Article 562).

votes cast, with one share being one vote, which sometimes leads to an absolute power of a majority shareholder over the minority shareholders.

When voting at a shareholders' meeting, shareholders should always have the corporate interest of the company in mind and act accordingly. The Supreme Court has defined the concept of "corporate interest" as "the collective pursuit of profit by all current and future shareholders", thereby opting for a traditional approach.[27]

Should a shareholder be found guilty of not acting in the corporate interest of the company, its liability may be engaged for abuse of power, on the basis of Article 1382 of the Belgian Civil Code (the general liability in tort provision). In that case, a fault must be proved, which can be a violation of the principle of good faith. A breach of a good faith obligation will be found if the following requirements are met:

(1) A shareholder exercises its rights with the mere intention to damage the other shareholder(s);
(2) A shareholder can make a choice between two different sorts of execution in the exercise of its rights both of which have the same effect and it chooses the execution that is most damaging to the other shareholder(s); and
(3) In the exercise of its rights, a shareholder damages the other shareholder(s) in such a way that is disproportionate in comparison with the benefits it receives.

Furthermore, the existence of damage and a causal relation between the fault and the damage occurred must be proven. Personal liability can result in damages if the nullity of the abusive decision does not fully repair the damage that was caused. The same liability for abuse of power can be invoked, under the aforementioned conditions, against the minority shareholder who is, e.g., purposely blocking a decision that requires a qualified majority, refusing to sell its shares to another shareholder.

Courts and tribunals enjoy a narrow margin of appreciation when assessing whether a shareholder abused its rights. Indeed, shareholders may legitimately claim that they exercised their rights in a normal and prudent way and in accordance with the provisions of the Companies Code. A precise assessment of what prudent and normal shareholders placed in the same circumstances would have done must be performed by the courts.

---

[27] Supreme Court (1ek.) AR C.12.0549.N, 28 November 2013.

Dispute Procedure

To increase foreseeability of the resolution of shareholders disputes, a Belgian Law of 13 April 1995 introduced new provisions in the Companies Code, with regard to the dispute procedure.[28] Prior to such provisions being added to the Companies Code, disputing shareholders were forced to resort to the dissolution of the company by a Court decision, if the cooperation between the shareholders became impossible.

A distinction must be made between "exclusion" and "withdrawal" of shareholders. Under the exclusion procedure, a shareholder holding 30 per cent of the share capital[29] or holding securities representing 30 per cent of the voting rights related to the total number of existing securities (or 20 per cent of the voting rights for the total number of existing securities if the company has issued securities that do not represent the capital) may request, before a Belgian court, the exclusion of another shareholder, for well-founded reasons.

A "well-founded reason" is a sufficiently serious and lasting disagreement between the shareholders, which jeopardizes or threatens to jeopardize the survival of the company. These include circumstances under which a shareholder can no longer reasonably be accepted as a shareholder or a shareholder can no longer reasonably be obliged to indulge the other shareholder as a shareholder of the company. Belgian courts are reluctant to rule in favor of an exclusion of a shareholder. They will usually avoid it if:

(1) There are other ways to resolve the problem;
(2) The plaintiff caused the conflict;
(3) The defendant has not committed a breach; or
(4) A particular breach was insufficient to constitute a "well-founded" reason.

The courts also will avoid the exclusion path if the plaintiff contributed to the well-founded reasons or the plaintiff has not proven well-founded reasons. If a plaintiff succeeds in an action for exclusion, a court will order the defendant to transfer its shares to the plaintiff at a price determined by the Court.[30] In a successful exclusion procedure, the court will order the plaintiff to purchase the defendant's shares for a price determined by the court.[31] This price is binding on all parties, even the

---

[28] Companies Code, Articles 334–342 and 635–644.
[29] These are shares whose nominal value or par value represents 30 per cent of the capital of the company.
[30] Companies Code, Article 640.
[31] Companies Code, Article 643.

plaintiff. A plaintiff may not unilaterally waive this order if it disagrees with the selling or purchase price.

The Companies Code only provides that the court determines the purchase price. However, it does not indicate how a court should determine the price. The court may determine the price itself, or ask for an expert's non-binding opinion (for example, an accountant or auditor). The moment the value of the shares is determined is crucial.

In most cases, this is the moment the procedure was started or the date on which the expert determines the price. However, the parties sometimes object to this valuation by claiming that the value of the shares had decreased between the defendants' breach and the court's decision (for example, by abuse of majority).

During the exclusion procedure, the defendant is not allowed to transfer or encumber its shares. Pursuant to the withdrawal procedure, any shareholder may, for well-founded reasons, request the other shareholders to buy out its shares. While the procedure is similar to the exclusion procedure, there are no thresholds to comply with. In addition, the court usually only takes the interests of the shareholders into account and not the interests of the company.

Liability of Shareholders in Listed Companies

In addition to the obligations pursuant to general corporate law, shareholders of listed companies face an additional set of obligations and related liabilities (criminal, civil, and administrative).

These are essentially different from the obligations mentioned above as they aim to protect the interests of the other (minority) shareholders rather than the interests of the creditors. In particular, they do so by prohibiting market abuse, imposing notification obligations for transactions executed by certain shareholders, and providing safeguards for minority shareholders in case of a public takeover.

Market Abuse

In General

Several provisions exist under Belgium corporate law, the aim of which is to protect the interests of the minority shareholders by prohibiting (prospective) shareholders to buy or sell shares (or abstain from doing so) in a number of cases. This is in stark contrast to non-listed companies where there are no such restrictions.

A shareholder, informed of the fact that the company in which it holds shares is about to lose an important client, may in principle still sell its shares to a third party without informing the latter thereof. Moreover, such third party shall in principle very often not be able to rely on the legal concepts of fraud and error as the courts are generally reluctant to accept such claims to the extent they are based on error or fraud relating to the qualities of the underlying company rather than the shares as such.

In practice, most sophisticated purchasers solve this issue by requesting that the sellers give representations and warranties. Most legislators have, however, come to the conclusion that the specific features of the financial markets (i.e., the fact that the purchaser and seller typically do not know each other and the absence of the possibility to negotiate representations and warranties) as well as their importance to the economy, require a different approach. Therefore, they have imposed a regulatory framework prohibiting insider trading and market abuse. Belgium is not different in this respect.

For more than a decade, this matter was largely governed by the Law of 2 May 2002. However, since the proper functioning of (equity) capital markets is essential for the implementation of the freedom of capital as set out in the Treaty on the Functioning on the European Union, this field of law has witnessed an ever increasing involvement of the EU. Eventually, this led to the introduction of Regulation 596/2014 on market abuse (the "MAR"), which creates a European-wide regulatory framework on market manipulation. Thus, the concepts of inside information and market abuse now have a uniform definition throughout the EU. Of course, this drastically reduces the role of the Law of 2 August 2002, which provides a "Belgian" definition.

In short, the MAR maintains a blanket prohibition on the use of inside information (including through an unlawful disclosure to a third party) and market manipulation. Inside information is defined as "information (1) of a precise nature, which (2) has not been made public, (3) relating, directly or indirectly, to one or more issuers or to one or more [shares], (4) and which, if it were made public, would be likely to have a significant effect on the prices of those [shares]".[32]

The MAR further lists a number of practices that qualify as market manipulation. These include entering into transactions that give

---

[32] Regulation 596/2014 of 16 April 2014 on market abuse, Article 7.

misleading signals to the market or place the price of shares at an artificial or abnormal level.[33] Shareholders that infringe upon these prohibitions could face hefty fines and even imprisonment.

The MAR expanded the toolbox of the public institutions in charge of enforcement and significantly increased the applicable fines by obliging the EU Member States to provide for maximum fines of at least €5,000,000 in the case of private individuals and even €15,000,000, or 15 per cent of the total annual turnover for legal entities as well as three times the amount of the profits gained or losses avoided because of the infringement.[34] The Belgian legislator, however, has not transposed all of these sanctions into Belgian law as yet.

Notification of Participations

Driven by the same objective that led to the prohibition of market abuse, the legislator introduced provisions to oblige shareholders in listed companies to divulge certain information relating to transactions they execute. Obviously, this also can be seen as a measure to ensure the smooth functioning of the financial markets. Indeed, information on a shareholder building up a stake in a company or disposing such stake is important for other shareholders.

Therefore, a shareholder must, pursuant to the Law of 2 May 2007, disclose its shareholding in a Belgian listed company to that company and the FSMA, if its stake represents five per cent or more of the total voting rights exercisable at the time of the acquisition.

This disclosure notification is once again required whenever the shareholding exceeds or drops below the threshold of five per cent or any other multiple of five per cent of the total voting rights.[35] This is the case regardless of whether such threshold is reached as a result of an acquisition or disposal of shares or a change of the breakdown of the voting rights (e.g., through an increase or decrease of the company's share capital).[36]

The company could decide to go even further and include lower or different notification thresholds (e.g., one per cent, three per cent, or 7.5 per cent) in its articles of association. The calculation of the thresholds must take into account the shareholdings of affiliates and parties acting in concert and will include financial instruments which, pursuant to a

---

33 Regulation 596/2014, Article 12.1(a).
34 Regulation 596/2014, Article 30.2(i).
35 Law of 2 May 2007, Article 6(1).
36 Law of 2 May 2007, Article 6(3).

formal agreement, grant the holder either the unconditional right to acquire securities carrying voting rights or the possibility of acquiring such rights at the shareholder's discretionary election.[37]

Additional disclosure obligations exist for persons that qualify as "insiders". In a number of cases, the Law of 2 May 2007 and its implementing royal decrees nevertheless provide for exemptions from the disclosure obligation (for example, for market making and trading book exemptions).[38] The disclosure notification must be made by the acquirer to the target and the FSMA promptly and no later than four trading days from the date of the event triggering the disclosure obligation.[39]

The target must publish the information contained in the notification within three trading days from the day of its receipt.[40] It is a criminal offence to fail to disclose this information which could also result in civil sanctions, such as the suspension of the voting rights attached to the relevant shares. Administrative fines also can be imposed by the FSMA.[41]

Liability upon Exit

Transfer of Restrictions

Legal Transfer Restrictions

As a general principle, the shares in a SA are freely transferrable.[42] In some particular cases, contractual or legal restrictions may, however, limit the possibility to transfer. As mentioned above, transfers of shares that are not yet fully paid up are, for example, only effective towards third parties after the publication of a list of the shareholders that have not yet paid up their shares, reflecting the transfer, in the Annexes to the *Belgian Official Journal*.[43]

Furthermore, profit shares can only be transferred, at the earliest, ten days after the deposit with the National Bank of Belgium of the second

---

37 Law of 2 May 2007, Article 6(5) and (6).
38 Law of 2 May 2007, Article 10.
39 Law of 2 May 2007, Article 12.
40 Law of 2 May 2007, Article 14.
41 Law of 2 May 2007, Article 26.
42 Companies Code, Article 476.
43 Companies Code, Article 506.

annual report following the profit shares issuance.[44] Any transfer before such deed can only be done pursuant to a public or private deed that must be notified by registered letter to the company. This restriction generally does not apply to listed companies.[45]

Another notable transfer restriction relates to shares issued to employees of the company. Such shares cannot be transferred during a period of five years[46] as of their issuance. In the same vein, shares acquired as a result of the conversion of warrants[47] within the framework of a public takeover bid (i.e., as a defense mechanism) are not transferrable for twelve months after the conversion.[48]

Contractual Transfer Restrictions

In addition to these legal restrictions, shareholders often wish to further limit the transferability of shares to avoid being confronted with an unknown third party as fellow shareholder in a company. This could be done by including transfer restrictions in the articles of association of the company or by entering into a shareholder agreement.

Shareholder agreements offer the advantage of being confidential[49] as opposed to limitations in the articles of association, which on the other hand have the benefit of automatically applying to all shares (or every share falling within the category to which a share transfer restriction is applicable). In any case, parties should take into account that the Companies Code regulates a number of (contractual or statutory) transfer restrictions. This is, in particular, the case for the approval clause, the pre-emption clause, and the lock-up clause.

An approval clause makes the transfer of shares subject to the prior approval of a corporate body of the company[50] or specific individual (usually another shareholder). This is slightly different from a pre-emption clause, pursuant to which the transferor must first offer its shares to the beneficiaries of the clause before being able to validly transfer its shares to a third party.

---

44 Companies Code, Article 508.
45 Companies Code, Article 509.
46 This does not apply in case of death (including death of a spouse), invalidity, termination of contract, or retirement of the employee.
47 This does not include warrants issued to members of the company's personnel.
48 Companies Code, Article 500.
49 This does not apply to listed companies, in which case the existence of such agreements must be made public (Article 506 of the Companies Code).
50 Shareholders' meeting or board of directors.

The beneficiaries of this clause usually have the right to then purchase the shares at the same price the third party was willing to pay or at a pre-set price. A lock-up clause, finally, is the most restrictive mechanism as it prohibits a shareholder from selling its shares altogether or at least precludes him from selling them to a number of designated individuals.

Due to their far-reaching consequences, the legislator decided to regulate these three types of clauses. Pre-emption and approval clauses are only valid if they do not result in the non-transferability of the shares for a period of more than six months as of the request for approval or the moment the shares were offered pursuant to the pre-emption clause.[51] A longer duration will automatically be reduced. Within the context of a public takeover bid, shareholders whose shares are subject to a pre-emption or approval clause must receive an offer to purchase their shares within five days after the notification of the bid to the company by the FSMA.[52]

Furthermore, a clause prohibiting the transfer of shares must be limited in time and justified in the interest of the company. The Companies Code does not provide a hard-and-fast rule as to the maximum duration of that limitation, but it is generally accepted that this duration is linked to the degree that the interest of the company justifies a lock-up of the shares. Parties typically justify the fact that a clause is in the interest of the company by referring to the importance of stability in the shareholders' structure of the company.

It could, for example, be argued that this is more the case for fledgling start-up than for an incumbent on the market. A clause that is not or no longer deemed to be in the interest of the company shall be deemed null and void.[53] If the clause is part of an agreement, the agreement shall remain valid unless this provision was considered fundamental to the parties. Moreover, it is generally accepted that the invalidity of the clause is absolute.

Other related mechanisms such as tag-along rights, drag-along rights, or call option rights are not explicitly mentioned in the Companies Code. However, to the extent they fall within the scope of the transfer restrictions set out above (which will very often be the case), they must comply with the same requirements as well as general corporate and contract law. In practice, this means that the scope of such clause also

---

51 Companies Code, Article 510.
52 Companies Code, Article 506.
53 Companies Code, Article 551(2).

must be limited in time and justified by the interest of the company. Further, if the agreement provides for a compulsory transfer of shares, the object of such transfer as well as the purchase price must be determined or at least determinable.[54]

As the Companies Code does not provide clear guidance on the sanctions in case of an infringement of valid restrictive clauses and case law is not always consistent on this point, the matter is highly debated in the literature. If a shareholder sells its shares notwithstanding a contractual or statutory restriction, he could in any case be held liable for a contractual breach against the transferee. Furthermore, the parties to the shareholder agreement could, within certain legal boundaries, include penalties, for example, obliging the shareholder that breached transfer restrictions to pay a lump sum to the other shareholders.

If the restrictions were included in the articles of association, the illegal sale may be unenforceable against the company, meaning that the faulty shareholder will still be considered as the legal owner. Pursuant to general civil law, the shareholder also is bound to repair the damage, which may result in the sale being void or, if such reparation is no longer possible, damages and interest could be granted to the beneficiary of the clause. Surprisingly, however, some courts have even gone beyond this and outright awarded the shares to the beneficiary of a preemptive clause. This approach appears to be debatable.

It is less clear to what extent a prospective transferee could be liable to the company and the beneficiary for breach of a transfer restriction. If such a clause is included in a shareholder agreement, neither the company nor the beneficiary can enforce this against a prospective transferee. Following a debatable decision of the Supreme Court,[55] the same principle applies to statutory clauses. However, if the transferee was aware of the existence of such clause but willfully ignored it, it could still be liable for third-party involvement in a contractual breach.

Finally, the Companies Code precludes parties to enter into shareholder agreements pursuant to which a shareholder would agree to vote in accordance with the instructions of a corporate body of the company or one of its subsidiaries or engage in approving proposals of corporate bodies of the company. Such agreements will automatically be deemed null and void, and any votes cast at the occasion of a shareholders' meeting pursuant to such agreement will be void.

---

54 Companies Code, Article 551(1) and (3).
55 Supreme Court, 5 May 1976, *Pas.*, 1976, I, at p. 957.

SCRL and SPRL

Transferability of shares in these two types of companies is more restricted. Subject to a number of exceptions, any transfer of shares in an SPRL must be accepted by half of the shareholders representing at least three-quarters of the shares, excluding the shares to be sold.[56] If the transferring shareholder does not obtain such approval, he can initiate legal proceedings before the competent court.[57]

If the court would come to the conclusion that the refusal was arbitrary, the other shareholder must find a buyer for the shares within three months, failing which the transferring shareholder can request the dissolution of the company. The shares in an SCRL are freely transferable between shareholders, whereas the shares can only be transferred to third parties if the transferee is listed in the articles of association or belongs to a specific category designated in the articles of association. In the latter case, a vote from the shareholders' meeting is nevertheless still required to approve a transfer.

Mandatory Transfer: Squeeze Out

Stand-Alone Squeeze Out

Pursuant to Article 513 of the Companies Code, a private individual or company that, acting alone or in concert,[58] holds 95 per cent of the voting securities in a company which made a public offering of securities, can force the minority shareholders to transfer their shares.

To that end, a specific procedure must be followed by the majority shareholder, which aims at making sure that the majority shareholder offers a fair price to the minority shareholders. For example, the price needs to be evaluated by an independent expert chosen by the majority shareholder and the minority shareholders have the opportunity to express concerns on the squeeze-out bid to the FSMA, which could in turn decide to withhold approval of the bid until such concerns (or concerns the FSMA raises itself) have been addressed.[59] At the end of this procedure, even the shares held by minority shareholders that did not offer their shares shall be deemed to be transferred to the majority shareholder.

---

56 Companies Code, Article 249.
57 Companies Code, Article 251.
58 Companies Code, Article 513, Paragraph 1.
59 Royal Decree of 27 April 2007, Article 10.

Squeeze Out after Public Takeover Bid

In addition to the stand-alone squeeze-out procedure, the legislation on public takeover bids also provides for a specific squeeze-out procedure as a back-end transaction after a public takeover bid. Pursuant to the Takeover Decree, a shareholder that has previously pursued a public takeover bid may demand that the remaining owners sell all their voting securities provided he holds 95 per cent of the voting securities (representing at least 95 per cent of the share capital).

In addition, he must have acquired at least 90 per cent of the shares to which the takeover bid was applicable. The latter requirement is not applicable in case of a mandatory takeover bid. The squeeze out must be initiated at the latest three months after the end of the acceptance period of the public takeover bid.

The procedure mentioned above is much simpler[60] compared to the stand-alone bid and, since the squeeze bid must be pursued under the same terms and conditions as the initial bid, the purchase price should not necessarily be in cash. After a period of acceptance which should last for a minimum of fifteen days,[61] the voting securities that have not been offered at the termination of the acceptance period will be deemed to have been transferred to the offeror.

Mandatory Acceptance of Shares

Following a public takeover, the minority shareholders also have the right to require the offeror to buy their securities after the end of the acceptance period to the extent the required conditions have been fulfilled. In such case, a shareholder must inform the offeror (or an individual designed by the latter) by registered letter of its intention to transfer the shares within three months following the takeover bid. Any such requests and resulting purchases must be notified by the offeror to the FSMA.[62]

Conclusion

The topic of shareholders' liability is vast and involves (sometimes) complicated features. In these difficult economic times, this topic

---

60 Royal Decree of 27 April 2007, Article 43.
61 Companies Code, Article 513, Paragraph 1.
62 Royal Decree of 27 April 2007, Article 44.

deserves special attention as shareholders are increasingly under scrutiny for their actions. While the basic principle of the "corporate veil" remains predominant in Belgian corporate law, the aim of this article has been to demonstrate that there are significant sources of liabilities for the shareholders, which might seriously undermine this basic principle.

The aim of this article also was to approach the topic of shareholders' liability in a horizontal way following a timeline, from the very beginning of the life of a company with the liability of founders, the common sources of liabilities that shareholders face during the lifetime of a company and, finally, through the liability they face upon exiting the company.

By doing so, this article has demonstrated that, in every step of the way, shareholders of Belgian limited-liability companies may either be held liable for the company's debts or engage their own liability on the basis of general principle of tort law or pursuant to specific provisions of the Companies Code or, in the case of listed companies, mostly on the basis of special laws derived from the EU.

With the growing number of major companies facing financial difficulties or engaging in restructuring operations, the topic of shareholders' liability should continue to gain visibility in the EU and in Belgium, and practitioners may have more occasions to write on this old and yet still very important issue.

Brazil

Adriana Camargo Rodrigues
Adriana Camargo Rodrigues Advocacia
São Paulo SP, Brazil

Introduction

Brazilian law contemplates two basic types of companies. i.e., the so-called company (*sociedade anônima*) and the partnership (*sociedade limitada*). Both types are governed by Federal Law. The company is treated as a combination of capital while the partnership is treated as a combination of persons. This difference is essential when it comes to personal liability of the members.

In the case of a partnership, liability may exceed the capital contribution, allowing the members to be pursued by creditors. In the case of a company, liability is limited to the capital contribution in most cases. Partner liability is governed by Decree Number 3708 of 10 January 1919 and the Civil Code, Law Number 10406 of 10 January 2002.

Shareholder liability is governed by Law Number 6404 of 15 December 1975, complemented by rules of the Civil Code, Law Number 10406 of 10 January 2002. This article deals solely with the liability of shareholders. The subject is vast and complex with countless material already produced on its various issues, from which few are addressed herein.

Allocation of Powers between Shareholders and Directors

In General

The allocation of powers between shareholders and directors is in part determined by law and in part by the statutes of the company.

Shareholders

The law guarantees to shareholders the powers to establish the statutes of the company and, in consequence, the powers and attributions of the board of directors. The powers of shareholders vary in accordance with the class of shares. The general meeting of shareholders has exclusive authority to amend the statutes, and to elect or discharge directors and auditors at any time.

In addition, shareholders have exclusive authority to receive the yearly account report drawn up by the company's directors and officers and decide on the financial statements presented by them, authorize the issuance of debentures, suspend the rights of a shareholder, resolve on the appraisal of assets contributed as capital by shareholders, authorize the issuance of founder shares, resolve on the company's transformation, consolidation, incorporation and divestment, dissolution and liquidation, and elect and discharge its liquidators, examine their accounts, and authorize the directors to file for bankruptcy or request reorganization.

Shareholders may decide whether the company's administration will be entrusted to its administrative council and its board of directors, or only to its board of directors. The administrative council is a deliberative body only. The company's representation is vested exclusively in the directors.

Administrative Bodies

The responsibilities and powers conferred by law upon administrative bodies may not be delegated to another body, either created by law or by the statutes. The administrative council must consist of at least three members, who must be elected at a general meeting of shareholders and who are subject to removal at any time by a general meeting.

The statutes of the company may establish a larger number of board members, eventually specifying a maximum and a minimum allowed. The statutes also may establish the procedures to choose and substitute the chairman of the board of directors by the meeting or by the board member. The statutes may determine the procedures for replacement of administrative council members and the duration of the mandate, which may not exceed three years. Reelection is permitted by law, but the statutes may decide differently.

The administrative council has powers to establish the strategy of the company's business, elect and discharge the directors and prescribe their duties, supervise the performance of the directors, examine books and records of the company at any time, request information on contracts signed or about to be signed, and take all other necessary action. The administrative council has powers to call a general meeting whenever deemed advisable, to give its opinion on the reports of the management and on the accounts of the board of directors and to select and discharge independent auditors.

Depending on the statutes, the administrative council may give its opinion in advance on actions or contracts, may decide whether to issue share or subscription bonuses, and may authorize the transfer of fixed assets and the creation of liens and obligations on assets of the company. Members of the administrative council may be domiciled abroad, but they must be elected among the shareholders of the company.

Board of Directors

The board of directors[1] must be composed of two or more directors, who must be elected by and may at any time be removed by the administrative council or, if none, by a general meeting of the shareholders. The statutes of the company may decide on a higher number of directors, and establish the procedures for their replacement and the duration of the mandate. The mandate may not exceed three years. Reelection is permitted by law, but the statutes may decide differently.

The duties and powers of each director may vary according to the rules established by the statutes. One-third of the members of the administrative council may be nominated to the board of directors and exercise both functions simultaneously. The by-laws may establish that a certain number of decisions be made at a meeting of the board of directors.

In the absence of a provision in the statutes or a resolution of the administrative council, each director has powers to represent the company and take such actions as are necessary for its operation. Within the limits of their duties and powers, the directors may appoint company proxies and must specify in the instrument of appointment the limits of authority and validity of the appointment. Exception is made to the appointment of attorneys to represent the company before court, in which case the term of validity may be undetermined. Members of the board of directors must be domiciled in Brazil and may be chosen outside the list of the shareholders.

Classes of Shareholders

In General

The statutes of the company must establish the number of shares into which the capital is divided and must establish whether or not the shares

---

1 Law Number 6404 of 15 December 1975, Articles 143–144.

must have a par value.[2] The statutes may create one or more classes of preferred shares with par value for a company whose shares have no par value.

The number and par value of shares may only be modified in the event of a change in the amount of capital or the monetary expression thereof, by shares division or consolidation or by cancellation of shares. The issuance of shares at a price below its par value is prohibited. The issue price of shares of no par value must be established by decision of the founders at the moment the company is formed, or by decision of the shareholders or the administrative council. The company may issue three types of shares: common, preferred, and the so-called founders' shares, each with advantages and disadvantages.

Common Shares

Unless otherwise specified in the statutes, all the shares issued by any company are common shares, all with equal rights, including right to vote and receive dividends.

There may be different classes of common shares, depending on their convertibility into preferred shares, on a requirement that the shareholder be a Brazilian citizen, or on the right to vote separately to fill certain positions in administrative bodies.

Preferred Shares

Preferred shares[3] have certain privileges, which may include priority in the distribution of fixed or minimum dividends, priority in the reimbursement of capital, or accumulation of the two. Regardless of having priority rights in the reimbursement of capital, preferred shares will only be accepted for trading in the Stock Exchange if they are afforded at least one of the following preferences or advantages: the right to have an interest on the divided to be distributed, corresponding at least to twenty-five per cent of the net income for the year; or the right to receive dividend at least ten per cent higher than the dividend assigned to each common share; or the right to be included in the public offering for alienation of control.

In addition, the statutes must indicate the preferences and advantages assigned to the shareholders without voting rights or with restricted

---

2 Law Number 6404 of 15 December 1975, Articles 15–19.
3 Law Number 6404 of 15 December 1975, Articles 17–19.

voting rights. The statutes may provide for one or more classes of preferred shares to have the right to elect one or more members of the administrative bodies by separate votes. The number of preferred shares without voting rights may not exceed fifty per cent of all issued shares.

Founder Shares

The company may at any time create negotiable securities of no par value and unrelated to the capital of the company that are called founder shares.[4] Founder shares must confer to their owner the right of credit to a possible participation in the annual profits of the company, but no voting rights are conferred.

The participation attributed to founder shares, including the right to form a redemption reserve, if any, may not exceed one-tenth of the company's profits. Founder shares may not carry any exclusive shareholder rights, except to inspect the actions of the company's officers.

The issuance of more than one class or series of founder shares is prohibited. The company may dispose of founder shares under the conditions established in the statutes of the company or as decided by the shareholders. Founder shares may be allocated to a founder, a shareholder, or a third party as remuneration for services rendered to the company.

Shareholder Voting

In General

A voting right is not inherent to all types and classes of shares. The company may have different classes of shares and the voting right of each class is established in the statutes.[5] Only the owner of a registered, endorsable, or book entry share may have the right to vote.

The shareholder must exercise the right to vote in the company's interest. The right to vote must be deemed abusive if it is exercised with the intent to cause damage to the company or to other shareholders, or to obtain an advantage for the shareholder or for a third party to which neither is entitled, and which results or may result in damage to the company or to other shareholders.

---

4 Law Number 6404 of 15 December 1975, Articles 46–51.
5 Law Number 6404 of 15 December 1975, Articles 110–115.

A shareholder may not vote in a general meeting on a resolution that relates to the evaluation report on the property transferred by that same shareholder to form the company's capital. A shareholder may not vote in a general meeting to approve the accounts presented by that shareholder while as a company officer or approve any resolutions which may benefit that shareholder while an officer or benefit a third company having conflicting interests with the company in question.

However, if all founders jointly owned a property that they transferred to form the company's capital, they may approve the evaluation report. A shareholder will be liable for any damages caused by abuse of voting rights, even if the vote does not prevail. Resolutions passed with the vote of a shareholder who has conflicting interests with the company may be voided. In such case, the shareholder must be liable for any damage caused and must be required to transfer to the company any benefits obtained.

Shareholder agreements regulating the exercise of voting rights or the exercise of control, as well as the purchase and sale of shares and the preference to acquire shares, must be respected by the company when filed in its head office. The commitments or encumbrances resulting from such a shareholders' agreement[6] may only be enforced against a third party after the agreement has been duly entered in the registry books of the company and on the share certificates, if any. Such agreements may not be invoked to exempt a shareholder either from liability when exercising the voting rights or from the controlling powers.

The mandate granted under a shareholder agreement to vote against or in favor of a resolution in a general or special meeting may not have a term longer than one year. The president of the meeting or of the decision-making body of the company may not compute a vote that infringes a shareholder agreement registered in the books of the company.

Failure to attend a general meeting or meetings of the company's management bodies, as well as failure to vote on matters specified in the shareholder agreement by any party or by members of the board of directors elected under the terms of the shareholder agreement, assures the damaged party the right to vote with the shares belonging to the shareholder who is absent and, in case of a member of the board of directors, by the board member elected by the votes of the damaged party.

---

[6] Law Number 6404 of 15 December 1975, Article 118.

Controlling Shareholder

A controlling shareholder is defined as an individual or legal entity, or a group of individuals or legal entities by a voting agreement or under common control, which have power enough to assure majority of votes in resolutions of general meetings.[7]

A controlling shareholder also may be an individual or legal entity, or a group of individuals or legal entities, with powers to elect the majority of the company officers. In practical terms, a controlling shareholder is the shareholder, or group of shareholders, with enough powers to direct the company activities and to guide the operations of any of the bodies of the company. A controlling shareholder must use its controlling power to make the company accomplish its purpose and perform its social role, and must have duties and responsibilities towards other shareholders of the company and the community in which it operates.

The controlling shareholder of a publicly-held company, and the shareholders or group of shareholders that elect a member of the board of directors, or of the administrative council, must immediately inform any changes in the respective ownership positions to the Brazilian Securities and Exchange Commission, or entities of the Exchange Market where the securities issued by the company are traded. A controlling shareholder must be liable for any damage caused by acts performed by the abuse of power. Abuse of power may take various forms, among which are:

(1) The guidance of the company towards an objective other than the company's purposes or towards an objective harmful to national interest;
(2) The use of the company to favor another company to the detriment of the shareholders' interest;
(3) The liquidation of a viable company or the transformation, merger, or division of a company in order to obtain an undue advantage to the detriment of other shareholders, the company, or its investors;
(4) The adoption of policies or decisions which are not in the best interest of the company;
(5) The election of a company's officer or administrative council member known to be unfit for the position; or
(6) The inducement of officers or administrative council members to unlawful action or contrary to the interests of the company.

---

[7] Law Number 6404 of 15 December 1975, Articles 116 and 117.

An officer or administrative council member committing an unlawful act is jointly and severally liable with the controlling shareholder. A controlling shareholder acting as officer or administrative council member cumulates the duties and responsibilities relating to that position.

Shareholder Meetings

The general meeting is called and opened in accordance with Law Number 6404 of 15 December 1975.[8] Specific rules may be established by the statutes. Certain decisions may only be taken at the general meeting,[9] such as the amendment of the statutes, the appointment of company officers, the approval of the yearly accounts, the issuance of debentures, and the suspension of the rights of a shareholder.

In addition, it is necessary to call a general meeting to resolve the company's transformation, consolidation, incorporation, and divestment, dissolution, and liquidation. In case of bankruptcy or reorganization, a general meeting must be called. However, in case of urgency, the filing for bankruptcy or the request for reorganization may be made by the officers, as agreed with the majority shareholder, if any, and a general meeting must be immediately called in order to ratify the decision.

Except if otherwise established by the statutes, the general meeting must be called by the administrative council, if any, or by the directors of the company if the company does not have an administrative council.[10] A general meeting also may be called by the administrative council, if any. Shareholders representing at least five per cent of the equity are entitled to call a general meeting should the company's officers delay the call for more than eight days after a request is presented by that shareholder. In the event the officers delay the call for more than sixty days, the general meeting may be called by any shareholder.

The call must be made by means of a notice published on at least three occasions which, in addition to the place, date, and time of the general meeting, must contain the agenda and, in the case of an amendment to the statutes, an indication of the topics to be amended. The first call of the general meeting must be made, in a closely-held company, at least eight days in advance counted from the date of publication of the first notice; if the meeting is not held, a new notice of the second call must be published at least five days prior to the meeting.

---

[8] Law Number 6404 of 15 December 1975, Article 121.
[9] Law Number 6404 of 15 December 1975, Article 122.
[10] Law Number 6404 of 15 December 1975, Articles 123 and 124.

In a publicly-held company, the first call must be made fifteen days in advance, and the second call eight days in advance. The general meeting is opened on first call with the presence of shareholders representing at least one-quarter of the voting capital; on the second call, it is opened with any number. Shareholders without voting rights may attend the general meeting and take part in the discussions of any of the matters being voted.

Except as otherwise established in the statutes, general meetings must be presided by a board composed of a chairman and a secretary, both chosen by the shareholders attending the meeting. The resolutions of a general meeting must be passed by simple majority of votes. Abstentions are not taken into account, except as otherwise established. The statutes of a closed-held company may increase the quorum required for certain resolutions.

In the event of an equal number of votes being cast in favor of or against a resolution, if the statutes do not provide for arbitration and do not contain any provision to the contrary, a general meeting must be called after a period of at least two months to vote the resolution; if the equality in votes persists and the shareholders do not agree to entrust the decision to a third party, it must be incumbent upon the court to decide the issue in accordance with the best interests of the company.

The proceedings and resolutions of the general meeting must be recorded in the appropriate book in minutes signed by the presiding board and by the shareholders attending the meeting.[11] For the minutes to be valid, it must contain the signature of as many shareholders as necessary for the resolution's approval. Attested or certified copies must be made of the minutes for legal purposes.

General Meetings

In General

There are two types of general meetings: the annual meetings, which are held yearly, and the extraordinary meeting, which may be called at any time. Both the annual meeting and the extraordinary meeting may be called and held together in the same place, on the same date, and at the same time, and may be recorded in a single set of minutes.

---

[11] Law Number 6404 of 15 December 1975, Article 130.

Annual Meeting

The annual meeting of shareholders must be held every year during the first four months after the closing of the fiscal year (31 December of each year). Incumbent to the annual meeting are the exam and approval of the financial statements, the destination of the net profits, and the election of officers and members of the administrative council and the administrative council, if any.

At least one month before the general meeting, the officers must give notice to the shareholders that the relevant documents are available for inspection, such as the management report, the financial statements, and the opinion of the independent auditors, among others, that are relevant or of interest to the shareholders.

The notices must indicate the place or places where the shareholders may obtain copies of such documents. The minutes of the annual general meeting must be registered at the Commercial Registry and published in the newspaper. Publication is not necessary for companies whose directors are the only shareholders.

Extraordinary Meetings

Any matter of interest to the company or the shareholders may be brought to the shareholders at any time by means of the convocation of an extraordinary meeting.[12] An extraordinary meeting called to amend the statutes must only be opened on the first call if shareholders representing at least two-thirds of the voting capital are present, but may be opened on the second call with any number.

Law Number 6404 of 15 December 1975 establishes that certain matters may be decided only by a specific number of votes. The approval of shareholders representing at least one-half of the voting shares must be necessary for a resolution merging the company with another company or authorizing the participation in a group of companies or the division or termination of the company.

Shareholders dissenting from certain decisions, such as a change in the company's purposes, have the right to withdraw and claim the reimbursement of shares within the next thirty days from the publication of the minutes of the general meeting.[13] A shareholder who fails to exercise the right to withdraw within the prescribed period will lose such right.

---

12 Law Number 6404 of 15 December 1975, Articles 135.
13 Law Number 6404 of 15 December 1975, Article 137.

Share Transfer Restrictions

A share is indivisible in relation to the company.[14] When a share belongs to more than one person, the rights conferred by it must be exercised by the representative of the co-holders. A share of a publicly-held company may only be traded after thirty per cent of its issue price has been paid. The non-compliance with this obligation voids the transaction.

The company may not trade on its own shares.[15] This prohibition does not apply in case of redemption, refund, or amortization operations. Nor does this prohibition apply in case of acquisition of shares to be held in the company's treasury or canceled. A company willing to acquire its own shares must obtain the previous approval of the Brazilian Securities and Exchange Commission. The company may not receive its own shares as a guarantee, except to guarantee the officers in the performance of the respective duties before the company.

Shares held in a company's treasury do not have the right to receive dividends or to vote. The ownership of registered shares is evidenced by the record of the same in the company's books or by the certificate supplied by the custody agent acting as fiduciary owner of the shares. The transfer of shares is enforceable before the company and third parties if recorded in the company's books, with the signature of both assignor and assignee.

The transfer of registered shares by inheritance, legacy, award, court order, or other judicial act or by any other means is accomplished with the record of the act in the company's books. The document authorizing the transfer must be kept in the company's files.[16] In the case of transfer of registered shares acquired at the Stock Exchange, the assignee must be represented by the brokerage company or Stock Exchange liquidation department, which may act without a power of attorney.

The statutes of the company may require all the company's shares, or one or more classes thereof, to be kept in deposit accounts in the name of their holders at an institution designated by the company, without issuing share certificates. Only financial institutions authorized by the Brazilian Securities and Exchange Commission may keep book entry share services. The company will be liable for losses and damages resulting from errors or irregularities in book entries.[17]

---

14 Law Number 6404 of 15 December 1975, Article 28.
15 Law Number 6404 of 15 December 1975, Article 30.
16 Law Number 6404 of 15 December 1975, Article 31, Paragraph 2.
17 Law Number 6404 of 15 December 1975, Article 34, Paragraph 3.

The statutes of a privately-held company may impose restrictions on the transfer of registered shares, provided that such restrictions are defined in detail and do not preclude their negotiability nor subject the shareholder to the arbitrary decision of the administrative bodies of the company or of the majority of shareholders.

A restriction on the transfer of shares created by an amendment to the statutes must only be applied to shares whose holders have expressly agreed to such a restriction, by requesting its record in the books of the company. By notice to the Stock Exchange on which its shares are dealt with and by publication of a notice, a publicly-held company may suspend the transfer, conversion, and division of its shares for periods not exceeding fifteen days each or a total of ninety days during the year. The provisions may not affect the registration of share transfers negotiated on the Stock Exchange prior to the beginning of the suspension period.

Rights in Proxy Voting

Persons attending a general meeting must produce proof of the respective shareholder status in accordance with certain rules of Law Number 6404 of 15 December 1975. Specific rules may be established by the statutes, such as share certificates or receipts of deposit or record.[18]

A shareholder may be represented at a general meeting by a proxy appointed less than one year before, who must be a shareholder, a company officer, or a lawyer.[19] In a publicly-held company, the proxy also may be a financial institution.[20] The legal representative of a shareholder must be authorized to attend general meetings. Before a general meeting is opened, the shareholders must sign the attendance book, indicating their name, nationality, and residence, as well as the number, type, and class of shares owned.

A shareholder resident or domiciled abroad must maintain a representative in Brazil empowered to accept service of process in proceedings based on Law Number 6404 of 15 December 1975. This proxy will exercise the voting rights of that shareholder.[21] The exercise of any shareholder right must authorize the service of process related to company matters against that shareholder in the person having exercised that right, irrespective of the content of the power of attorney or any other empowering document.

---

18 Law Number 6404 of 15 December 1975, Article 126.
19 Law Number 6404 of 15 December 1975, Article 126, Paragraph 1.
20 Law Number 6404 of 15 December 1975, Article 126, Paragraph 1.
21 Law Number 6404 of 15 December 1975, Article 119.

Access to Company Information

A company may have an administrative council and the statutes must make provision for its operation. The committee may be either permanent or appointed for a specific fiscal year, at the request of the shareholders.[22] The administrative council must be composed of at least three and not more than five members and an equal number of alternates, who must be elected at a general meeting and who may or may not be shareholders.

When not operating on a permanent basis, the administrative council must be appointed by the general shareholders' meeting at the request of shareholders representing at least one-tenth of the voting shares or five per cent of the nonvoting shares, and each period of operation must terminate at the first annual general meeting held after its appointment.

The request for the administrative council to operate, even if the subject is not included in the call notice, may be made at any general meeting, which must elect the members of the committee. Certain rules must be observed in appointing the administrative council. The holders of preferred shares without voting rights or with restricted voting rights must be entitled to elect one member and his alternate in a separate election.[23]

The minority shareholders must have the same right, provided they jointly represent ten per cent or more of the voting shares. Notwithstanding the provisions of the previous item, the other shareholders with the right to vote may elect the effective members and the alternates, who, in any event, must be equal in number to those elected under the above, plus one. The members of the administrative council and their alternates must hold office until the next annual general meeting held after their election, and may be re-elected.

The members of the administrative council and their alternates must exercise their positions until the first general meeting which takes place after election, reelection being permitted. The duties of a member of the administrative council may not be delegated. Only a person who resides in Brazil and is a university graduate or has held a position of company officer or administrative council member for at least three years may be elected to the administrative council.[24]

In a place where there are not enough persons qualified to hold such a position, a judge may excuse the company from meeting the

---

22 Law Number 6404 of 15 December 1975, Article 161.
23 Law Number 6404 of 15 December 1975, Article 161, Paragraph 4.
24 Law Number 6404 of 15 December 1975, Article 162.

requirements. A member of an administrative body and an employee of the company or of a controlled company or a company in the same group, and the spouse or any relative up to the third degree of a company officer, may not be elected to the administrative council. Among other obligations, the administrative council must supervise the acts of any officer, and the acts of any director, and ensure that they comply with their legal and statutory duties.

It also must give an opinion on the annual report of the management, as well as on any proposals of the administrative bodies to be submitted to a general meeting. The administrative council must report any error, fraud, and criminal act which may be discovered in regards to any officer or members of the administrative bodies. If the administrative bodies delay the calling of the annual meeting for more than one month, the administrative council must call the annual meeting. The same applies in case of urgent matters, when an extraordinary meeting must be called.

The administrative bodies must provide the members of the administrative council with copies of the minutes of their meetings and of the balance sheets and other financial statements and performance reports of the company. Upon request of any of its members, the administrative council must request clarification or information from the administrative bodies, as well as the draft of special financial or accounting statements. If the company has independent auditors, the administrative council, by request of any of its members, may demand that they provide information considered necessary and investigate specific facts.

In order to perform its obligations, the administrative council may, if the company has no independent auditors, select an accountant or an auditing firm, establishing reasonable remuneration in accordance with current market standards and compatible with the economic resources of the company. This remuneration must be paid by the company. Upon request of shareholders representing at least five per cent of the capital, the administrative council must supply information on matters within its competence.[25]

If the administrative council wishes to ascertain a fact where clarification is needed, it may justifiably obtain expert advice. The members of the administrative council, or at least one of them, must attend the general meetings and must respond to inquiries presented by any shareholder. The opinions and statements of the administrative council, or of any of its members, may be presented and read at the general

---

25 Law Number 6404 of 15 December 1975, Article 163, Paragraph 6.

meeting, irrespective of publication, even if the matter has not been included in the agenda.

The members of the administrative council must have the same duties as the officers and must be liable for any damages resulting from any failure to comply with their duties. The members of the administrative council must perform their duties in accordance with the company's interests. Any action that causes damage to the company or its shareholders or officers must be deemed abusive, as must be deemed abusive the exercise of duties so as to obtain any personal or third-party advantages to which they have no right and which cause damage to the company, its shareholders, or its officers.

A member of the administrative council may not be liable for the illegal acts performed by other members, except if personal liability is attributed to such acts. The members of the administrative council must be jointly and severally liable for omissions in performing their duties, but any dissenting member must be exempt from such liability if he causes his dissent vote to be recorded in the minutes of an administrative council meeting and informs the managing bodies and the general meeting about it.

The members of the administrative council must immediately inform any changes in their ownership position to the Brazilian Securities and Exchange Commission or to entities of the Exchange Market where the securities issued by the company are traded. In addition to the above, any shareholder must have the right to inspect the records and books of the company in the period precedent to the general meeting, in connection with the matters to be discussed in that given meeting.

Inspection of Shareholder Lists

In General

A person may obtain certified copies of the entries made in the shares registry book and in the shares transfer book, as long as it is necessary to the defense of personal rights or the elucidation of personal interest or the interest of any shareholder or the capital market, being the company authorized to be reimbursed for the costs of such copies.[26] The denial of such request must be subject to appeal to the Securities and Exchange Commission.

Additionally, as already mentioned, any shareholder whose shares with or without voting rights represent one-half per cent or more of the

---

26 Law Number 6404 of 15 December 1975, Article 100, Paragraph 1.

capital must be entitled to request a list of the addresses of the shareholders for the purpose of being represented in the shareholders' meetings, giving the possibility that the shareholder may inspect the list of shareholders of the company.[27]

Right to Make Business Proposals

As noted, the administrative council of the company is responsible for the conduction of business activities of the company. If the company does not have an administrative council, the board of directors undertakes this function.

A proposal, however, must be approved by the share-holders and a meeting must be called for that purpose. Shareholders representing at least five per cent of the equity may call a meeting if the board of directors fail to do so when requested by them.[28]

Approval of Business Decisions

Not all business decisions must be submitted to the approval of the shareholders before being implemented. Certain business decisions, such as a merge or the liquidation of the company, however, must be previously approved by the shareholders. An extraordinary meeting must be called to that purpose.

Derivative Suits

Shareholders may sue the company for non-compliance with corporate governance rules. There also is the possibility to file a motion on behalf of the company to obtain compensation for damages that the company incurred because of the violation of corporate governance rules.[29]

If all shareholders were affected by the damages as a result of the company's violation of corporate governance rules, the filing of class actions to recover said damages is possible. The right to sue the company's officer or controlling shareholder is guaranteed by law, which provides civil liability for the company's controller when any misconduct is proved.

---

27 Law Number 6404 of 15 December 1975, Article 126, Paragraph 3.
28 Law Number 6404 of 15 December 1975, Article 123.
29 Law Number 6404 of 15 December 1975, Article 159.

In most cases, these lawsuits involve public companies and disputes are disclosed to the public. The officers have duties and responsibilities to the company and its shareholders, including the duty to be diligent and loyal. The misuse of the powers entrusted to the officers will entail liability suits.

Officer Duties

Duty of Diligence

In the exercise of his duties, a company's officer must employ the care and diligence which an industrious and honest individual customarily employs in the administration of his own affairs.[30] An officer must use the powers conferred upon him by law and by the statutes to achieve the company's purposes and to support its best interests, including public interests and the role of the company in the community.

An officer elected by a group or class of shareholders must have the same duties toward the company as any other officers and may not fail to fulfill such duties, even if contradictory to the interests of the shareholders who elected him. An officer is prohibited from performing any act of generosity to the detriment of the company.

Without the prior approval of the shareholders or the administrative council, any officer is prohibited from borrowing money or property from the company or using its property, services, or taking advantages for his own benefit or for the benefit of a company in which he or a third party has an interest.

Additionally, any officer is prohibited to receive from third parties any kind of advantage, except if expressly authorized by the statutes or by the shareholders in a general meeting. Any sums received in violation to the above belong to the company. In view of the company's responsibilities towards the community, the administrative council or the board of directors may authorize reasonable gratuities to benefit the employees or the community.

Duty of Loyalty

The officers must serve the company with loyalty, must treat its affairs with confidentiality, and may not use any commercial opportunity which

---

30 Law Number 6404 of 15 December 1975, Article 153.

may come to their knowledge for their own benefit or of a third party.[31] The officers may not fail to exercise or protect the company's interests.

The officers of publicly-held companies must treat in confidence any information not yet revealed to the public, which they obtained by virtue of their position and which may significantly affect the value of securities of the company. The officers must ensure that the duties mentioned above are not infringed by a subordinate or third party enjoying their confidence. A person detrimentally affected in a purchase or sale of securities effected in violation of the provisions mentioned above, may claim indemnity from the person responsible for the infringement.[32] An officer receiving confidential information not yet revealed to the public may not make use of such information to obtain any advantages for himself or for third parties by purchasing or selling securities.

Conflicts of Interest

An officer may not take part in any corporate transaction in which he has an interest which conflicts with an interest of the company, nor in the decisions made by the other officers on the matter.[33] He must disclose this circumstance to the other officers and must cause the nature and extent of his interest to be recorded in the minutes of the administrative council, or board of directors' meeting.

Notwithstanding compliance with the disclosure obligation, an officer may only contract with the company under reasonable and fair conditions, identical to those which prevail in the market or under which the company would contract with third parties. A matter effected otherwise than in accordance with the above is voidable and the concerned officer must be obliged to transfer to the company all benefits which he may have obtained or will obtain in such business.[34]

Duty to Inform

Upon signing the nomination document, the officer of a publicly-held company must declare the number of shares, subscription bonuses, options to purchase shares, and convertible debentures issued by the company, by a controlled company, or by a company belonging to the same group, which he owns.

---

31 Law Number 6404 of 15 December 1975, Article 155.
32 Law Number 6404 of 15 December 1975, Article 155, Paragraph 3.
33 Law Number 6404 of 15 December 1975, Article 156.
34 Law Number 6404 of 15 December 1975, Article 2, Paragraph 2.

At the request of shareholders representing five per cent or more of the capital, an officer of a publicly-held company must disclose to the annual general meeting the number of securities issued by the company or by a controlled company or a company belonging to the same group which he has acquired or disposed of, either directly or through other persons, during the previous fiscal year.[35]

The same obligation applies in case of options to purchase shares which the officer has acquired or exercised during the previous fiscal year, and in case of direct or incidental fringe benefits or advantages which he has received or is receiving from the company and from associated or controlled companies or companies belonging to the same group, as well as in case of any other matter which is relevant to the company's activities. A clarification offered by an officer may, at the request of any shareholder, be put into writing, authenticated by the board of the general meeting, and copies thereof furnished upon request.

The disclosure of the above matters may only be utilized in the legitimate interests of the company or of a shareholder, under risk of personal liability for misuse. The officers of a publicly-held company must immediately inform the Stock Exchange and publish in the press any resolution of a general meeting or of the company's administrative bodies or any relevant fact which occurs in its business affairs, which may substantially influence the decision of market investors to sell or buy securities issued by the company.

The officers may refuse to give such information or refrain from publishing it, should they feel that its disclosure would subject a legitimate interest of the company to risk.[36] In such an event, the Securities and Exchange Commission, at the request of the officers, any shareholder, or on its own initiative, must then decide whether the information should be provided and the officers held liable.

Officers of a publicly-held company must immediately inform, as specified by the Securities and Exchange Commission and the Stock Exchanges or any organized Exchange Market entities where the securities issued by the company are traded, of any changes to their ownership positions in the company.

Officer Liability

An officer may not be personally liable for the commitments he undertakes on behalf of the company and acts practiced in the ordinary

---

35 Law Number 6404 of 15 December 1975, Article 157, Paragraph 1.
36 Law Number 6404 of 15 December 1975, Article 157, Paragraph 5.

course of business. The officer must, however, be liable for losses and damages caused by acts practiced beyond his authority or in violation of the law or of the statutes of the company.

An officer may not be liable for unlawful acts of the other officers, except when acting in collusion with them, when neglecting to investigate such acts, or when, despite his knowledge, he fails to take preventive action. A dissenting officer must be exempt from liability when he makes his dissent to be recorded in the minutes of the meeting of the administrative body. If this is not possible, the officer must immediately inform the administrative body, the administrative council, or the shareholders about his dissent in writing in order to be exempted from liability.

The officers must be jointly and severally liable for losses and damages caused by failure to comply with the duties to ensure the normal operation of the company, even when in accordance with the statutes such duties do not apply to all officers. In a publicly-held company, the liability described above must be restricted to those officers who have the specific responsibilities for the performance of such duties.

An officer who knows of any failure to comply with such duties by his predecessor or by an officer responsible under the above, and who fails to bring such fact to the knowledge of the shareholders, must become jointly and severally liable for such non-compliance.[37] Anyone who acts in violation of the law or of the statutes of the company with the intention of obtaining undue advantages either for himself or for a third party must be jointly and severally liable with the officer.

Liability Action

By a resolution passed in a general meeting, the company may bring an action for civil liability against any officer for the losses caused to the company's property.[38] The resolution may be passed at an annual general meeting and, if included in the agenda or arising directly out of any matter included therein, at an extraordinary general meeting.

The officer or officers against whom the legal action is to be filed must be replaced at the same general meeting. A shareholder may bring the action if proceedings are not initiated within three months from the date of the resolution at the general meeting. Should the general meeting

---

37 Law Number 6404 of 15 December 1975, Article 158, Paragraph 4.
38 Law Number 6404 of 15 December 1975, Article 159, Paragraph 6.

decide not to initiate a proceeding, it may be initiated by shareholders representing at least five per cent of the capital.

Any damages recovered by proceedings initiated by a shareholder must be transferred to the company, but the company must reimburse said shareholder for all expenses incurred up to the limit of such damages. The officer may be excused by court judgment if the court understands that he acted in good faith and in the interests of the company.[39] The action initiated on behalf of the company may not preclude any action available to any shareholder or third party directly harmed by the acts of the officer.

Technical and Consultative Bodies

The obligations referred to above apply to the members of everybody created by the statutes.

Distributions

Income

Income will be deducted before any profit-sharing assignment, by accrued losses and by the provision for income tax. Losses of a particular fiscal year must be absorbed by retained earnings, by profit reserves, and by the legal reserve, in that order.[40]

Subject to the statutes, the company must present to the general meeting, together with the financial statements of the fiscal year, a proposal on the intended use of the net profit. Before any other use, five per cent of the net profit must be allocated to form the so-called Legal Reserve, which may not exceed twenty per cent of the capital. The company may refrain from allocating resources to the legal reserve during any fiscal year in which the balance of such reserve, taken together with the amount of the capital reserves, exceeds thirty per cent of the capital.

The legal reserve is intended to guarantee the capital and may only be utilized to offset losses or to increase the capital. The statutes may create extraordinary reserves. Upon a proposal by the administrative bodies, a general meeting may decide to withhold a portion of the net

---

[39] Law Number 6404 of 15 December 1975, Article 159.
[40] Law Number 6404 of 15 December 1975, Articles 189–199.

profit, according to the capital budget previously approved by that general meeting. The budget submitted by the administrative bodies with the justification for the proposed retention of profits must include all the sources and application of either fixed or working capital, and may cover up to five fiscal years, except in the event of an investment program executed over a longer period of time.

The budget may be approved in a general meeting. The balance sheet for the fiscal year, revised annually when applicable for more than one fiscal year, also must be approved in a general meeting. The allocation of profits to constitute reserves or the retention of profits as mentioned above may not be approved in each fiscal year if detrimental to the distribution of compulsory dividends.

Reserves

The company may only pay dividends by debiting net profits, retained earnings, or profit or capital reserves.[41] Notwithstanding any appropriate criminal sanctions, the officers and administrative council members must be jointly liable to reimburse the company for the amount distributed in excess of the legal or approved amounts.

The shareholders, however, must be under no obligation to repay the dividend they received in good faith.[42] Bad faith must be presumed when the dividend is distributed without the preparation of the balance sheet or without observing it. In every fiscal year, the shareholders must be entitled to receive a compulsory dividend equivalent to the portion of the profits as may be stated in the statutes.

The statutes may prescribe the dividend as a percentage of the profits or of the capital, or establish other criteria for its determination, provided they are prescribed adequately and in detail and do not subject the minority shareholders to the discretion of the administrative bodies or of the majority. When the statutes are silent and the general meeting resolves to amend the statutes in order to regulate compulsory dividends, the compulsory dividend may not be less than twenty-five per cent of the net profit.

As long as no shareholder opposes it, a general meeting may resolve to distribute a dividend which is less than the compulsory dividend or to retain the entire net profit. The dividend prescribed may not be compulsory in a fiscal year in which the administrative bodies notify

---

41 Law Number 6404 of 15 December 1975, Articles 201–205.
42 Law Number 6404 of 15 December 1975, Article 201, Paragraph 2.

the general meeting that its payment would be incompatible with the financial standing of the company.[43] The administrative council, if in operation, must deliver an opinion on any such notice and, in a public company, the officers must forward to the Brazilian Securities and Exchange Commission, within five days of holding the general meeting, an explanation justifying the notice.

A company which prepares a balance sheet every half year by virtue of any legal or statutory provision may, by resolution of the administrative bodies, if so authorized in its statutes, declare a dividend from the profit ascertained in such balance sheet. Where in accordance with statutory provision, a company may prepare a balance sheet and distribute dividends at shorter intervals. The total dividend paid in each half year of any fiscal year may not exceed the amount of the capital reserves. The statutes may authorize the administrative bodies to declare an interim dividend from the accrued profits or profit reserves existing in the last annual or semi-annual balance sheet.

Dividends

A company must pay a dividend to the person who is registered as the owner or the beneficiary of usufruct of the share on the date on which the dividend is declared. The dividend may be paid by a check sent by post to the address provided to the company by the shareholder, or by a credit to a bank account opened in the name of the shareholder.

The dividend paid in respect of shares held in the custody of, or on deposit at, a bank must be paid by the company to the financial depositary, which must be responsible for its transmission to the holders of the deposited shares. Except as otherwise resolved by the general meeting, the dividend must be paid within sixty days from the date on which it is declared and, in any event, during the fiscal year.[44]

Shareholders and Tender Offers

The acquisition of control in a Brazilian publicly-held company may be accomplished through purchase of a controlling stake directly from existing controlling shareholders, or purchase of outstanding shares

---

43 Law Number 6404 of 15 December 1975, Article 202, Paragraph 2.
44 Law Number 6404 of 15 December 1975, Article 205, Paragraph 3.

from different shareholders which represent, in the aggregate, a controlling stake, where no specific shareholder or group of shareholders holds enough shares to control the company.[45] The potential purchaser may acquire control by simply negotiating a private acquisition with the controlling shareholders, provided that minority shareholders' rights to tag-along and disclosure duties are observed.

The transfer of control occurs when controlling shareholders directly or indirectly assign, by a single transaction or series of transactions, voting shares, securities convertible into voting shares, or subscription rights to voting shares or to any type of securities convertible into voting shares as a result of which a third party acquires control of the publicly-held company. The purchaser must ensure that all non-controlling holders of the targeted voting shares have the opportunity to sell their stake at a price equivalent to at least eighty per cent of the price paid per share to the controlling shareholders under the same payment conditions offered to controlling shareholders.

In order to grant minority shareholders tag-along rights, a mandatory tender offer must be implemented by the purchaser for the acquisition of up to all voting shares held by non-controlling shareholders of the targeted stake. Only voting shares are granted tag-along rights. However, it is not uncommon for publicly-held companies to grant such rights to preferred shares or to increase the tag-along percentage to one hundred per cent of the total price paid by the purchaser to the controlling share-holders. The majority of such cases refer to companies listed for trading based on different corporate governance levels.

The tag-along tender offer must be filed for registration with the Securities and Exchange Commission within thirty calendar days of the execution of a binding instrument of sale of shares representing the controlling stake. Due to certain characteristics of the local Exchange Market, acquisition of control directly through market transactions is still uncommon. Nonetheless, such acquisitions may be performed by means of either a voluntary tender offer, which would be an unsolicited offer, or the acquisition of shares in the Stock Exchange market.

The voluntary tender offer may comprise one or more types of shares (i.e., only common shares or preferred shares, or both) and must contemplate an amount of shares sufficient to assure the purchaser. Although there is no preset maximum amount of shares for a voluntary tender offer, most publicly-held companies, without clearly identifiable controlling shareholders, have by-laws provisions that compel a

---

45 Law Number 6404 of 15 December 1975, Articles 254–263.

purchaser to extend its offer to all shareholders. Anyone who intends to acquire control of a publicly-held company must deal with at least one tender offer. In a private transaction, a tag-along tender offer will apply in relation to minority shareholders.

Tender offers are processed in very similar ways regardless of their nature and whether or not they are subject to registration with the Securities and Exchange Commission. The tender offer begins with the disclosure and publication of a tender offer notice and instrument, which must disclose all necessary information in order to allow shareholders to assess whether to accept such offer and specify all terms and conditions applicable to it. In addition, a single tender offer may be formulated to accomplish two or more different purposes, such as tag along and delisting, provided that such purposes are compatible with each other.

A tender offer must be intermediated by a brokerage house, a securities dealer, or a financial institution with an investment portfolio which, among other obligations, must assure the financial settlement of the transaction. The price applicable to a tender offer will vary depending on its purpose. In a transaction for acquisition of control in the market, the voluntary tender offer will have a price freely set by the interested party. In a tag-along tender offer the price must be equal to at least eighty per cent of the price per target share paid by the purchaser to the controlling shareholders.

Conclusion

The subject is vast and may be examined from various perspectives, each with their own aspects. As seen above, the liability of the shareholder is limited to the amount of capital subscribed but may be mitigated under certain circumstances, particularly in case of abuse or misuse of the voting rights, entailing civil and criminal lawsuits.

Croatia

Dionis Jurić, Antonija Zubović, and Edita Čulinović Herc
University of Rijeka Faculty of Law
Rijeka, Croatia

Introduction

In December 1993, the Croatian Parliament enacted a new Companies Act[1] that was modelled on German and Austrian company law. The fundamental principles set forth in the Companies Act include a uniform code that regulates both partnerships and companies. The Companies Act, moreover, regulates groups of companies, mergers, divisions, conversions of companies, and the legal status of foreign companies.

It was revised several times from 2003 to 2015 with contemporary changes in European Union (EU) company law. In this way, the Companies Act was harmonized with contemporary European Directives and regulations on Company Law. The Act on the Introduction of *Societas Europea* and the European Economic Interest Grouping was introduced in 2007.[2]

The number of registered joint-stock companies is 1,361, of which 983 are active joint-stock companies (March 2016).[3] They constitute 0.7 per cent of the registered companies in Croatia. The number of listed companies on the Zagreb Stock Exchange (ZSE) was 163 (26 companies on the Official Market, 104 companies on the Regular Market, and 33 companies on the MTF) (December 2015).[4] The total market capitalization of the ZSE in 2015 was HRK 208.85-million, and the turnover of transactions was HRK 3.5-billion.

The current and former workers of the companies usually participate in the ownership structure of the companies. Management board and supervisory board members also own shares in companies, mostly as a

---

1 Companies Act, *Official Gazette*, Numbers 111/93, 34/99, 121/99, 52/00, 118/03, 107/07, 146/08, 137/09, 125/11, 152/11, 111/12, 68/13, and 110/15.
2 Act on Introduction of the *Societas Europea* and the European Economic Interest Grouping, *Official Gazette*, Numbers 107/07 and 110/15.
3 Central Bureau of Statistics, see http://www.dzs.hr/.
4 Zagreb Stock Exchange, Trading Summary 2015, see http://zse.hr/UserDocsImages/reports/ZSE-2015-eng.pdf, at pp. 14–16.

result of the privatization rather than remuneration of the members of management boards in shares or options.

The Corporate Governance Code was adopted in 2007 by the Financial Services Supervisory Agency (HANFA). The Code is based on the principle "comply or explain"; if a listed public company does not comply with a recommendation, it must provide reasons for such exception. In December 2010, HANFA and the ZSE enacted the new Cor-porate Governance Code 2010, which entered into force on 1 January 2011. Rules of the Code 2010 were harmonized with the Capital Market Act,[5] the Companies Act, and the Listing Rules of the ZSE, which were enacted and revised from 2007 to 2010. Code 2010 is mandatory for all listed companies except for investment companies.

Croatia transposed the provisions of the Shareholders' Rights Directive,[6] the Transparency Directive,[7] and the Takeover Bids Directive.[8] Provisions of the Shareholders' Rights Directive and the Transparency Directive are implemented into Croatian law by virtue of the Companies Act and the Capital Market Act, while the provisions of the Takeover Bids Directive are implemented by virtue of the Takeover Act.[9]

The main goal of these modifications was a higher protection of the minority shareholders. This protection is realized by the provisions of exercising of voting rights ("control rights") and economic interests ("economic rights" or "ownership rights") in the company. In addition, the Takeover Act imposes an obligation on the controlling shareholder to launch the takeover bid if a certain percentage of voting rights is acquired in the respective listed joint-stock company. Therefore, shareholders are given a chance to exit their investment by accepting the takeover bid.

---

5 Capital Market Act, *Official Gazette*, Numbers 88/08, 146/08, 74/09, 54/13, 159/13, 18/15, and 110/15.
6 Directive 2007/36/EC of the European Parliament and of the Council of 11 July 2007 on the exercise of certain rights of shareholders in listed companies, OJ L 184, 14 July 2007, at pp. 17–24.
7 Directive 2004/109/EC of the European Parliament and of the Council of 15 December 2005 on the harmonization of transparency requirements in relation to information about issuers whose securities are admitted to trading on a regulated market and amending Directive 2001/34/EC, OJ L 390, 31 December 2004, at pp. 38–57.
8 Directive 2004/25/EC of the European Parliament and of the Council of 21 April 2004 on takeover bids, OJ L 142, 30 April 2004, at pp. 12–23.
9 Act on the Takeover of Joint Stock Companies, *Official Gazette*, Numbers 109/07, 36/09, 108/12, 90/13, 99/13, and 148/13.

Allocation of Powers between Shareholders and Directors

In General

Croatian corporate governance has features of the "block holder" model. In 1993, Croatia accepted a mandatory two-tier board system for all joint-stock companies. As a consequence of harmonization of Croatian company law with European Directives and Regulations, since the revision of the Companies Act in 2007, it has been possible to introduce a one-tier board system. However, only two listed companies have a one-tier board system.[10]

There are significant differences between the two-tier and one-tier board systems. In the two-tier system, the management board is responsible for the management of the company's business and its representation. The authority of the management board to represent the company may not be restricted. However, in relation to the company, the members of the management board must comply with the restrictions lawfully imposed on them by the articles of association, decisions of the supervisory board, general meeting, and rules of procedure of the management board (Article 242 of the Companies Act).

According to Article 243 of the Companies Act, the management board has the competence to prepare, at the request of the general meeting, decisions and bylaws whose adoption is within the competence of the general meeting, to prepare contracts that may be signed only with the consent of the general meeting, and to enforce decisions adopted by the general meeting within its competence. The management board convenes sessions of the general meeting and prepares the agenda.

The Companies Act prescribes the situations when the management board has the obligation to submit the reports to the supervisory board. It must submit periodical reports on current and future business activities. Furthermore, the supervisory board may require the management board to report on other matters of importance for business activities and the condition of the company, and it may at any time request the management board to provide information on matters related to the business activities of the company which either have or may reasonably be expected to have a material impact on the condition of the company.

---

10 Annual Report on Corporate Governance 2014, see http://www.hanfa.hr/EN/nav/109/godisnje-izvjesce---engleski.html.

In addition, the management board has the obligation to prepare for the general meeting an annual report on the company's condition and a consolidated annual report in case of affiliated companies. In a case of insolvency or over-indebtedness, the management board is obliged, without delay and, at the latest, three weeks after the occurrence of the event that is the cause of bankruptcy, to request initiation of bankruptcy proceedings.

In the one-tier system, the board of directors manages the business of the company and fixes principles for performance of the company's business, supervises executive directors, and represents the company towards executive directors. Furthermore, the board of directors is obliged to convene sessions of the general meeting and prepare the agenda when the interests of the company so require. It submits a written report to the general meeting with regard to the supervision of executive directors and takes measures for systematic control of the management of the company.

In a case of insolvency or over-indebtedness, the board of directors is obliged to request the initiation of bankruptcy proceedings. According to Article 272h, Paragraph 5, of the Companies Act, the board of directors and executive directors adopt annual accounts of the company. However, the articles of association may determine that the adoption of annual accounts is in the competencies of the general meeting.

Another difference between the two-tier system and one-tier system lies in the fact that in a two-tier system the supervisory board may revoke its decision on the appointment of members of the management board or its chairman for which there must be a just cause. This, for example, may be a gross violation of duty, inability to orderly conduct the business of the company, or non-issuance of clearance by the general meeting, unless such vote was made for manifestly unfounded reasons. On the other hand, in a one-tier board system, autonomy of executive directors is weakened because they must manage the company in accordance with decisions of the board of directors and they can be removed from the position without just cause at any time.

It may be determined either by the articles of association or by a decision of the supervisory board that particular operations are to be carried out only upon consent of the supervisory board. Therefore, the supervisory board gives consent to a member of the management board to carry out activities which are competitive to the business of the company or to conclude contracts with the company. It also gives consent to the company for granting loans to management board members, procurators, and their immediate family members. The board of directors has similar powers with regard to executive directors in the one-tier board system.

Shareholders exercise their rights with respect to the company through the general meeting. Members of managerial and supervisory bodies of the company must participate in the work of the general meeting. The general meeting decides upon issues explicitly stipulated by the Companies Act and the articles of association of the company, and in particular on:

(1) Election and revocation of membership on the supervisory board and board of directors, unless they have been appointed;
(2) Distribution of profits;
(3) Issuance of clearance to members of managerial and supervisory bodies;
(4) Appointment of mandatory auditors;
(5) Amendment of the articles of association of the company;
(6) Increase and reduction of the share capital of the company;
(7) Appointment of special auditors;
(8) Listing and delisting of company's shares on the regulated market; and
(9) Dissolution of the company.

Furthermore, the general meeting approves reorganization measures (mergers, divisions, conversions, and transfer of assets) and entrepreneurial contracts. It also adopts decisions on the assertion of the claim against members of managerial and supervisory bodies of the company for indemnity caused by their malpractice.[11]

Shareholders' Right to Make Business Proposals and Give Approval of Business Decisions

The general meeting shall decide upon issues related to the management of the company's business affairs only if requested to do so by the management board or executive directors.[12] This usually refers to cases when the management board or executive directors do not receive from the board of directors or supervisory board prior approval for certain types of jobs, which they should have requested under the articles of association.

---

11 Companies Act, Article 273a.
12 Companies Act, Article 275.

In order for a decision to be reached at the general meeting, the management board or executive directors must put the issue on the agenda of the general meeting. However, the general meeting may refuse to decide on what the management, i.e., executive directors, have requested.[13]

The general meeting must decide on such consent with at least three-fourths of all votes. The articles of association may require a larger majority for that decision and may impose additional requirements.[14] If a decision is reached at the general meeting, this decision is binding for all bodies of the company. Thus, the general meeting cannot interfere in the management of the company unless the management itself would request that the general meeting decide on some question about the company's business.

In doctrine and jurisprudence, the view is emphasized that, in taking measures to deeply penetrate the membership rights of shareholders, so that it cannot be expected that it can reach a decision on its own, the management board is obliged to seek the consent of the general meeting, although this is not explicitly prescribed by the Companies Act.[15]

Shareholders may only indirectly affect business operations of the company. Thus, minority shareholders may initiate convening of the general meeting and amendment of the agenda. Furthermore, the articles of association may prescribe that certain shareholders may appoint a certain number of members of the supervisory board or the board of directors.[16] The right to appoint members of supervisory bodies of the company may be given only to certain shareholders or to holders of certain shares. In the first case, when the right is given to certain shareholders, the entitled shareholders must be listed by name in the articles of association. When this right is given to the holders of certain shares, the articles of association must individualize these shares.

The holders of certain shares may be entitled by the articles of association to appoint members of supervisory bodies of the company

---

13 The general meeting is not required by law to engage in a discussion and decision-making on the question of running the company's business. The management board and executive directors may request a decision of the general meeting in order for them to be exempted from responsibility within the company. However, it is necessary to emphasize that the decision of the general meeting does not relieve them of the responsibility toward the people outside the company. Companies Act, Article 252, Paragraph 5, and Article 272.1, Paragraph 9.
14 Companies Act, Article 263.
15 *Holzmüller, Entscheidungen des Bundesgerichtshofes in Zivilsachen* (BGHZ), Bd. 83, at pp. 122–144.
16 The shareholders may not appoint more than one-third of members of supervisory bodies of the company. Companies Act, Articles 256 and 272c.

provided that such shares may be transferred only with the consent of the company. Such shares may not constitute a special class of shares. The shareholders may affect the composition of the management board or executive directors in this way, because supervisory bodies of the company have the power to appoint these persons. However, since Article 227, Paragraph 2, of the Companies Act prescribes that the consent of the company for the transfer of shares may be required only for materialized shares, it follows that in the company's articles of association the right to the appointment of supervisory board members may be given only on the basis of materialized shares, but not dematerialized shares.

Therefore, the articles of association cannot give the right to appoint members of the supervisory board to the holders of shares of listed companies. If the company's articles of association were to provide such a provision, it would be null and void. There is no obstacle to appointing a shareholder for a member of the management board or an executive director if he meets criteria for appointment governed by the Companies Act or the articles of association.

Shareholders have the right to submit a counterproposal to the management proposal, i.e., the executive directors, and/or the supervisory, i.e., the management board, on a particular item of the agenda with explanation.[17] Listed companies are obliged to publish draft resolutions on the company's Internet site.

However, if shareholders fail to meet the prescribed deadline to make a counterproposal, this does not mean that they have lost their right to make counter-proposals at the general meeting. The provision of Article 282, Paragraph 2, of the Companies Act prescribes the cases when the company is not obliged to give a statement about the shareholders' counterproposals. The general meeting is authorized to adopt decisions regarding those to:

(1) Issue shares, convertible bonds, and variable interest rate bonds;
(2) Approve contracts by which the company acquires objects or rights from its founders or shareholders whose aggregate shareholding equals at least one-tenth of the share capital of the company and, where these contracts are concluded in the period of two years after the establishment of the company, the company pays the price which is equal to or higher than one-tenth of the share capital;

---

17 The law does not stipulate a deadline in which the counterproposal must be made available to the prescribed persons. Therefore, the management board, i.e., executive directors, would need to make it available without delay after receipt, but only if it is received within the period in which the shareholder may place it.

(3) Consent to waiving a company's claim for compensation of the damage or negotiating a settlement of the claim against founders and members of managerial or supervisory bodies of the company;
(4) Consent to acquisition of own shares and authorize the management board or the board of directors to withdraw own shares by decrease of the share capital of the company;
(5) Grant remuneration to members of the supervisory bodies of the company;
(6) Assert a claim against members of managerial and supervisory bodies of the company for indemnity caused by their malpractice;
(7) Repeal preferred shares;
(8) Transfer minority shareholder shares to the majority shareholder; and
(9) Approve contracts on transfer of the company's entire assets or assets higher than the value of one-quarter of the share capital if this would mean a significant change in the structure of the company to another entity.

The general meeting also may take decisions to exclude priority rights of shareholders at the subscription of new shares in case of the share capital increase; continue the company under liquidation; approve entrepreneurial contracts and their amendment or cancellation; integrate the company into another domestic company; and approve mergers, divisions, and conversions of the company.

Allocation of Powers between Shareholders and Directors in Takeover Process

Croatia has adopted a board neutrality rule and has determined measures that may be taken only with the approval of the shareholders of the target company. According to Article 42, Paragraph 1, of the Takeover Act, target managerial or supervisory bodies may not, without prior approval of the general meeting:
(1) Increase the share capital;
(2) Enter into extraordinary business operations;
(3) Act or enter into operations that could significantly jeopardize future business of the target company;
(4) Decide on the target's acquisition or sale of treasury shares; and
(5) Take actions that would frustrate the bid.

According to Article 42, Paragraph 2, of the Takeover Act, which is in line with Article 9, Paragraph 3, of the Takeover Bids Directive, the decisions of the management or supervisory board that were adopted prior to the date of receipt of the notification or announcement of the same, but that have not been entirely implemented, must be granted an additional approval by the general meeting of the offeree company prior to implementation unless these decisions relate to the regular business operations of the offeree company and their implementation could not impede or frustrate the takeover bid.

The decision of the target's general meeting approving the above-listed decisions of managerial and supervisory bodies will be effective only if passed by a three-quarters majority of the share capital represented at the general meeting when adopting the decision.[18] The decisions of the managerial and supervisory bodies of the target company on taking anti-takeover (defensive) measures in the period from the notification about the occurrence of the obligation of publishing the takeover bid, i.e., their publishing, until the publication of the report on the takeover, are null and void in the event of failure to obtain the approval of the general meeting of the target company.[19]

However, the decision of the target company's managerial and supervisory bodies to search for another bidder (i.e., a "white knight") would not be prohibited and would not require shareholder approval.

The breakthrough rule has been transposed into Croatian law with Articles 43 and 44 of the Takeover Act. According to Croatian law, these provisions apply only if the offeree company has incorporated them into the company's articles of association. The general meeting of the target company makes the decision on the application of the breakthrough rule with the majority of votes representing at least three-quarters of the share capital represented at the general meeting.[20]

According to the Takeover Act, the breakthrough rule is effective upon the announcement of a takeover bid.[21] Thereby, those provisions of the breakthrough rule that apply throughout the duration of the takeover process differ from those provisions applicable upon completion of the takeover. Therefore, during the period for acceptance of the takeover bid, the restrictions on the transfer of shares of the offeree company to the offeror may not have effect, as determined by the articles of association of the offeree company, an agreement between the offeree company

---

18 Takeover Act, Article 42, Paragraph 5.
19 Takeover Act, Article 42, Paragraph 6.
20 Articles of association may determine the greater majority or the fulfillment of additional conditions.
21 This makes the breakthrough rule applicable only to future cases, which narrows the possibility of applying this rule.

and shareholders of the offeree company, or an agreement between shareholders of the offeree company.[22]

According to Article 44, Paragraph 3, of the Takeover Act, restrictions on voting rights provided in the articles of association of the offeree company, the agreement between the offeree company and shareholders of the offeree company, and the agreement between shareholders of the offeree company may not have effect at a general meeting of shareholders that decides on defensive measures. This allows the participation of all shareholders of the target company in dealing with the takeover bid.

Where, after the takeover bid, the offeror holds 75 per cent of voting shares of the offeree company at the first general meeting convened at the request of the offeror for the purpose of amending the articles of association and/or appointing and/or removing from office members of the supervisory board any restrictions on the transfer of shares and restrictions on voting rights determined by the articles of association of the offeree company, an agreement between the offeree company and shareholders of the offeree company, or an agreement between shareholders of the offeree company, will not have effect.

If, pursuant to these provisions, certain rights are forfeited, the offeror is obliged to pay an appropriate indemnification in cash. A right to indemnification may be demanded in court only within two months from the date when the rights were forfeited.[23] Croatia has failed to regulate the application of the principle of reciprocity if the offeror does not apply the board neutrality rule and the breakthrough rule.

Classes of Shareholders

Since 2007, companies may issue only registered shares. Depending on the form of shares, companies are allowed to issue materialized or dematerialized shares. However, listed companies and financial institutions must issue dematerialized shares. According to Article 490 of the Capital Market Act, a dematerialized share is kept as an electronic record of a securities account in the computer system of the central depository, which is operated by the Central Depository and Clearing Company.

---

22 Takeover Act, Article 44, Paragraph 2.
23 Takeover Act, Article 44, Paragraph 6.

Companies may issue ordinary or preference shares. Ordinary shares are shares that entitle the holder to vote in the general meeting of the company, receive a portion of company profits (dividends), and receive a portion of the remainder of the company's assets in the event of liquidation or bankruptcy. Preference shares give certain privileges, such as the right to dividends in previously defined amounts or percentages of nominal share amounts, the right of priority in collecting payments of dividends or remainders of liquidation or bankruptcy estate, or other rights in accordance with the law and the articles of association of the company.

Croatian law permits the issuing of only non-voting preference shares, and it is not allowed to issue non-voting shares without preference. A non-voting preference share may be cumulative or participative. A cumulative non-voting preference share provides its holder, in compliance with the decision on issuing shares, with the right to receive cumulated unpaid dividends before the ordinary shareholders have received these dividends. A participating non-voting preference share entitles its holder to an additional amount of dividend in addition to the dividend belonging to ordinary shares, in compliance with the decision on issuing shares.

Issuing of non-voting shares should be provided for in the articles of association, and their total amount is limited to half of the share capital of the company. The articles of association cannot include provisions that deprive holders of non-voting shares of other control rights except voting rights.

However, if the non-voting preference shareholders are not paid, or only partially paid, their preference dividend and, if this failure has not been made up for in the following year along with the amount of the dividend they are due to receive for that year, they acquire the voting right at the general meeting of the company and may keep it as long as they have not received all dividends to which they are entitled.[24] In this situation, they acquire voting rights automatically, i.e., without the need to make a special decision.

According to Croatian law, preference shares may be converted into ordinary shares by a decision made at the general meeting, which must be reached by a majority of three-quarters of the votes at the general meeting. However, such a decision cannot be made without the special consent of preference shareholders.[25] The conversion of ordinary shares

---

[24] Companies Act, Article 296, Paragraph 2.
[25] Companies Act, Article 279.

into non-voting preference shares can only be done by amending the articles of association, whereby it is necessary that it complies with the limitations for their issue.

In the case of a takeover, the decision to convert ordinary shares into non-voting preference shares significantly affects the position of the potential bidder in a manner that reduces the number of shares that he wishes to acquire since he is generally only interested in shares carrying voting rights. According to Article 169 of the Companies Act, multiple voting rights shares are not permitted. According to the Central Depository and Clearing Company, in June 2016, only 24 listed public companies issued and listed preferred shares on the ZSE.[26]

Shareholder Meetings

Convocation of Shareholder Meetings

The general meeting must be convened as stipulated by the Companies Act and articles of association of the company and where interests of the company require. The management board or executive directors must convene the annual general meeting immediately after receiving the report of the supervisory board or the board of directors on annual accounts, annual report of the company, and decision proposal on distribution of profits.

According to Article 277 of the Companies Act, the annual general meeting must be held in the first eight months of the financial year. The management board or executive directors bring the resolution on convening of the general meeting.[27] The notice on convening shall include all conditions to be fulfilled in order to participate therein and to exercise the voting rights. These conditions may be stipulated by the articles of association (i.e., the duty of shareholders to notify their attendance on the general meeting in advance, to provide evidence of their right to participate, or to vote in the general meeting).

In the case of listed companies, the notice on convening of the general meeting must contain additional information determined by the Companies Act. The notice on convening of the general meeting must

---

26 Central Depository and Clearing Company, Securities list, see http://www.skdd.hr/portal/f?p=100:31:996993962426701.

27 The resolution must include the company name and registered seat of the company and time and location of the general meeting, and indicate the agenda of the general meeting.

be published in the *Company Gazette*, together with the draft resolutions to be adopted at the meeting. If the shareholders are known to the company by name, the general meeting may be convened by a registered mail whereby the day of the letter dispatch is deemed the day of the announcement of the notice.

The Companies Act stipulates the deadline for convening the general meeting. It must be convened not less than one month prior to the day of the meeting.[28] The deadline may be extended by the number of days fixed for notification of attendance or providing the evidence of right to participate or to vote in the general meeting of shareholders.[29]

Finally, minority shareholders who hold shares which constitute one-twentieth of the share capital of the company may initiate convening of the general meeting and amendment of the agenda. It must be noted that this threshold could only be lowered by the articles of association, not increased.[30] Therefore, the position of the shareholders may only be made easier, not more difficult.

Minority shareholders must submit a written request and state the purpose and reasons for convening of the general meeting. They file the request to the management board of the company. They continue to be protected with the provision that provides them with the possibility to address the court in case the management board fails to comply with their request. The court may authorize minority shareholders to convene the general meeting themselves or to publish the items to be resolved at the general meeting.[31] The court also may appoint the chairman of the general meeting.

Right to Include Items on Agenda and Table Draft Resolutions

Minority shareholders are given the right to put items on the agenda of the general meeting and table draft resolutions. The shareholders may do so before the publication of the invitation to participate in and the agenda of the general meeting,[32] as well as after the publication of the invitation and the agenda (amendment of the agenda).[33]

---

28 The day on which the notice on convening of the general meeting is published is not included in the calculation of the required period.
29 Companies Act, Articles 277 and 279.
30 The provision of the articles of association that would prescribe a higher threshold for the convening of the general meeting would be null and void.
31 The company must bear the costs of convening and holding of the general meeting as well as the legal costs.
32 Companies Act, Article 278, Paragraph 2.
33 Companies Act, Article 280, Paragraph 1.

Shareholders whose aggregate shareholding equals one-twentieth of the share capital of the company are entitled to put items on the agenda.[34] If they amend the agenda, each new item must be accompanied by an explanation and a resolution proposal. The request to put items on the agenda must be received by the company not less than twenty-four days prior to the general meeting and, in relation to the listed public companies, not less than thirty days prior to the general meeting.[35] If minority shareholders request amendment of the agenda, this must be published simultaneously with the notice on convening of the general meeting or in any other manner without delay after receiving such request.

Article 280, Paragraph 4, of the Companies Act stipulates that the general meeting cannot decide on the agenda items that are not properly announced. Therefore, if the management board refuses to disclose what the shareholders are requiring or if it fails to do so within the prescribed period, the agenda cannot be amended and the general meeting will decide on the agenda published in the invitation in which it was convened. The shareholder's request then remains a proposal for the convening of the new meeting.

Shareholder Voting

In General

The Shareholders' Rights Directive was implemented by amendments to the Companies Act in 2009, which came into force on 1 May 2010. Although the Shareholders' Rights Directive regulates only listed companies, Croatia broadened its scope to all companies, and there are special rules imposed for listed companies.

Shareholders may exercise their voting rights at the general meeting in person or through a proxy. Voting rights must be proportionate to the nominal value of shares or number of shares without nominal value.

---

[34] This right will be held by the shareholders regardless of whether they requested the convening of the general meeting or not or whether it is convened under the conditions prescribed by the Companies Act.

[35] If a listed company adheres to the legal time limits on the publication of a call to the general meeting (one month before the meeting), shareholders, at the moment when they have received an invitation, must submit an application for putting items on the agenda.

In non-listed companies, it is possible to introduce voting caps in the articles of association. However, limitations applying only to individual shareholders are not permitted.

The general rule states that the right to vote is acquired by full payment of shares. If the articles of association do not provide that the voting right is acquired prior to the full payment of shares and if no share has been fully paid yet, the ratio of voting rights is determined in proportion to the amount of contributions paid. In such cases, the payment of the minimum contribution will give the right to one vote and the fractions of the vote are taken into consideration only to the extent that they result in full votes for the shareholder entitled to vote. According to the Companies Act, by pledging the share, the shareholder does not forfeit his voting rights.

Under Article 279, Paragraph 2, of the Companies Act, a company in its articles of association may require a shareholder to apply for the general meeting in order to be able to participate and/or vote in it. The application form should reach the company at the latest six days prior to the general meeting if a shorter closing date is not otherwise provided for in the articles of association. If identification of the shareholder is required, the deadline for the convocation of a general meeting (at least a month prior to the date of the general meeting) is extended by the length of the registration (identification) period.

The law does not stipulate that a proxy form may be requested within this period; therefore, the company could not lay this down in its articles of association. Thus, the application is relevant and, if a shareholder wants to be represented by a proxy at the general meeting, the proxy must present a proxy form to the general meeting. Otherwise, the shareholder would be unlawfully deprived of the right to exercise management rights at the general meeting.

Decisions at the general meeting are reached by a simple majority vote. Article 289 of the Companies Act provides companies with the opportunity to prescribe with their articles of association the necessary representation of shareholders at the general meeting in order for the decisions made at it to be valid.

The articles of association may prescribe a quorum as a prerequisite for the adoption of all or some decisions. When the articles of association prescribe a quorum for all decisions, in convening the general meeting, it must be determined when to hold the next general meeting in case the requirement of a quorum is not fulfilled at the convened meeting.[36]

However, the Companies Act does not stipulate the minimum time that should pass until the new meeting, but it could be held on the same day, but at a different time. The Companies Act further states that such a meeting can make valid decisions regardless of the number of present shareholders.[37] The determination of a quorum does not affect the majority included in decision making.

Shareholders are allowed to conclude shareholder voting agreements.[38] The Companies Act permits companies to offer to their shareholders any form of participation in the general meeting by electronic means.[39]

The articles of association cannot prescribe that the right to participate in the general meeting can only be achieved by electronic means; nor may they authorize the management board to so decide. According to the Annual Report on Corporate Governance, in 2014, only four listed public companies enabled voting of shareholders by electronic means in six general meetings that were held. Shareholders did not use this option.[40]

Rights in Proxy Voting

Croatian law on voting by proxy is in accordance with the Shareholders' Rights Directive. As has been mentioned, a shareholder may exercise his voting rights at the general meeting through a proxy. Croatian law prescribes specific requirements for exercising the voting right by proxy for the listed companies.

Listed companies are obliged to state in the convocation of the general meeting the procedure for voting by proxy with reference to proxy forms to be used and the manner in which proof of proxy appointment may be submitted to the company by electronic means, and the procedure for voting in writing or by electronic means if the articles of association provide a certain form for exercise of voting rights.[41]

---

36 If it is not specified in the convocation for the general meeting that a new one will take place in the case that the quorum is not met, but that condition has been fulfilled and the main meeting is held, the decisions reached at the meeting are not null and void due to the mentioned omission in the convocation. Decision of the High Commercial Court of 11 December 2007 adopted in Case Number Pž-6317/05.
37 Companies Act, Article 289, Paragraph 2.
38 Companies Act, Article 293.
39 Companies Act, Article 274.
40 Annual Report on Corporate Governance 2014, see http://www.hanfa.hr/EN/nav/109/godisnje-izvjesce---engleski.html, at p. 38.
41 Companies Act, Article 277, Paragraph 4.

Immediately after the convocation of the general meeting, listed companies are obliged to take all necessary measures to make available on their websites the forms to be used to vote by proxy or by correspondence or by electronic means, unless those forms are sent directly to each shareholder. This ensures that shareholders have access to information necessary for exercising their membership rights. However, failure to do so does not render decisions reached at the meeting null and void.

A shareholder may give proxy to one or more persons. Where more than one proxy holder has been appointed by a shareholder, the company may refuse to accept one or more of such proxy. Unless the oral form has been provided for by the articles of association, a written form is necessary for granting and revoking a proxy and proof of appointment of the proxy holder. In the case of listed companies, it is possible at least by electronic means to forward proof of a proxy appointment. According to Article 291 of the Companies Act, a proxy must be submitted to the company, and the company must hold it for safekeeping for not less than three years.

The proxy form is generally submitted by the proxy before the general meeting.[42] In Croatian courts, the view has been taken that it is not possible to set a time limit within which it is necessary to submit a proxy or to link its submission to the application for participation in the general meeting if the obligation to notify is determined by the articles of association.[43] The proxy can be revoked at any time.

According to Article 434, Paragraph 4, of the Capital Market Act, the issuer must ensure that shareholders may exercise their rights by proxy, subject to the law of the country in which the issuer is incorporated.[44] By transposing of the Takeover Bids Directive into Croatian law, protection is provided to the shareholders of the target company, stipulating that a company must facilitate the issuance of proxies to vote at the general meeting of shareholders which decides on defensive measures for shareholders, if this is possible under the law and articles of association.[45]

---

42 The collection of proxies should be entrusted to an independent third party since, if the proxy is submitted before the general meeting, the management board is able even before voting to find out how it will be voted.
43 Decision of the High Commercial Court of 4 June 2002 in Case Number Pž-1740/02.
44 Article 434, Paragraph 5, of the Capital Market Act explicitly prescribes further obligations to the issuers.
45 Takeover Act, Article 42, Paragraph 4.

Voting by Credit or Financial Institution

Croatian law regulates voting by credit[46] or financial institutions, shareholders' associations, custodians of shares, and other persons who, by virtue of the work, offer shareholders' voting at the general meeting. This position of a credit or financial institution, when it votes based on shares that are not owned by it but are subscribed in the register under its name, differs from the position in which it may exercise the voting rights on the basis of shares not owned by it and in respect of which it does not appear as their holder on the register of shares.

In the first case, the credit or financial institution will not require authorization to vote at the general meeting; in the second case, it is allowed to exercise voting rights only if it has been appointed as a proxy holder in relation to this. A proxy may be granted to only one specific credit or financial institution, which shall be required to keep the proxy appointment so that it can be verified. The statement of will by which a proxy is granted must be complete and may be related only to the statements of will concerning the exercise of voting rights.

Under Croatian law, the provision on the limitation of the duration of the proxy given to credit and financial institutions for fifteen months has been deleted. Thus, the authorization is valid until its revocation. However, credit and financial institutions are required to clearly and on an annual basis bring to the attention of the shareholder the possibility of revoking the appointment of or changing a proxy holder at any time. Furthermore, the shareholder must be provided a form designed to facilitate the giving of instructions on the voting on resolutions from individual agenda items, the granting and revocation of a general proxy, and the giving and modification of orders.[47]

Credit and financial institutions must vote in accordance with the received instructions. However, credit and financial institutions need not actively seek instruction on how to vote. Where the shareholder does not give explicit voting instructions, a general proxy may entitle a credit or financial institution to exercise the right to vote only as specified in the proposals of that institution on how to vote or in proposals of managerial and supervisory bodies of the company. In the event of discrepancies

---

46 The concept of credit institution is defined by the Law on Credit Institutions, *Official Gazette*, Number 59/13, 19/15, which in Article 3, Paragraph 1, Point 28, refers to Article 4, Paragraph 1, of the Regulation (EU) 575/2013 of the European Parliament, and of the Council of 26 June 2013 on prudential requirements for credit institutions and investment firms and amending Regulation (EU) 648/2012, OJ L 176, 27 June 2013.

47 Companies Act, Article 292, Paragraph 1.

between those proposals, a credit or financial institution must exercise the right to vote in the manner specified in the proposal of the supervisory board or the board of directors.

Article 292, Paragraph 3, of the Companies Act states that, if the shareholder has not given to the credit or financial institution instructions on the exercise of voting rights, the credit or financial institution must exercise it in accordance with its proposal, unless, as required, it may conclude that the shareholder, if he knew of the state of affairs, would approve of such voting.

A credit or financial institution may depart from its own proposals, but it also can deviate from the received instructions. The law states that if, when voting, the credit or financial institution disobeys the shareholder's instruction or, if there was no such instruction, departs from the proposal that it itself announced, it will be required to inform the shareholder and state the reasons therefore.[48]

A credit or financial institution wishing to exercise, on the basis of a granted proxy, the right to vote in accordance with its own tabled proposals will be required to make the proposals in respect of resolutions from individual agenda items available in due time.[49] In respect of the proposals, it must act in the interests of the shareholders.

The Companies Act provides three situations when a credit or financial institution is obliged to inform a shareholder about a possible conflict of interest. The first situation is when a member of the managerial and supervisory bodies or an associate of a credit or financial institution is a member of the managerial and supervisory bodies or an associate of the public company or vice versa.

In the other two cases, a shareholder should be informed if the credit or financial institution owns a share in the public company which by law it is required to report to the competent supervisory authority or it forms a consortium with the public company which during the previous five years took upon itself the last issue of the company's securities.

A decision of the general meeting may be contested if a credit or financial institution not subscribed in the share register voted at the general meeting and did not have the authorization to vote. However, the decision of the general meeting may not be contested if a credit or financial institution voted at the general meeting that, although being

---

[48] The law does not state the reasons why a deviation from the given voting instructions would be justified.
[49] Since the Companies Act states that these proposals must be made available to the shareholders, the view is taken that it would be enough to publish them on the website of the credit or financial institution.

subscribed in the register of shares, exercised its voting rights but did not have the authority of a person whose shares are in custody.

A decision may not be contested if the credit or financial institution voted contrary to the received instructions. According to Article 292 of the Companies Act, provisions that regulate voting by credit or financial institutions must apply appropriately to shareholders' associations.

Share Transfer Restrictions

The Companies Act accepts freedom of transferability of shares. While the transfer of materialized shares is governed by the Companies Act, the transfer of the dematerialized shares is governed by the Capital Market Act. A key difference between the materialized and dematerialized shares lies in the ability to prescribe limits on the transfer of shares.

A company may provide with its articles of association that consent of the company is required to transfer the materialized registered shares. On the other hand, this restriction is not possible for the transfer of dematerialized shares. Therefore, since listed companies are allowed to issue only dematerialized shares, these companies may not prescribe in their articles of association that the transfer of shares requires the consent of the company.

If the transfer of shares requires the approval of the company, approval is provided by the management board or executive directors of the company. However, the articles of association can give this authority to the supervisory board, board of directors, or the general meeting. The articles of association also may determine the reasons for refusing the consent for transfer of shares. If the reasons are not determined in the articles of association, the consent may be denied only for the reason of protecting the company's interest (e.g., a change of shareholders' structure may endanger a company's aim or its economic existence). The articles of association cannot specify more stringent reasons for denial of the consent for transfer of shares.

The company may require from the acquirer to declare whether he acquires shares for himself or for the account of another. The approval for the transfer of shares may be denied if the acquirer refuses to provide this information or declares that shares are acquired for the account of another. If shares are acquired through inheritance, universal succession of the entity, or sale in enforcement or bankruptcy proceedings, the company may refuse the consent for transfer of shares only if it offers to the acquirer redemption of the shares at market value. The acquirer may reject this offer within one month from the date of receipt of the offer. If he fails to reject the offer, it is considered that he had accepted the offer.

An acquirer cannot exercise membership rights from the shares before obtaining consent for the transfer of shares. If shares are acquired through inheritance, a universal succession of the entity, or sale in enforcement or bankruptcy proceedings, the acquirer cannot exercise voting rights in the company. The company must give consent within one month from receipt of the request from the acquirer.

According to Article 227 of the Companies Act, if the company does not give the consent by the deadline or refuses to give the consent because of reasons that are not listed in the articles of association of the company or in the Companies Act, it is considered that the consent is given.

Access to Corporate Information

Shareholders exercise their right to corporate information at the general meeting. They collect information on corporate business through the report of the supervisory board or the board of directors on annual accounts, annual report of the company, and decision proposal on distribution of profits which are prepared by the management board or executive directors.

Since the day of the announcement of the notice on convening of the general meeting, the annual accounts and proposals must be displayed to shareholders for insight in the business premises at the company's registered seat when they are the issue of discussion and decisions at the general meeting. In addition, upon request of each shareholder, a copy of the indicated documents must be placed at his disposal.

At the general meeting, the management board or executive directors must provide each shareholder, at his request, with relevant information regarding the company business where necessary for proper evaluation of the items on the agenda. The duty to provide information also extends to legal and business relationships of the company with affiliated companies.

When information has been provided to a shareholder outside the general meeting, such information must be presented at the general meeting to each shareholder in the company upon his request even if the particular information is irrelevant for the evaluation of the items on the agenda. In addition, if information is denied to a shareholder, he may request that his question and the reason for being denied the information be included in the minutes taken at the general meeting.

The chairman of the general meeting may be authorized to set an appropriate time limit for the realization of the shareholder's right to pose questions and for debate in the articles of association or in the general meeting's rules of procedure. He also must have this authority if this is not prescribed by the articles of association or the general meeting's rules of procedure, if he deems the time limit necessary for the orderly functioning and reasonable duration of the general meeting.[50]

The Companies Act prescribes situations when the management board or executive directors are entitled to deny information. These are usually information which could incur damage to the company. However, if the management board or executive directors are obliged to provide the shareholder with the information, but they fail to do so, the shareholder may file a request to the court to decide whether the management board or executive directors are obliged to provide him with relevant information.

This request may be filed by any shareholder who did not get information if a decision was adopted at the general meeting concerning the item on the agenda to which the requested information is related. The same request may be also filed by any shareholder who attended the meeting and expressed his disagreement with the decision and if this disagreement was recorded in the minutes of the meeting. The request will be made within fifteen days following the general meeting at which such information was denied to the shareholder. If the court accepts the request, notice may be given outside of the general meeting.

Minority shareholders may initiate the appointment of special auditors. If the general meeting refuses to appoint special auditors, they will be appointed by the court upon request of minority shareholders whose aggregate shareholding equals at least one-tenth of the share capital of the company, provided there is a reasonable doubt that there have been irregularities in the process of the establishment of the company or that the law or the articles of association have been violated.[51] At the request of any shareholder, the management board or executive directors must provide a copy of the report of the special auditors. The management board or executive directors are obliged to include the report in the agenda of the next general meeting.

---

50 Companies Act, Article 287.
51 The applicants must deposit their share certificates with the company, the notary public, or the financial institution dealing with safekeeping of securities until their request is decided on. They also must prove that they have been shareholders in the company for at least three months prior to the date of the holding of the general meeting.

Inspection of Shareholder List

The Companies Act imposes on companies the obligation to keep a share register. The management board or executive directors are authorized and responsible for its keeping. The duty to keep the share register depends on the form of shares. If the company issues dematerialized shares, keeping of the share register is optional. These shares are kept as an electronic record of a securities account in the computer system of the central depository, which is operated by the Central Depository and Clearing Company.

The legal holder of a dematerialized share (shareholder) is the person in whose name a securities account is opened with the central depository on which a dematerialized share is entered. If the company issues registered shares without share certificates or registered shares with share certificates (materialized shares), keeping of the share register is mandatory. In relation to the company, only the person who has been entered in the share register is considered a shareholder.

When the share is transferred, this must be recorded in the share register upon request of the previous or new shareholder and submission of the evidence of share transfer. If, in the company's opinion, a person has been unjustifiably entered into the share register as a shareholder, the company is authorized to delete the entry, but only upon prior notice addressed to the shareholder and offer of an appropriate time limit for a complaint.

Each shareholder can require information from the share register with regard to him or other shareholders in the company. The company may use information from the share register only in the achievement of their tasks in relation to the shareholders. According to Article 226 of the Companies Act, data cannot be used for other purposes if the shareholder is opposed.

Each holder of dematerialized shares may demand access to the data.[52] Each person who proves his legal interest has the right of access to the data and the right to a copy of documents which were a basis for performed entries.

It must be noted that the Central Depository and Clearing Company is not given the power to judge based on the principle of opportunity if someone will be allowed access to the data entered in the accounts or

---

[52] The scope of this provision should be extended to all persons who have the right of access to the data.

not, but must allow access to anyone who has the right to access, if the prerequisites required for the formation of that right have been met.

Derivative Suits

According to Croatian law, shareholders cannot directly assert the claim against members of the management board or executive directors, members of the supervisory board or the board of directors, and founders of the company for the company's account. Members of managerial and supervisory bodies are liable to the company for performance of their duties.

In the case of an untimely initiation of bankruptcy proceedings, members of the management board or board of directors are liable to insolvency creditors of the company for inability to settle their claims in bankruptcy proceedings.[53] In cases where the management board members or executive directors have grossly violated their duty to act as a prudent businessman, creditors of the company may assert the claim for compensation of damage if they are unable to settle their claim from the company.[54]

The general meeting of the company adopts the decision on the assertion of the claim against members of the management board or executive directors, members of the supervisory board or board of directors, and founders of the company by simple majority. Minority shareholders whose shares represent at least one-tenth of the share capital of the company also may request adoption of such decision if they provide that they have been company shareholders for a minimum of three months prior to the general meeting which decides on their request. The claim must be asserted in six months from the adoption of the decision by the general meeting.

The company is represented in litigation by the management board or executive directors, or by the supervisory board or board of directors, or by special representatives appointed by the general meeting. If so decided by the general meeting, or if the stated minority shareholders have requested filing of the claim, the commercial court may appoint other representatives of the company, upon the proposal of the stated minority shareholders or shareholders holding shares which account

---

53 Companies Act, Articles 251 and 272h.
54 Companies Act, Article 252.

for a minimum of HRK 8-million of a company's share capital where the court considers that this will be useful for the fulfilment of the company's claim. If the court accepts the claim, the costs of the procedure will be borne by the company.

Minority shareholders whose shares represent at least five per cent of the share capital or a pro rata amount of HRK 4-million may ask the court to appoint a special representative if the claim has not been asserted by representatives of the company within six months from the adoption of a decision by the general meeting. They may do so if there are facts that justify the suspicion that the company suffered damages by improper conduct or by gross violation of the law or the articles of association. An appointed special representative must assert the claim for the company's account if he estimates that there are prospects for success in litigation.

If the company fails to succeed or only partially succeeds with his claim, the aforementioned minority shareholders who requested filing of the claim will be jointly and severally liable to compensate the company thereby for costs caused to the extent that they are higher than what is obtained in litigation. If the claim is rejected, minority shareholders are obliged to compensate all costs of the litigation, court expenses related to the appointment of representatives, as well as the costs and fees paid for the representatives' work.[55]

Distribution of Profits

The management board or executive directors create the policy of distribution of profits in the company. They prepare annual accounts, annual report of the company, and a decision proposal on the distribution of profits in accordance with the Accounting Act (Article 300a of the Companies Act).[56] Listed companies, financial institutions, and large entrepreneurs and medium-sized entrepreneurs are obliged to audit their annual accounts.[57] A mandatory auditor is appointed by the general meeting.[58] The supervisory board or board of directors instructs the auditor to examine the annual accounts.[59]

---

55 Companies Act, Article 273a.
56 Accounting Act, *Official Gazette*, Numbers 78/15 and 134/15.
57 Accounting Act, Articles 3–5 and 20.
58 Companies Act, Article 275.
59 Companies Act, Articles 263 and 272h.

The management board or executive directors must submit annual accounts and annual report of the company, together with the decision proposal on distribution of profits, without delay to the supervisory board or board of directors.[60] They must inspect annual accounts and the proposed decision on distribution of profits and prepare a written report. The report must be submitted to the management board or executive directors within a month after submission of annual accounts and decision proposal on distribution of profits.

If the supervisory board or the board of directors does not submit the report on inspection, the management board or executive directors must give them additional time for the submission. The additional time may not be more than a month. According to Article 300c of the Companies Act, if they do not submit the report within the additional time, it will be deemed that annual accounts are not approved. If the supervisory board or board of directors gives consent on annual accounts, it will be deemed that they are adopted by managerial and supervisory bodies of the company.[61]

The general meeting may adopt annual accounts only if this power is transferred to it by the decision of managerial and supervisory bodies of the company or if the supervisory board or board of directors do not give their consent to annual accounts. The management board or executive directors must submit adopted annual accounts to the judicial register and convene the general meeting without delay.[62]

The general meeting adopts the decision on the distribution of profits by simple majority in accordance with the proposal of the management board or executive directors. Adopted annual accounts, annual report of the company, the report on the inspection of the supervisory board or board of directors, and the decision proposal on the distribution of profits will be presented to the shareholders. The management board or board of directors may propose the distribution of profits to the shareholders, the transfer of profits to the company's reserves, or the retaining of profits in the company's assets.

The order and manner of use of the company's profits is regulated by the Companies Act. The management board or executive directors must first use net profits realized in the current financial year to cover transferred losses from previous financial years; to contribute five per cent of profits accrued during the current financial year, reduced by the

---

60 Companies Act, Article 300b.
61 Companies Act, Article 300d.
62 Companies Act, Articles 277 and 300d.

amount of loss in the previous year to statutory reserves until such reserves together with the capital reserves have reached the level of five per cent of the share capital of the company or a higher amount prescribed by the articles of association; to contribute a certain amount of profits to the reserves for its own shares if the company has acquired or intends to acquire its own shares; and to contribute a certain amount of profits to reserves envisaged by the articles of association.[63]

The general meeting or managerial and supervisory bodies of the company may contribute an additional amount of profits to other company's reserves after adoption of annual accounts, with certain statutory limitations. The shareholders will be entitled to charge their dividends unless the general meeting, in compliance with the Companies Act and the articles of association, decides that the profits will be used for contribution to other company reserves or that the profits may not be distributed amongst shareholders (retained profits).

Only those profits shown in the profit and loss account of the company and part of retained profits may be distributed amongst shareholders. Except for cases of reductions of subscribed capital, no distribution to shareholders may be made when, on the closing date of the last financial year, the net assets as set out in the company's annual accounts are, or following such a distribution would become, lower than the amount of the subscribed capital plus those reserves which may not be distributed under the law or the articles of association.

Where the uncalled part of the subscribed capital is not included in the assets shown in the statement of financial position, that amount will be deducted from the amount of subscribed capital. The amount of a distribution to shareholders may not exceed the amount of the profits at the end of the last financial year plus any profits brought forward and sums drawn from reserves available for this purpose, less any losses brought forward and sums placed in reserve in accordance with the law or the articles of association.[64]

The management board or executive directors, with consent of the supervisory board or board of directors, may pay interim dividend if they are empowered to do so by the articles of association. According to Article 221 of the Companies Act, payment of interim dividend must meet three conditions:

(1) Interim accounts must be drawn up, showing that the funds available for distribution are sufficient;

---

[63] Companies Act, Article 220.
[64] Companies Act, Article 220.

(2) The amount to be distributed may not exceed half of profits, less sums to be placed in reserves pursuant to the requirements of the law or the articles of association; and

(3) The amount to be distributed may not exceed half the profits realized in the previous financial year.

The participation of shareholders in the profit is determined according to the company's share capital which accounts for their shares. However, if contributions into the share capital are not paid in full or if they are not paid in equal proportions for all shares, the shareholders must participate in the distribution of the profits in proportion to their payments. Contributions paid in the course of the current financial year will be taken into account, depending on the period of time which passed since paying the contribution. A different method of distribution also may be determined by the articles of association of the company (e.g., preferred shares).[65]

A distribution made contrary to the Companies Act must be returned by shareholders who have received it if the company proves that those shareholders knew of the irregularity of the distributions made to them, or may not in view of the circumstances have been unaware of it. The company's claim towards shareholders also may be asserted by its creditors if the company is incapable to settle their claims. Claims asserted on the grounds of the unlawful distribution of profits must cease to be valid five years upon receipt of payment.[66]

Minority shareholders may contest the general meeting's decision on the distribution of profits if it does not allow distribution of profits among the shareholders, despite the fact that such distribution should be done taking into account business results of the company. An action to contest the decision may be filed by shareholders whose shares account for at least one-twentieth of the share capital or at least HRK 4-million, or by the supervisory board or board of directors of the company. The action may be filed if the right to distribution of profits is not excluded by law or the articles of association and within thirty days following the date when the decision was adopted.[67]

This enables the protection of minority shareholders towards the majority shareholder. Nullity of the decision on adoption of annual accounts, which was brought by the general meeting or by managerial

---

[65] Companies Act, Article 223.
[66] Companies Act, Article 224.
[67] Companies Act, Article 365.

and supervisory bodies of the company, affects the validity of the general meeting's decision on the distribution of profits.[68]

Shareholders and Tender Offers

Takeover Regulation

Takeovers are regulated by the Takeover Act. The Takeover Act covers only takeovers of listed companies. Croatia has implemented the mandatory bid rule in Article 9 of the Takeover Act. In Croatian law, the control threshold has been set at 25 per cent + 1 of voting shares since 1997. Non-voting shares are not covered by this rule.

The Takeover Act gives the possibility to cover non-voting shares with the takeover bid but only when this bid is published for voting shares. Therefore, the decision to cover non-voting shares depends on the offeror since he is obliged to publish a bid only for voting shares.

The Takeover Act, in accordance with the Takeover Bids Directive, contains provisions on price in the takeover bid. According to Article 16 of the Takeover Act, the offeror and persons acting in concert with him must offer an equal price for all the shares of the same class. The price in the takeover bid may not be lower than the highest price at which the offeror and the persons acting in concert with him have acquired the voting shares within a year before the obligation was created.

However, if the average price of shares realized on stock exchange and regulated public markets is higher than this price, the offeror must offer a higher price, calculating the average price for every individual stock exchange or regulated public market, as a weighted average of all the prices realized on the stock exchange or regulated public market within three months before the obligation to announce that a takeover bid was created. Furthermore, if the bidder, or a person acting in concert with him, within one year after the expiration of the validity of the bid, acquires additional shares of the target company for a price that is higher than the price set forth in the bid, the bidder would be obliged to pay the difference in price to all shareholders who have accepted the bid within seven days from the acquisition of the additional shares.

However, this provision does not apply to the acquisition of shares through reorganization measures (e.g., mergers and divisions), through

---

[68] Companies Act, Article 359.

an increase of the share capital of the target company, or through an acquisition of the target company's shares in lieu of the payment of a dividend. The purchase price for shares in a takeover bid can be paid either in cash, substitute shares, or a combination of both. When offering substitute shares or a combination of cash and shares, the bidder also must offer cash as an alternative.[69]

The bidder will be obliged, within 30 days following the date required to announce the takeover bid, to submit to HANFA an application for approval of the announcement of a mandatory bid. HANFA must issue a decision within fourteen days following receipt of the application. The bid must remain open for at least twenty-eight days from its announcement. However, the deadline for the validity of a mandatory bid and a competing bid cannot be longer than sixty days from the announcement of the first mandatory bid.

Within ten days after announcement of the bid, the management board of the target company must issue an advisory opinion. Within five days after the announcement of the bid and before the opinion is published, the management board of the target company must submit its opinion to the target company's workers' representatives or to the workers directly, who can give their opinion on the bid within the next three days. If the management board of the target company receives the workers' opinion on time, it is obliged to attach it to its opinion on the bid. The management board is obliged to submit its opinion on the bid to HANFA and to the operator of the regulated market no later than the day on which the publication of the opinion is ordered.

If persons who are obliged to publish a takeover bid fail to do so, HANFA is entitled to initiate an administrative procedure in which it will determine the obligation to publish a takeover bid. Persons who are obliged to publish a takeover bid pursuant to the law cannot exercise their voting rights arising from all the acquired shares of the target company. It also is possible to initiate misdemeanor proceedings. In addition, there is protection for minority shareholders who have the right to demand a mandatory conclusion of an agreement on shares sale, subject to the conditions according to which the takeover bid had to be announced.[70] Thus, each shareholder of the target company is authorized to initiate proceedings before the Commercial Court to enable shareholders to sell their shares.

---

[69] The Takeover Act explicitly prescribes that substitute shares must be: a) listed on either the same market or another market having at least the same level of transparency; b) of the same type and class; and c) without any encumbrances.

[70] Takeover Act, Article 49.

Squeeze-Out and Sell-Out Rights

Croatian law recognizes the right to demand transfer of shares from minority shareholders (squeeze-out) and the right to require redemption of the shares of minority shareholders to major shareholders (sell-out). However, while the squeeze-out right is regulated by the Companies Act and the Takeover Act, the sell-out right of a minority shareholder is only recognized by the Takeover Act.

According to the Takeover Act, squeeze-out and sell-out rights are to be applied only if the takeover of the offeree company has been previously carried out. Therefore, if following the end of bidding the bidder and persons acting in concert together hold at least 95 per cent of voting shares in the target company, the bidder may require all remaining minority shareholders to sell him their voting shares at a fair price. The offeror must have a right to a transfer of such shares of minority shareholders within three months after expiry of the period for acceptance of the takeover bid.[71] He also has the right to acquire remaining non-voting preference shares, but only if they were acquired during the bid term.

Thus, if he holds 95 per cent of the voting shares but not this percentage of non-voting shares, he cannot squeeze out the shareholders of non-voting shares but only those who hold voting shares. The same view was taken by the Croatian legislator regarding sell outs. Thus, it can be concluded that, if non-voting shares were not covered by the takeover bid, squeeze-out or sell-out rights do not apply to them, which puts them in an unequal position with shareholders who hold voting shares. Their unfavorable position is especially prominent in the inability to exercise the sell-out right.

The offeror does not gain its right to squeeze out the minority shareholders by simply reaching the threshold, but is entitled to submit a request to the Central Depository and Clearing Company. The offeror must, when submitting the request, notify minority shareholders, the target company, the operator of the regulated market, and HANFA. He also must publish the request to exercise the squeeze-out right.

The offeror's right to transfer shares at a fair price is explicitly stipulated. According to Croatian law, a fair price must imply a price determined in a takeover bid, increased by a difference in price if the offeror or the person acting in concert with the offeror acquires the shares of the offeree company that were subject to a bid, within one year from

---

[71] The Takeover Act provisions are in accordance with the Transparency Directive.

the date of expiry of the period for acceptance of the bid, at a price higher than the one in the bid. Unlike the Takeover Bids Directive, the presumption of a fair price in Croatia is applicable to both voluntary and mandatory bids.

The Takeover Act also determines the moment for the Central Depository and Clearing Company to carry out a transfer of shares from the shareholders' account to the offeror's account and to pay out the minority shareholders. This is due after it has established that, following a takeover bid, the offeror and persons acting in concert with the offeror hold a minimum of 95 per cent of voting shares of the offeree company and 95 per cent of preference shares without voting rights, that the offeror has secured consideration for the shares that are subject to the request, and that three months have not expired after the end of the period for acceptance of the takeover bid. All of the conditions must be cumulatively met for the Central Depository and Clearing Company to transfer the shares to the offeree's account and finalize the pay-out to the minority shareholders.

In the sell-out procedure, if, following the takeover bid, the offeror and persons acting in concert with the offeror hold a minimum of 95 per cent of voting shares in the target company, the minority shareholders may require that the offeror buy all their remaining voting shares at a fair price within three months from expiry of the period for acceptance of the takeover bid. The period for the minority shareholders to claim their sell-out right is the same as that for the offeree to claim its squeeze-out right. The deadline is preclusive so that minority shareholders cannot demand the purchase of their shares upon its expiry.

The Companies Act, in Articles 300f-k, regulates the procedure for the transfer of minority shareholders' shares to a majority shareholder (squeeze-out). In accordance with Article 300f of the Companies Act, the general meeting, upon the request of a shareholder in possession of at least 95 per cent of the share capital (i.e., the major shareholder),[72] may reach a decision upon which the shares of minority shareholders, with corresponding severance payment due in cash, are to be transferred.

The major shareholder submits a request to convene the general meeting of the management board. The Companies Act is silent as to the form of the request. The management board decides upon the request for a call of the general meeting and is not obliged to seek consent of the

---

72 It must be a single person. Several shareholders may not be treated as major shareholder, even if they are acting in concert.

supervisory board.[73] The general meeting may reach a decision by simple majority if the company's charter does not require a larger majority or additional conditions. The majority shareholder is obliged to pay out the corresponding severance pay for the shares, in cash, to the minority shareholder(s). The amount of money, in accordance with the Companies Act,[74] is to be set by the majority shareholder alone.

In accordance with the principle of the equal position of the shareholders, the amount of severance pay must be equal for all shareholders. Potential differences could appear if pledged shares are in question. Furthermore, the adequacy of the severance pay must be reviewed by one or more experts appointed upon the majority shareholder's request by the court in the non-litigation procedure.[75] The moment the ruling on the share transfer is filed in the court register, all of the minority shareholder's shares are *ex lege* transferred onto the major shareholder. Therefore, the entry in the court register has a constitutive character.

Entrepreneurial Contracts and Reorganization Measures

In case of the conclusion of the control agreement and the profit transfer agreement (entrepreneurial contracts), they must include the duty of the controlling company to buy shares of shareholders of the controlled company on their request in exchange for adequate compensation defined by the agreement. The compensation can be paid either in substitute shares of the controlling company or in cash.

If the agreement does not include provisions on the compensation or if it is inadequate, each shareholder of the controlled company will be entitled to request the court to decide on the adequate compensation within three months from the entry of the agreement in the judicial register. In such case the court must determine payment of the compensation in cash unless the agreement provides payment of the compensation in substitute shares of the controlling company. The court decision must apply to all shareholders of the controlled company.[76] Shareholders of the integrated company have a similar right to compensation for their shares in case of integration of companies.[77]

---

[73] The stated consent can be required by means of a company's charter or the general meeting's decision.
[74] Companies Act, Article 300g.
[75] High Commercial Court, Judgment of 19 January 2005, Number Pž-7584/04.
[76] Companies Act, Article 492.
[77] Companies Act, Article 504a.

Shareholders of a public company which underwent certain reorganization measures (merger by acquisition of a company to a limited-liability company, crossborder mergers, or conversion of a company to a limited-liability company) may request compensation for their shares under certain conditions. Each shareholder who has voted against the reorganization measures on the general meeting may request the company to buy his shares by paying him compensation in cash.

The shareholder may request compensation within two months after the announcement of the entry of a reorganization measure in the judicial register. A shareholder may waive this right by an explicit statement in writing. The shareholder and the company must agree on the amount of compensation in cash. If no such agreement is reached within thirty days of the date when the shareholder submitted the request, the company must pay to the shareholder an adequate compensation determined by the court, upon the proposal made either by the shareholder or by the company.

The decision of the general meeting on the consent for such reorganization measures cannot be contested on the grounds that the compensation has not been paid or is inadequate.[78] In the case of the division of a company, each shareholder who has voted against the division on the general meeting may request the recipient company to buy his shares by paying him a compensation when shares in the recipient companies are allocated to the shareholder of the company being divided otherwise than in proportion to his rights in the share capital of that company; when the transfer of shares in the recipient company is restricted; and when the recipient company has a different legal form than the company being divided.[79]

The company must offer adequate compensation within one month from the date of receipt of the request. The decision of the general meeting on consent for a division cannot be contested on grounds that compensation has not been offered or is inadequate. In such case, the shareholder who submitted the request to the company on time may demand the court to decide on the adequate compensation until expiration of a deadline for the acceptance of the offer.[80]

---

[78] Companies Act, Articles 534, 549g, and 562.
[79] A shareholder may request the compensation within two months after announcement of the entry of a division in the judicial register.
[80] Companies Act, Article 550k.

Germany

Anette Kespohl
Weitnauer
Munich, Germany

Introduction

The most common corporations in Germany are the limited-liability company (*Gesellschaft mit beschränkter Haftung*, GmbH) and the stock corporation (*Aktiengesellschaft*, AG).[1] As of 31 December 2014, 522,573 GmbHs and 7,747 AGs were registered.[2] The GmbH is governed by the Act on Limited-Liability Companies, and the AG by the Stock Corporation Act and, if listed, by several capital market related statutes.

The GmbH is the typical legal form for small and medium-size enterprises, subsidiaries, and affiliates. Listed companies must have the legal form of an AG, but this form also is eligible for non-listed entities. The establishment of both types of companies requires a notarial deed, and both come into existence as a corporation upon their registration in the commercial register. The liability of the corporation is limited to its assets, except for scenarios described below.

A GmbH has one or more managing directors (*Geschäftsführer*) who run the business. An AG has a management board (*Vorstand*), consisting of one or more individuals who run the business, and a supervisory board (*Aufsichtsrat*), consisting of one or more individuals who supervise the *Vorstand*. In AGs of a certain size, between 30 per cent and 50 per cent of the seats of the *Aufsichtsrat* are to be given to representatives of the employees (known as "co-determination").

Allocation of Powers between Shareholders and Directors

In General

Whereas the shareholders of a GmbH are quite powerful *vis-à-vis* the *Geschäftsführer*, the power in the AG is balanced between *Vorstand*, *Aufsichtsrat*, and shareholders' meeting.

---

1 Other corporation forms are the KGaA, REIT-AG, UG, and SE.
2 See www.destatis.de/DE/Zahlen&Fakten.

GmbH

In a GmbH, the shareholder(s) appoint(s) the *Geschäftsführer*. The *Geschäftsführer* is the legal representative of the GmbH. Unless otherwise stipulated in the articles of association (*Satzung*), he has unlimited power to engage in all kinds of business transactions within the GmbH's defined purpose, without being obliged to seek approval by the shareholder(s).

In practice, in more than eighty per cent of all GmbHs all *Geschäftsführer* also are shareholders.[3] In scenarios where the *Geschäftsführer* is not a shareholder or a minority shareholder only, the *Satzung* will typically provide for a catalogue of business transactions which require shareholder approval.

The only scenario in which the GmbH is not represented by the *Geschäftsführer*, but by the shareholders, is in transactions between the GmbH, on the one hand, and the *Geschäftsführer*, on the other hand, e.g., his employment contract. The shareholders can give instructions to the *Geschäftsführer*, which he must comply with. This is the reason why most group companies are set up in the form of a GmbH.

AG

In an AG, the shareholders appoint the *Aufsichtsrat*, which in turn appoints the *Vorstand*. The *Vorstand* represents and runs the AG in its own right. His powers are not limited by law and can hardly be limited by the *Satzung*. The *Satzung* may define measures/transactions, which require approval by the *Aufsichtsrat*, but not by the shareholders.

Shareholders are well advised not to exercise any influence on the *Aufsichtsrat* or the *Vorstand*, since that may entail damage claims of the AG against them.[4]

Classes of Shares

GmbH

By statute, the GmbH has one class of shares only. The shares are called *Geschäftsanteile*. A *Geschäftsanteil* must have a nominal value to be

---

[3] Baumbach/Hueck, *GmbHG* (20th ed., 2013, Number 4, before Section 35 of the Act on Limited-Liability Companies.
[4] Stock Corporation Act, Section 117.

expressed in Euros (minimum €1). It represents a fraction of the nominal capital (*Stammkapital*) of the GmbH (minimum €25,000). The *Geschäftsanteile* can have different nominal values, but the nominal values of all *Geschäftsanteile* must add up to the nominal amount of the nominal capital.[5]

Upon establishment of a GmbH, and in cases of capital increases, the *Geschäftsanteile* must be issued at full nominal value. It is, however, permitted to add an *Agio*,[6] which the shareholder must pay in addition to the nominal amount, and which is to be entered into the books of the company as capital reserve (*Kapitalrücklage*).

In the *Satzung* or in a separate shareholders' agreement (*Gesellschaftervereinbarung*), the shareholders may set out that certain *Geschäftsanteile* bear certain rights, e.g., preferred dividends, a preferred fraction of the purchase price in case of a trade sale of the company, or the right to nominate a *Geschäftsführer*, and thus *de facto* create preference shares. Typically, a GmbH does not issue share certificates for its *Geschäftsanteile*, but they are mandatorily registered in the commercial register files, including their owners.

AG

The minimum nominal capital (*Grundkapital*) of an AG is €50,000.[7] It can be higher, but must be in full Euro. The shares (*Aktien*) can be designed as nominal value shares (*Nennbetragsaktien*) or as no-par shares (*Stück-aktien*). The no-par shares have no nominal value. All no-par shares represent the same fraction of the company's nominal capital.

In case of *Nennbetragsaktien*, the fraction of the company's nominal capital is determined by the nominal amount of the *Nennbetragsaktien* pro-rated by the company's nominal capital. *Aktien* cannot be split. An AG can only have *Nennbetragsaktien* or *Stückaktien*. Both classes of shares can be designed as bearer shares (*Inhaberaktien*) or registered shares (*Namensaktien*).[8] Both classes of shares can be designed as ordinary shares (*Stammaktien*) or preference shares (*Vorzugsaktien*). Shares may be issued at nominal value or with an *Agio*, but not below par.

---

[5] Act on Limited-Liability Companies, Section 5, Paragraphs 2 and 3.
[6] "Agio" is a term used in commerce for exchange rate, discount, or premium; here it means premium.
[7] Stock Corporation Act, Section 7.
[8] Stock Corporation Act, Section 23, Paragraph 2, Number 5.

Shareholders' Meetings

GmbH

The shareholders of a GmbH pass their resolutions in shareholders' meetings, which are held as physical meetings, but may also be held via telephone or in writing, if either the *Satzung* so provides, or if all shareholders participate in the "meeting" and agree to its form. Every shareholder has a right to participate and to speak, even if he has no voting right.

The shareholders' meeting is called by the *Geschäftsführer* at least once a year to resolve on the financial statements of the preceding year, when necessary, and when it becomes evident that the company is in a pre-insolvency condition. Shareholder(s) holding minimum 10 per cent of the nominal capital may ask the *Geschäftsführer* to call a shareholders' meeting for good reason. If the *Geschäftsführer* does not comply with the request, the shareholders may call the shareholders' meeting themselves.

AG

The shareholders of an AG also may exercise their shareholders' rights in shareholders' meetings physically, or — *Satzung* permitting — in writing, or even electronically. The members of the *Vorstand* and of the *Aufsichtsrat* have the right and the duty to participate. Every shareholder may participate, even if he holds non-voting shares.

The shareholders' meeting is called by the *Vorstand* in the situations prescribed by statute or *Satzung* or "if the company's good so requires". Shareholders who solely or jointly represent five per cent of the company's nominal capital can request the *Vorstand* to call a shareholders' meeting. If the *Vorstand* does not comply with the request, the local court may — upon application of those shareholders — empower them to call the shareholders' meeting. The shareholders' meeting makes decisions on:
(1) Appointment of the members of the *Aufsichtsrat* (to the extent they are not being appointed by the employees under the various co-determination statutes);
(2) Appropriation of the balance sheet profit;
(3) Discharge of the members of *Vorstand* and *Aufsichtsrat*;
(4) Appointment of the auditors;

(5) Changes to the *Satzung*;
(6) Measures to increase or decrease the capital; and
(7) Liquidation of the company.[9]

The shareholders' meeting may decide on management issues only upon request by the *Vorstand*.[10] Legal practice has developed implied competencies of the shareholders' meeting. It must decide on actions of fundamental relevance for the company, such as the sale of a major part of the business[11] or downgrading or delisting of listed companies.[12]

Shareholder Voting

GmbH

By statute, the number of voting rights equals the number of the nominal capital — each €1 of a *Geschäftsanteil* equals one vote.[13] In the *Satzung*, the shareholders may deviate from the statutory principle.

For example, the *Satzung* can provide for voting rights per capita, grant multiple voting rights to certain *Geschäftsanteile*, and define others as non-voting in full or in part.

AG

The *Satzung* may create non-voting shares. All voting shares have the same rights; multiple voting-rights are not permitted.[14] The principles are:
(1) No share without a voting right;
(2) No voting right without a share; and
(3) All shares have equal voting rights.

Non-voting shares may be issued only if combined with a dividend preference. As long as a due dividend has not been paid out, the voting right is revived.

---

9 Stock Corporation Act, Section 199, Paragraph 1.
10 Stock Corporation Act, Section 119, Paragraph 2.
11 This practice is widely accepted.
12 This practice is disputed in legal literature.
13 Act on Limited-Liability Companies, Section 47, Paragraph 2.
14 Stock Corporation Act, Section 12, Paragraph 2.

Rights in Proxy Voting

GmbH

Section 47, Paragraph 3, of the Act on Limited-Liability Companies states that "Proxies require written form in order to be valid."

That means that proxy voting is permitted. However, in practice, many *Gesellschaftsverträge* set out that only shareholders may participate in shareholders' meetings, sometimes accompanied by a lawyer or auditor, but that the voting right may not be exercised by a third party, with the exception of another shareholder.

AG

Proxy voting is permitted. Listed companies must indicate in the invitation to a *Hauptversammlung* the form for and the procedure of proxy voting.[15] It is common to grant proxies to banks. Section 135 of the Stock Corporation Act sets out in great detail how a bank must or may not exercise a proxy.

Share Transfer Restrictions

GmbH

According to Section 15, Paragraph 1, of the Act on Limited-Liability Companies the shares in a GmbH are alienable and hereditary. The *Gesellschaftsvertrag* can make a transfer subject to certain provisos, in particular to the approval by the company,[16] and most *Gesellschaftsverträge* actually do so. The transfer as such requires a notarial deed, which limits the marketability of *Geschäftsanteile*.

AG

Bearer shares are, by definition, freely transferable. As for registered shares, the *Satzung* can provide that their transfer requires the company's

---

15 Stock Corporation Act, Section 121, Paragraph 3, Subparagraph 2.a.
16 Act on Limited-Liability Companies, Section 15, Paragraph 1.

approval.[17] The approval is being granted by the *Vorstand*. The *Satzung* can, however, stipulate that the *Aufsichtsrat* or the shareholders' meeting resolve on the granting of the approval. The *Satzung* can set out the reasons for a denial of the approval.[18]

Access to Corporate Information

In General

Both GmbHs and AGs must publish their financial statements.

GmbH

On access to corporate information, Section 41a of the Act on Limited-Liability Companies clearly states:

> "(1) Upon request, the *Geschäftsführer* without delay must inform each shareholder about the matters of the company and grant access to the books and records.
>
> "(2) The *Geschäftsführer* may deny information and access only, if there is a concern that the shareholder will use them for purposes unrelated to the company, and thereby cause a substantial disadvantage to the company or a related company. The refusal requires a resolution by the shareholders.
>
> "(3) The *Satzung* may not deviate from these provisions."

AG

A shareholder of an AG must inform the AG in writing, if and as soon as he owns more than one fourth of the shares of such company and, once he has had such shareholding, if and as soon as it decreases below twenty-five per cent. The AG in turn must publish the aforementioned information in the usual publication devices.[19]

If and as soon as the AG itself owns more than one-fourth of another corporation with its seat in Germany, or a majority of another enterprise,

---

17 Stock Corporation Act, Section 68, Paragraph 2.
18 It is disputed whether transferability can be ruled out completely.
19 Stock Corporation Act, Section 20.

it must inform such corporation or enterprise. The same applies if and as soon as the shareholding decreases below the above-mentioned thresholds.[20]

The access to corporate information in an AG is exercised in a more collective way than in a GmbH. Section 118, Paragraph 1, 1st Sentence, of the Stock Corporation Act stipulates:

> "The shareholders exercise their rights in company matters in the shareholders' meeting, unless otherwise provided by statute."

Corporate documents, such as financial statements, are typically available for inspection in the corporation's premises and/or published on the corporation's website.

Inspection of Shareholder Lists

GmbH

The shareholders of a GmbH and their shareholding are listed in the so-called *Gesellschafterliste*, a document that must be prepared, updated, and filed with the commercial register by the *Geschäftsführer*. It can be inspected by every shareholder but, since it is a public register, also by every third party.

AG

An AG, having issued *Namensaktien*, must maintain a register of such shares.[21]

It is up to each holder of a *Namensaktie* to keep the register up to date in that respect, since only if and to the extent registered, can he exercise the shareholder rights *vis-à-vis* the company. A shareholder can demand from the AG to inform him about the data registered about him in the register.[22] A (corporate) right to inspect the register as a whole does not exist.[23] Non-listed companies may set out in their *Satzungen* that a shareholder can inspect the whole register, not only his entry.

---

20 Stock Corporation Act, Section 21.
21 This is often done by a service provider on behalf of the company.
22 Stock Corporation Act, Section 67, Paragraph 6, Sentence 1.
23 Section 810 of the Civil Code grants a general right to inspect third party documents in defined cases of legal interest.

Right to Make Business Proposals

GmbH

A formal procedure for the making of business proposals and how they must be considered by the *Geschäftsführung* does not exist. *De facto* the shareholders can make such proposals and even instruct the *Geschäftsführung* accordingly.

AG

As the AG is managed by the *Vorstand*, which is supervised by the *Aufsichtsrat*, there is no room for business proposals by the shareholders, and thus no formal procedure. In the annual shareholders' meeting, shareholders can make such proposals orally, but will hardly be considered.

Approval of Business Decisions

GmbH

In the *Satzung* of a GmbH, it can be set out, which business decisions require prior approval by the shareholder(s). If a *Geschäftsführer* enters into a transaction without having obtained such approval, the company is bound by his action, but he is liable for damages *vis-à-vis* the company.

AG

According to Section 76, Paragraph 1, of the Stock Corporation Act, the *Vorstand* runs the company on his own responsibility. "Own responsibility" means that he is not bound by instructions of the *Aufsichtsrat*, or the shareholders' meeting, let alone a single (majority) shareholder.

The *Vorstand* can put certain matters to the decision of the shareholders' meeting,[24] but not vice versa. The *Vorstand*'s right and obligation to represent the company *vis-à-vis* third parties cannot be limited.[25]

---

[24] Stock Corporation Act, Section 119, Paragraph 2.
[25] Stock Corporation Act, Section 82, Paragraph 1.

Derivative Suits

GmbH

A shareholder can challenge resolutions of the *Gesellschafterversammlung* in court. Unlike the Stock Corporation Act, the Act on Limited-Liability Companies does not contain provisions on the procedures.

It is, however, widely held that such suits are possible in the GmbH as well, and that the procedure is to be seen analogously to the procedure in the AG (see text, below).

AG

The Stock Corporation Act distinguishes between a rescission claim (*Anfechtungsklage*)[26] and a voidance claim (*Nichtigkeitsklage*).[27] By way of an *Anfechtungsklage*, a resolution that has certain defects in form and/or in substance can be challenged, but remains valid and in force if not or not successfully challenged.

By way of a *Nichtigkeitsklage*, the shareholder claims the confirmation by the court that a resolution has been invalid from the outset. Both claims must be filed with the Regional Court (*Landgericht*) of the company's seat. The court ruling takes legal effect on all shareholders.[28]

In recent years, so-called "critical" or "predatory" shareholders had raised *Anfechtungsklagen* at random. Since pending derivative suits prevented, e.g., the registration and execution of a capital increase, the companies were inclined to pay off such shareholders, irrespective of whether their claim had any merits. Certain legislative changes have put an end to that business model.

Distributions

GmbH

The shareholders are entitled to the annual profit plus profit carried forward minus loss carried forward, to the extent the resulting amount is

---

26 Stock Corporation Act, Section 246.
27 Stock Corporation Act, Section 249.
28 Stock Corporation Act, Section 248.

not barred from distribution by statute, *Satzung*, or individual resolution of the shareholders' meeting to allocate it to capital reserve or profit carried forward.[29] All *Geschäftsanteile* have the same (proportionate) rights to dividends. The *Satzung* may provide for a different standard of distribution.[30]

AG

In an AG, the *Aufsichtsrat* approves the annual accounts (unless the *Vorstand* and the *Aufsichtsrat* jointly decide to derogate the decision to the *Hauptversammlung*).[31] The *Hauptversammlung* is bound by the approved annual accounts and resolves on the appropriation of the net profit (*Bilanzgewinn*), indicating:
(1) The amounts or assets to be distributed to the shareholders;
(2) The amounts to be allocated to profit reserve; and
(3) The profit carried forward.[32]

The amount so calculated is distributed to the holders of the preference shares (if any) upfront, and then to the holders of the ordinary shares. The shares of one and the same class of shares must be treated equally.

Shareholders and Tender Offers

GmbH

For the GmbH, there is no formal procedure for a tender offer, and tender offers are unheard of.

AG

The same holds true for the AG whose shares are not listed on a stock exchange. Tender offers for shares in listed companies are governed by the Security Acquisition and Takeover Act (*Wertpapierübernahmegesetz*). It sets out in detail the procedures for voluntary and mandatory offers.

---

29 Stock Corporation Act, Section 29, Paragraph 1.
30 Act on Limited-Liability Companies, Section 29, Paragraph 3.
31 Stock Corporation Act, Section 172.
32 Stock Corporation Act, Section 174.

A shareholder who has obtained the control of a listed AG must make an offer to the other shareholders to also acquire their shares. Control is defined as holding 30 per cent or more of the target's voting rights.[33] If, after a voluntary or mandatory offer, the offeror holds a minimum of 95 per cent of the votes of the nominal capital, he can squeeze out the remaining shareholders.[34]

Shareholders' Duties

GmbH

The shareholder of a GmbH must contribute the nominal amount of his share in cash or in kind, and an *Agio*, if so agreed. As to the company, he also may become liable for non-paid nominal amounts of the *Geschäftsanteile* of other shareholders. An obligation to provide cash or kind over and above the agreed nominal amounts (and the *Agio*, if any) exists only if stipulated in the *Satzung*.

AG

The shareholder's main duty is to contribute in cash or in kind the par value of his share(s).[35] In scenarios where the transfer of shares requires a company's approval, the company may levy ancillary duties on the shareholder.[36] Case law has established an implied duty of good faith vested in every shareholder.

Claims of Company against Its Shareholders

There is always an interim period between the establishment of a company and its registration in the commercial register. Only upon registration does the barrier between shareholder(s) and company become fully effective. If in such interim period the value of the contributed assets (or cash) decreases below the amount of the nominal capital, the shareholders are liable towards the company to make good the difference.

---

33 Security Acquisition and Takeover Act, Section 29, Paragraph 2.
34 Security Acquisition and Takeover Act, Section 39a.
35 Stock Corporation Act, Section 54.
36 Stock Corporation Act, Section 55.

The same applies if a shareholder does not pay in the nominal amount of his share(s). In addition, if the nominal capital is paid back to the shareholders, they are obliged to pay it in again. Such claims will usually be raised by the receiver, if the company becomes insolvent.

Piercing Corporate Veil

Since the statutory provisions for establishment and capitalization for both types of corporations are quite rigid, there is hardly any need to hold the shareholders personally liable. If the capital contributions have been fully paid up, and no repayments to the shareholders have occurred in violation of applicable laws, the company's creditors can only hold the legal entity itself liable.

Legal literature and jurisprudence acknowledge a piercing of the corporate veil on an exceptional case-by-case basis only. The basic idea is that a shareholder should not invoke the principle of separation of company, on the one hand, and shareholder, on the other hand, if such invocation would constitute an abuse of the legal form or infringe the concept of good faith. Examples are the receipt of bribes by the company instead of the shareholder,[37] or the GmbH commissioning a renovation of the shareholder's house,[38] or non-existing accounting leading to a lack of transparency of the company's assets.[39]

It is being disputed whether so-called "Cinderella companies", which are dramatically under-capitalized from the outset, are a scenario to make the shareholders liable for the company's debt. The concept of "existence destruction" also is being discussed in various shapes and forms.

The Federal Supreme Court has rejected that concept, and replaced it by a liability of the shareholder *vis-à-vis* the company.[40] In a ruling in 2012,[41] the Federal Supreme Court decided that shareholders who have resolved on the redemption of another shareholder's share(s) are personally liable for his compensation payment if the corporation itself is not in a position to pay it.

---

[37] RG DR 1940, 580.
[38] BGH DB 1988, 1848.
[39] BGH ZIP 2008, 308 (310).
[40] BGHZ, NJW 2007, 246.
[41] BGH NZG 2012, 259.

Conclusion

GmbHs are widely spread. The statutory provisions governing them may to a large degree be varied by agreement. The shareholders have a rather strong influence on the management of the company. AGs are less common.

The statutory provisions governing them allow only minor variations by agreement. The shareholders' influence in an AG is minor. It is being managed by the *Vorstand* in its own right and controlled by the *Aufsichtsrat*. The *Aufsichtsrat* may be co-determined.

Indonesia

Iswahjudi A. Karim, Karen Mills, and Margaret Rose
KarimSyah Law Firm
Jakarta, Indonesia

Introduction

Business practices in modern countries are carried out through various organized and systematic entities. The entities recognized by Indonesian law include cooperatives (*Koperasi*), foundations (*Yayasan*), partnerships (*Persekutuan*), firms (*Firma*), limited partnerships (*Persekutuan Komanditer / CV*), and limited-liability companies (*Perseroan Terbatas / PT*). Among the various business entities as stated, the limited-liability company is the most preferable and by far the most common.

Limited-liability companies have enjoyed the most rapid and comprehensive growth and development. Formerly, limited-liability companies were regulated under both the original Dutch-based Indonesian Commercial Code, Articles 36–56 and the Indonesian Civil Code, Chapters 8 and 9. However, the existing regulations were not able to keep up with modern business requirements, and the Government has continued to issue new regulations regarding limited-liability companies.

In 1982, Law Number 3 was enacted regarding company registration. In 1995, a new comprehensive law was promulgated regulating most matters concerning the limited-liability company, being Law Number 1 of 1995 regarding limited-liability companies, which has been amended by Law Number 40 of 2007 (the "Company Law"). Shortly thereafter, Law Number 8 of 1997 was enacted regarding company documents and, in 2003, Law Number 19 of 2003 regarding state-owned companies was promulgated.

The Company Law, Article 1, Paragraph (2), states that the company's organs consist of the general meeting of shareholders, the board of directors, and the board of commissioners. The general meeting of shareholders, consisting of the owners of the company, is vested with authority not provided to either the board of directors or board of commissioners, within limits stipulated in the Company Law or in the articles of association of that company.[1]

The general meeting of shareholders also is entitled to obtain information in relation to the company from the board of directors and/or board of commissioners in accordance with the agenda as long as it does not contravene with the company's interests. The general meeting of shareholders represents the capital of the company's owners.

Therefore, it may be concluded that the general meeting of shareholders acts in the interest of the shareholders. The board of directors is responsible to perform the company's management and operations and must act in the interests of the company itself. The board of commissioners has a supervisory role over the board of directors, in effect to ensure that shareholder interests are represented.

Shares and Shareholders

In General

Payment for shares in a company is made in the form of money. However, it is possible for payment to be made in other forms, such as tangible or intangible goods that are able to be valued in monetary terms and are actually received by the company. Other forms of shares payment must be accompanied with details of value or price, type, status, place or domicile, and other information deemed necessary to clarify the deposit of capital.

Matters concerning shares and shareholders are explicitly regulated in the Company Law and implicitly in other regulations. Shares owned by the shareholders are considered as ownership proof, and shares issued by the company must be identified as the shareholders' payment receipt. Each share (or each share in each class of shares) has one, or equal, voting right within the class. The shareholder's responsibility is limited by the number of the shares owned. The shares generally provide voting rights in the general meeting of shareholders. They also provide the right to receive dividends proportional to the number of shares owned. Under the Company Law, shareholders are entitled to:

(1) Attend and cast votes in the general meeting of shareholders;

---

1 Company Law, Article 75, Paragraph 1.

(2) Receive dividends and the proportional share of any remaining assets resulting from a liquidation process;
(3) File a lawsuit against the company if the shareholder suffers a loss as a result of actions performed by the company which are considered unfair and unreasonable;
(4) Request the company to purchase their shares at a reasonable price in the event of certain specified corporate transactions; and
(5) Exercise the pre-emptive right to subscribe to newly issued shares, proportionally.

As stipulated in the Company Law, Article 3, Paragraph (1), "[t]he company's shareholders are not personally liable for any legal agreements entered into on behalf of the company and are not liable for any company losses exceeding their owned shares". However, the Company Law also provides a provision related to "Piercing the Corporate Veil" in Article 3, Paragraph (2), stating that shareholders may be personally liable towards the company in case of the occurrence of any of the following events:
(1) The requirements for the company as a legal entity were not completed;
(2) The shareholders, whether directly or indirectly, in bad faith, took advantage of the company for their own interest;
(3) The shareholders were involved in an unlawful act conducted by the company; or
(4) The shareholders, whether directly or indirectly, have unlawfully misapplied the company's assets leading to an inadequacy of the assets in order to settle the company's debts.

The Company Law and Law Number 8 of 1995 (the "Capital Market Law") also regulate various issues related to shares and shareholders.

Shareholders' Authority

The Company Law specifically regulates the authority provided to the general meeting of shareholders, board of directors, and board of commissioners. Each performs its own role in the company in accordance with its respective authority, each of which differs from the others. These roles are normally also set out in the company's articles of association.

As noted above, the board of directors is responsible for conducting management and operational functions inside the company, and represents the company with respect to external parties. However, certain

actions or decisions within the company may not be taken by the board of directors without prior consent from the general meeting of shareholders, according to the Company Law. Under the Company Law, the actions or decisions that require consent or approval of the general meeting of shareholders include being related to the following events:
(1) Amendment to the articles of association;[2]
(2) Capital increase;[3]
(3) Capital reduction;[4]
(4) Annual financial statement approval and management discharge;[5]
(5) Appropriation of profit;[6]
(6) Transfer of company assets and rendering of the company's assets as collateral, which constitute more than fifty per cent of the net company assets;[7]
(7) Appointment and termination of board of directors and board of commissioners;[8]
(8) Merger, acquisition and consolidation;[9] and
(9) Company dissolution.[10]

Shareholders may add additional restrictions on corporate actions performed by the board of directors in the company's articles of association. The board of directors in public companies must comply with the regulation issued by the Financial Services Authority (*Otoritas Jasa Keuangan*), wherein shareholder approval is required for certain corporate actions, including conflict-of-interest transactions and material transactions. Approval of the board of commissioners also may be required for certain activities of the board of directors, and these are within the shareholders' authority to determine and set out in the articles of association.

Classification of Shares

As stated in the Company Law, Article 53, the articles of association determine one or more classifications of shares. Each share of the same

---

[2] Company Law, Article 19.
[3] Company Law, Article 41.
[4] Company Law, Article 44.
[5] Company Law, Article 69.
[6] Company Law, Article 71.
[7] Company Law, Article 102, Paragraph 1.
[8] Company Law, Articles 94–105 and 111–119.
[9] Company Law, Article 123.
[10] Company Law, Article 142.

classification must be provided with equal rights. If there is more than one classification of shares, the articles of association must designate one class as common shares. There are two types of shares, namely:
(1) Common shares — Owners of common shares have the right to participate in the company's decision-making by casting votes in the general meeting of shareholders. They also are entitled to obtain profit from the company, either in the form of dividends or capital gain. Each share must have the same nominal value and carry the same rights, interest, and obligations for the owners in accordance with the articles of association. In accordance with the Company Law, Article 52, the holders of common shares have the right to attend and cast votes in the general meeting of shareholders, to receive dividends and remaining asset distribution from a liquidation process, and to perform any other rights in accordance with the prevailing law.
(2) Preferred or priority shares — Preferred or priority shares benefit from a privilege not provided to common shares. Based on the Company Law, Article 53, Paragraph (4), the classification of shares besides common shares is shares with or without voting rights, shares with prerogative rights to nominate candidates for the board of directors and/or the board of commissioners, shares including the right to exchange one class of shares for another after a designated time or upon a designated occurrence, shares that provide priority rights to the owner with respect to receipt of dividends, and shares that provide priority rights to the owner with respect to distribution of the remaining assets from a liquidation process.

All shares must be registered in the name of the owner both in the company's register book and set out in the articles of association, or an amendment thereto, registered with the Ministry of Law and Human Rights and published in the *State Gazette* (*Berita Negara*). Bearer shares are not recognized in Indonesia. The registration of public company shares is conducted by the Central Securities Depository (*Kustodian Sentral Efek* / KSEI).

Transfer of Shares

Article 56 of the Company Law provides that the transfer of rights of shares must be performed by transfer of a rights deed. The deed may be made before a notary public or privately; in either case, the deed must be registered with the Ministry of Law and Human Rights and published in the *State Gazette*.

Basically, shareholders are free to transfer their shares, but there may be some prerequisites. The procedure of share transfer in a limited-liability company is subject to the company's articles of association. Share transfer may be subject to prior consent from other shareholders, prior consent from the company's organs (general meeting of shareholders, board of directors, or the board of commissioners), and/or prior consent from a governmental institution in accordance with the law.[11]

Approval or refusal for a transfer of shares by the company's organs must be provided in writing within ninety days from the date the request for approval is received by the company's organs. If no written statement is provided by the company within the determined period, an automatic approval from the company's organ is considered given regarding the transfer of shares.

In the case of issuance of new shares, each shareholder has the pre-emptive right to subscribe to newly issued shares in accordance with their respective proportion for the equivalent class of shares. New shares may be issued to a third party if the existing shareholders have waived their pre-emptive rights.[12] Provisions regarding pre-emptive rights also are regulated by the Capital Market and Financial Institution Regulatory Board (*Badan Pengawas Pasar Modal dan Lembaga Keuangan / Bapepam-LK*), now known as the Financial Services Authority (*Otoritas Jasa Keuangan*).[13]

While foreign interests are not restricted in ownership of shares listed on the Stock Exchange, shares in regular private Indonesian companies may only be held by Indonesian individuals or legal entities. In general, in most fields, foreign interests may hold shares in specific Indonesian companies designated as foreign investment limited-liability companies (PT PMA, *Penanaman Modal Asing*), pursuant to the Foreign Investment Law, Law Number 25 of 2007, replacing Law Number 1 of 1965. Periodically, the government issues a Negative Investment List (*Daftar Negatif Investasi* / DNI), setting out relevant sectors that are allowed and/or restricted to foreign investment, including its respective proportion to investment.[14]

---

11 Company Law, Article 57.
12 Company Law, Article 58.
13 Bapepam-LK Regulation Number IX.D.1.
14 Capital Market Law, Article 12, Paragraph 1; Government Regulation Number 44 of 2016.

Restrictions on transfer of shares may be agreed between or among the shareholders in the articles of association or in a shareholder agreement. Provisions regulated in the shareholder agreement must be set forth in the company's articles of association. Amendments covering the shareholder's proportion of shares in a company must be notified by the company through a notary public or directly to the Ministry of Law and Human Rights and published in the *State Gazette* once the parties have executed the transfer deed. An increase in the company's authorized capital requires Ministry of Law and Human Rights approval.

An increase in issued and paid-up capital must be notified to the Ministry of Law and Human Rights once the new shareholder has injected additional funds for the subscription of new shares. Any increase or decrease of capital or change of shareholders in a PMA company must first obtain approval of the Investment Coordinating Board (BKPM). Prior consent also may be required for any amendments to the shareholder's composition in certain business fields. For example, financial institutions whether bank or non-bank require prior consent for any change. The Company Law regulates transfer of shares as follows:

(1) Transfer of shares is performed by executing a deed of share transfer and providing a copy of the deed to the company;

(2) The board of directors must register every transfer, including the date of transfer, in the shareholder register (and update the special register, if applicable) and may notify amendments to the Ministry of Law and Human Rights within thirty days of the date of the transfer of shares being recorded;

(3) Transfers of shares in public companies shall be made in accordance with the prevailing Capital Market Law;[15] and

(4) The articles of association may provide additional requirements for a transfer of shares, such as an offer to shareholders of a certain class of shares, an offer made to employees, and the requirement to seek consent from third parties or the general meeting of shareholders. Shares can be pledged, unless otherwise provided under the articles of association. Pledges over shares must be registered in the shareholder register. A pledge is a security instrument only and voting rights on pledged shares remain with the shareholder.

---

15 Transfer of shares in public companies is scriptless, conducted by a broker, and must be registered.

Shareholder Voting Rights and Quorum

Basically, provisions regarding voting rights and quorum are stipulated in the company's articles of association. However, the legal basis of the stipulation is regulated in the Company Law. If possible, resolutions should be attempted to be agreed by consensus of all shareholders.

If no consensus can be reached, a vote is taken and the resolution will pass if favored by more than fifty per cent of the share/votes cast unless the articles of association require a greater percentage. The Company Law also requires a greater percentage for certain matters, such as amendment to the articles of association and merger or dissolution of a company. In addition, shareholders may conclude a resolution by circular resolution, without holding a general meeting of shareholders, as long as all of the shareholders are in agreement. The resolution will have the same legal force as the general meeting of shareholders' resolution.[16]

Each share will carry one vote, unless otherwise determined in the articles of association. Nonetheless, the vote may not apply with respect to company shares that are controlled by the company itself (treasury shares, which are limited to no more than 10 per cent of the total), parent company shares that are controlled whether directly or indirectly by a subsidiary, or company shares that are controlled by another company whose shares are directly or indirectly owned by the company.[17] Following are the specific quorum and voting requirements for certain corporate actions of the general meeting of shareholders:

(1) Amendments to the articles of association — Amendments to the articles of association must be conducted through a general meeting of shareholders wherein at least two-thirds of the entire company's shares with voting rights are present or represented in the general meeting of shareholders. The amendment will be considered valid if approved by at least two-thirds of the votes cast, unless a greater percentage is required under the articles of association. If the quorum is not reached at the first meeting, a second general meeting of shareholders may be held. The second general meeting of shareholders must be valid and authorized to conclude a resolution if at least three-fifths of the entire company's shares with voting rights are present or represented. The amendment will pass if approved by at least two-thirds of the

---

16 Company Law, Article 91.
17 Company Law, Article 84.

votes cast, unless otherwise determined by the articles of association. If the quorum cannot be reached in the second general meeting of shareholders, the company may request the chairman of the District Court whose jurisdiction covers the company's domicile to determine the quorum for a third general meeting of shareholders.[18]

(2) Merger, consolidation, acquisition, bankruptcy, and/or dissolution — A merger, consolidation, acquisition, bankruptcy, and/or dissolution of the company, as well as the transfer or pledge of more than 50 per cent of the company's assets as security for a loan, in one or more related or unrelated transactions, must be approved through a general meeting of shareholders wherein at least three-quarters of the entire company's shares with voting rights are present or represented. The action will require approval of at least three-quarters of the votes cast, unless a higher percentage is required under the articles of association. If the quorum is not reached, a second general meeting of shareholders may be held, in which the quorum must be two-thirds of the total shares with voting rights and approval by at least three-quarters of the votes cast.[19]

(3) Increase of issued and paid-up capital — An increase of issued and paid-up capital must be approved through a general meeting of shareholders wherein at least more than half (simple majority) of the entire company's shares with voting rights are present or represented in the general meeting of shareholders. The increase will be considered valid in terms of approval by more than half of the casted votes, unless otherwise determined by the articles of association.[20]

Quorum and Voting in Conflict-of-Interest Transactions

The Financial Services Authority also regulates voting rights and quorum requirements for certain corporate actions specifically for public companies. The requirements are stipulated in Financial Services Authority Regulation Number 32/POJK.04/2014 regarding the implementation of general meetings of shareholders in public companies.

---

18 Company Law, Articles 86–88.
19 Company Law, Articles 89–102(1).
20 Company Law, Article 42.

In addition, there are certain transactions that require approval from an independent shareholder through a general meeting of shareholders. These include conflict-of-interest transactions. A conflict-of-interest transaction is a transaction where the economic interest of a director, commissioner, or majority shareholder is not the same as, or is not in harmony with, that of the company, so that the transaction may cause a loss to the company.

In a conflict-of-interest transaction, the attendance (for quorum purposes) and votes cast by the shareholders with a conflict of interest are not calculated. This means that a quorum is reached if shareholders holding more than 50 per cent of the total shares owned by the independent shareholders, and those free of conflict of interest, attend the general meeting of shareholders. Even where the percentage of the shares owned by the independent shareholders is less than 50 per cent of the total issued shares of the company, the approval must be granted if more than 50 per cent of the shares owned by the independent shareholders are cast in favor. The approval is not required for the following transactions:

(1) A facility application provided by the company or a company controlled by the company to the commissioners, directors, or majority shareholders, where the majority shareholder also is an employee, provided that the application is considered relevant to their responsibilities within the company, in accordance with the company's policy, and has been approved by the general meeting of shareholders;

(2) A transaction between the company and any of its employees, directors, or commissioners, or between the company and the employees, directors, or commissioners of a controlled company, or transactions between the controlled company and the employees, directors, or commissioners of the controlled company, as well as transactions between the controlled company and company's employees, directors, or commissioners, provided that the transaction has been approved by the general meeting of shareholders, including all benefits provided by the company or the controlled company to its employees, directors, or commissioners with the same terms and in accordance with the company's policy;

(3) Remuneration, including salary, pension fund contribution, and/or special benefits granted to commissioners, directors, and majority shareholders who also are employees, if the total amount has been disclosed in the annual financial statement;

(4) A transaction with continuous nature which commenced following a public offering which has fulfilled the requirements of the prevailing regulations and that transaction's terms and conditions do not inflict any loss to the company;
(5) A transaction conducted by the company, the value of which does not exceed 0.5 per cent of the paid-up capital of the company, provided that the 0.5 per cent of the paid-up capital does not exceed Rp. 5-billion; or
(6) A transaction conducted in compliance with the law or a court judgment.[21]

Rights in Proxy Voting

A shareholder with voting rights may appoint a representative (proxy) to attend a general meeting of shareholders on its behalf by providing a power of attorney. The proxy may cast its votes in accordance with the representative proportion of shares owned by the shareholder.

However, if the shareholder decides to attend the general meeting of shareholders in person, the proxy may not be recognized in the general meeting and the power of attorney will be invalid, whereby the power of attorney is valid for one meeting only. Nor may an employee or member of the board of directors or board of commissioners act as proxy to vote on behalf of a shareholder to vote in the general meeting of shareholders.[22]

Shareholder Meetings

In General

Shares provide their owners the right to attend a general meeting of shareholders and cast votes in the meeting following its registration in the shareholder register. Only listed shareholders are entitled to participate in a general meeting of shareholders. Under the Company Law, a general meeting of shareholders consists of annual general meetings of shareholders and extraordinary general meetings of shareholders.

A general meeting of shareholders must be held at the company's domicile as it is determined in the articles of association. A general

---

[21] Bapepam-LK Regulation Number IX.E.1.
[22] Company Law, Article 85.

meeting of shareholders also may be held elsewhere within Indonesia. It also is required to provide minutes of a meeting, approved and signed by the general meeting of shareholder participants. A general meeting of shareholders may be held as long as more than half of the total number of shares with voting rights are present or represented in the general meeting of shareholders, unless a greater percentage is otherwise provided by the law and/or the articles of association.

Agenda

A general meeting of shareholders may be called by the board of directors, board of commissioners, or one or more shareholders who jointly represent one-tenth or more of the total number of shares with voting rights, unless otherwise determined in the articles of association.[23] The notice should include the agenda, which gives the structure and the issues to be discussed at the general meeting of shareholders.

The annual general meeting of shareholders must be held no later than six months following the end of the company's fiscal year. At the annual general meeting of shareholders, the board of directors is required to present the company's annual report, including an audited financial statement. The report should have obtained prior consent from the board of commissioners and be accepted by the shareholders at the annual general meeting, which acceptance absolves the board of directors from liability.

Other matters commonly resolved in annual general meetings of shareholders are dividend distributions, amendments in the board's structure, auditor's appointment, election of directors and commissioners whose terms have expired or who have resigned, compensation provided to the board of directors and board of commissioners, and statutory reserve allocations. An extraordinary general meeting of shareholders may be held any time required by the shareholders or by the board of directors. No specific provisions are regulated in the Company Law regarding the agenda for an extraordinary general meeting of shareholders.

Notice

In accordance with the Company Law, notice of a general meeting of shareholders must be made through registered mail and/or publication

---

23 Company Law, Article 79.

in at least two daily newspapers. Notice is to be delivered to the shareholders at least fifteen days prior to the date of the general meeting of shareholders.

A shareholder seeking to hold an annual general meeting of shareholders must request that notice be sent by the board of directors or, if the board of directors fails to deliver it, to the board of commissioners. If neither send the notice, a shareholder may request the chairman of the District Court within the company's domicile to authorize the shareholder to deliver the notice. For publicly listed companies, an early announcement is required to be made prior to the general meeting of shareholders' notice delivery in accordance with the Capital Market Regulation.[24]

Media

In accordance with Article 77 of the Company Law, a general meeting of shareholders also may be conducted through teleconference, video conference, or other electronic media that enables the general meeting of shareholder participants to see and hear each other during the meeting.

Inspection of Shareholder Lists

Every shareholder has the right to examine, search, and copy the list of shareholders. Shareholders are entitled to verify the accuracy of information in the list regarding themselves and their holdings. They also are entitled to submit an objection to any irregularity in the list and request an amendment to correct information or add missing information.

The board of directors is obligated to provide and maintain a list of shareholders that must contain, for each shareholder, shareholder's name and address; amount, number, and date of the share's acquisition, along with its classification, if more than one type of shares was issued; paid-up amount of each share; if the shares are pledged, the name and address of the individual or legal entity who is entitled to the share's pledge rights, including the date the pledge was acquired and its registration; and information regarding other forms of payment made for the shares, if not paid in currency, as stipulated in Article 34 of the Company Law.[25]

The board of directors also is required to maintain a special list containing information regarding shares owned by members of the board

---

[24] Company Law, Article 83.
[25] Company Law, Article 50.

of directors and board of commissioners, including relatives, in the company and/or related companies, along with the date the shares were acquired. The shareholders' list must be made available at the company's domicile to enable the shareholders to inspect the related information.

The board of directors must actively revise and/or record amendments made to the shareholder list from time to time. This will apply as long as the Capital Market Law does not otherwise apply, in which case the provisions stipulated in Article 50, Paragraphs (1), (3), and (4), will apply to listed companies.

Upon written request from the shareholders, the board of directors must allow the shareholders to examine the list (register of shareholders and special register), minutes of general meetings of shareholders, and annual reports. Members of the board of commissioners have the right to inspect this list, as well as all other corporate documentation.

Acquisition and Tender Offers

Acquisition and tender offers are regulated by Financial Services Authority Regulation Number IX.H.1 In a tender offer performance, the new controlling shareholder is required to:
(1) Deliver an announcement text of the tender offer to the Financial Services Authority, containing a tender offer disclosure attaching the related documents, no later than two business days follow the takeover announcement;
(2) Deliver any amendments and/or additional information including documents attached to the announcement text above, no later than five business days following the receipt of request from the Financial Services Authority;
(3) Announce information disclosure regarding tender offer in at least one Indonesian daily newspaper no later than two business days following the receipt of a letter from the Financial Services Authority, stating that the new controlling shareholder may announce information disclosure regarding the tender offer;
(4) Perform a tender offer for thirty days commencing one day following the day of the announcement;
(5) Complete the tender offer transaction by delivering the money, no later than twelve business days following the expiration of the offering period as determined in point 4, above; and
(6) Deliver the tender offer result report to the Financial Services Authority no later than five business days following the expiration of the transaction completion, as determined in point 5, above.

The disclosure announcement is required to contain the acquisition background and information regarding the shares, including the amount and percentage of shares that are to be purchased and the amount and percentage of the target company's shares, whether directly or indirectly owned by the new controlling shareholder, including options to purchase or rights to receive dividends or other benefits and the power to cast votes in the taken-over public company's general meeting of shareholders.

Distributions

The Company Law requires that a company reserve a certain amount from its net profit each year, not to exceed twenty per cent of the issued and paid-up capital, as a reserve fund to ensure the company has gained profit in the same year.[26] Dividends may only be distributed among the shareholders if the company has gained positive profit balance.

A company may distribute interim dividends prior to the end of the company's financial year as long as it is regulated in the company's articles of association. The distribution may be made only if the company's total net assets are not less than the company's issued and paid-up capital plus the mandatory reserves. The distribution may not interfere with the company's activities or cause the company to be unable to perform its obligations towards any creditor. Distribution of interim dividends is based on the board of directors' decision with prior consent from the board of commissioners. If there is a loss suffered by the company at the end of the company's fiscal year, distributed interim dividends must be returned to the company by the shareholders.

The board of directors and board of commissioners will be jointly and severally liable for the company's losses if shareholders are not able to return distributed interim dividends. Dividends that are not collected for five years after the determined date must be placed in the special reserve fund. The general meeting of shareholders may determine the procedure to collect dividends that were placed in the special reserve fund. Dividends that were placed in the special reserve fund and are not collected within ten years will be owned by the company.

---

[26] Company Law, Article 70.

Derivative Suits and Put Option

Derivative Suits

A company's actions that may be considered detrimental to the shareholders or the company itself include amendments of the articles of association, transfer or placing any security right over the company's assets that are valued at more than fifty per cent of the company's total net assets, or merger, consolidation, acquisition, or spin-off.[27]

Under the Company Law, one or more shareholders who represent one-tenth of the total shares with legal voting rights may file a lawsuit within the District Court against the board of directors for its negligence.[28] One or more shareholders who represent one-tenth of the total shares with legal voting rights may submit a request to the District Court to investigate the company to obtain required information for some specific reason.[29]

One or more shareholders who represent one-tenth of the total shares with legal voting rights may submit a request within the District Court to dissolve the company if it is deemed to not be able to continue its businesses.[30] Such shareholders may request the convening of a general meeting of shareholders.

If the board of directors or the board of commissioners fails to perform the call for a general meeting of shareholders within thirty days, the shareholders requesting the general meeting of shareholders may submit a request to the District Court to permit shareholders to perform the call for a general meeting of shareholders.[31] One or more shareholders who represent one-tenth of the total shares with legal voting rights may file a lawsuit at the District Court against the board of commissioners for its negligence.[32]

Put Option

Detrimental actions resulting from a merger, consolidation, acquisition, or spin-off may not be contested by the minority shareholders. However, they are entitled to request that the company repurchase the shares

---

27 Company Law, Article 62(1).
28 Company Law, Article 97(6).
29 Company Law, Article 138.
30 Company Law, Article 114.
31 Company Law, Articles 79 and 80.
32 Company Law, Article 114(6).

owned by them at a reasonable price, wherein the nominal value of the repurchase may not exceed ten per cent of the company's issued capital.

The repurchase may not cause the net assets of the company to become less than the subscribed capital added with the mandatory reserves set aside.[33] If exceeded, the company is required to strive to enable the remaining shares to be purchased by a third party.

Business Plan

The annual business plan of a company is regulated by Article 63 of the Company Law. The board of directors is required to prepare the business plan prior to the commencement of the upcoming financial year. The business plan must contain the company's annual budget and activities to be performed by the company for the upcoming financial year.

The business plan must be delivered by the board of directors to the board of commissioners or to the general meeting of shareholders, as determined in the articles of association. The articles of association may designate whether the business plan requires approval from the board of commissioners or the general meeting of shareholders, unless otherwise determined by the law. If the articles of association require the business plan to be approved by the general meeting of shareholders, the plan must be reviewed in advance by the board of commissioners.[34]

Under Article 65 of the Company Law, it is possible to apply the previous year's business plan if the board of directors fails to deliver the business plan to the board of commissioners or the general meeting of shareholders in accordance with the articles of association. This condition occurs if the board of directors fails to complete the business plan for the upcoming financial year or the board of directors does not submit the prepared business plan to the board of commissioners or the general meeting of shareholders for approval.

In this case, all provisions and activities that must be applied in the upcoming financial year must be based on the previous business plan. If the board of directors has prepared and delivered the business plan to the board of commissioners or the general meeting of shareholders, but it has not yet been approved, the previous business plan will apply for the upcoming financial year.

---

33 Company Law, Article 37.
34 Company Law, Article 64.

Access to Corporate Information

In accordance with the Company Law, the board of directors is responsible for disclosure and transparency. The shareholders are entitled to obtain certain information in relation to the company upon written request. The board of directors shall disclose any information related to the company to the shareholders through a general meeting of shareholders as long as the disclosed information is in accordance with the meeting agenda and does not contravene the company's interests.[35] The board of directors also is required to allow the shareholders to examine the shareholder list, shareholder special list, minutes of the general meeting of shareholders, and annual reports.

In addition, under the Financial Services Authority Regulation,[36] information or material facts that may affect the share price must be disclosed to the public not later than two business days from the date the information or facts become available. Such information or material facts would relate to the following:

(1) Merger, consolidation, or joint venture;
(2) Tender offers to purchase another company's shares;
(3) Purchase of shares with material value;
(4) Splitting or incorporation of shares;
(5) Distribution of interim dividends;
(6) Delisting and re-registration of shares in the stock exchange;
(7) Extraordinary dividend income;
(8) New material invention or product;
(9) Sale of additional shares to the public;
(10) Amendment in the public company's management;
(11) Purchase/buy back of debt securities;
(12) Purchase of crucial assets;
(13) Labor dispute;
(14) Material lawsuit against the public company, the board of directors, or the board of commissioners;
(15) Accountant replacement;
(16) Trustee replacement;
(17) Share administration replacement;
(18) Amendment of the company's fiscal year book;
(19) Amendment of the currency applied in the financial statement;
(20) Restrictions on the company's business activities;

---

35 Company Law, Article 75(2).
36 Financial Services Authority Regulation Number 31/POYJ.04/2015.

(21) Amendment of the published financial projection;
(22) Debt restructuring;
(23) Suspension of part or the entire business segment;
(24) Material impact on the company resulting from an event of *force majeure*; and/or
(25) Other material information or facts.

In accordance with Article 138 of the Company Law, a company may be inspected in order to obtain data or information if there is suspicion that the company has committed an act that is considered a violation of the law and is detrimental to the shareholders or other third parties, or members of the board of directors or board of commissioners of the company have committed an act that is considered a violation of the law and is detrimental to the shareholders or other third parties.

The inspection must be carried out by submitting a written request, together with the reasons to the District Court covering the company's jurisdiction. The request may be submitted by one or more shareholders representing at least one tenth of the total number of shares with voting rights; other parties based on the regulations, articles of association, or contract with the company, who have been provided with the authority to apply the request; or the public prosecutor's office for the public interest.

Conclusion

Principally, shareholder liability is based on the shares invested in the company as it is implied in the Company Law and the Commercial Code. Shareholders may not be personally liable for any action made by and on behalf of the company and for any loss suffered by the company exceeding their owned shares.

However, the shareholders may be personally liable for the company's loss if otherwise determined by the prevailing law. Any action or decision made by the shareholders must be in accordance with the prevailing law and regulations.

Mexico

Vanessa Romero
Cannizzo, Ortiz y Asociados, S.C.
Mexico City, Mexico

Introduction

Private law in Mexico is governed by a general principle known as autonomy of will (*principio de autonomia de la voluntad*), pursuant to which individuals are free to waive any right granted by law, provided that such waiver does not directly affect public interest or rights of a third party.[1] In view of the foregoing, all provisions referred to hereunder must be understood as waivable within the aforementioned limits.

Pursuant to the General Law of Commercial Companies, there are several types of companies and partnerships that may be created with a separate legal personality from that of their shareholders or partners. For companies, capital stock is integrated by shares, including those for a:

(1) Stock company (*sociedad anónima*);
(2) Simplified stock company (*sociedad por acciones simplificada*);
(3) Special partnership with shares (*sociedad en comandita por acciones*); and
(4) Promotion of investment stock company (*sociedad anónima promotora de inversion*).

For partnerships, capital is integrated by equity quotas, including those for a:

(1) Limited-liability company (*sociedad de responsabilidad limitada*);
(2) General partnership (*sociedad en nombre colectivo*); and
(3) Special partnership (*sociedad en comandita simple*).

All the aforementioned companies and partnerships also may be incorporated as companies and partnerships with variable capital stock[2] (*sociedades de capital variable*). In the variable capital companies and partnerships, capital may be increased through new contributions made

---

[1] Federal Civil Code, Article 6. Article 78 of the Code of Commerce provides that, in commercial conventions, each party obliges himself in the terms evident to which such party wished to be bound.
[2] General Law of Commercial Companies, Article 1.

by the shareholders or partners or by admission of new shareholders or partners, or reduced by the partial or total withdrawal of contributions without further conditions.[3] All increases or decreases of capital must be recorded in a special registry book kept by the company or partnership for such purpose.[4]

Companies and partnerships with variable capital will be governed by the same provisions as the corresponding kind of company or partnership and by the stock company's (*sociedad anónima*) provisions in relation to the balance sheets and the administrator or manager liabilities.[5]

Commercial companies and partnerships may perform all mercantile acts required to develop their corporate purpose, unless they are forbidden by law or their by-laws and articles of incorporation and association.[6] Companies and partnerships must be incorporated before a public notary or commercial public notary (*corredor público*); the latter may not authorize the corresponding incorporation if the by-laws and articles of incorporation and association contravene the law.[7]

Companies and Partnerships

Legal Personality

Commercial companies and partnerships acquire legal personality independent from that of their shareholders or partners when recorded in the Public Registry of Commerce (*Registro Público de Comercio*).[8] However, companies and partnerships not recorded in the Public Registry of Commerce also are treated as legal entities if they act as such towards third parties.

In this case, the persons who acted on behalf of the company and partnership as representatives or attorneys-in-fact will be liable before third parties for their activities in a jointly and unlimited manner, without prejudice to any criminal liability which they may incur if such acts cause harm to the third parties.[9] Shareholders or partners not liable

---

3 General Law of Commercial Companies, Article 213.
4 General Law of Commercial Companies, Article 219.
5 General Law of Commercial Companies, Article 214.
6 General Law of Commercial Companies, Article 4.
7 General Law of Commercial Companies, Article 5.
8 General Law of Commercial Companies, Article 2.
9 General Law of Commercial Companies, Article 7.

for the non-recordation of company and partnership with the Public Registry of Commerce may claim damages payment from the guilty parties and from those who acted as representatives or attorneys in fact of the irregular company or partnership.

Companies and partnerships recorded with the Public Registry of Commerce cannot be declared null and void unless they engage in illegal activities; in such case, they must be immediately liquidated upon request of any person.[10] The liquidation will consist of the disposal of the assets of the company and partnership to pay its debts, while any surplus must be applied to extinguish any civil liabilities or, if there is none, turned over to the Public Charity (*Beneficencia Pública*) of the domicile of the company and partnership.

Types of Companies and Partnerships

Companies

Stock Company. A stock company may not have less than two shareholders.[11] No mandatory minimum capital stock may be provided by law; however, minimum capital must be determined upon incorporation.[12] It may be incorporated either by the persons subscribing the deed of incorporation (founders) appearing before a public notary, a commercial public notary (*corredor público*), or through public subscription pursuant to the Securities Market Law[13] (*Ley del Mercado de Valores*).[14]

Simplified Stock Company. A simplified stock company may be incorporated with one or more shareholders (they must be individuals having an advanced electronic signature in force who are not simultaneously shareholders and partners of another company and partnership which the shareholder controls or manages).[15] No mandatory minimum capital stock is provided by law; however, minimum capital must be determined upon incorporation.

---

10 General Law of Commercial Companies, Articles 2 and 3.
11 General Law of Commercial Companies, Article 89.
12 General Law of Commercial Companies, Article 91.
13 *Official Gazette of the Federation*, 30 December 2005 (last modification, 10 January 2014).
14 General Law of Commercial Companies, Article 90.
15 General Law of Commercial Companies, Article 260.

The total annual income of the company may not exceed MXN 5-million (amount to be updated on an annual basis on 1 January each year, pursuant to the factor to be published by the Ministry of Economy (*Secretaría de Economía*) in December of each year). The company does not need to be incorporated through a public deed. It can be incorporated through the online system of the Ministry of Economy. Once the company has been incorporated, the Ministry of Economy will record it with the Public Registry of Commerce.

Special Partnership with Shares. A special partnership with shares may not have less than two partners. No mandatory minimum capital is provided by law; however, minimum capital must be determined upon incorporation. Active or general partners (*socios comanditados*) may not engage in businesses similar to that of the partnership without the unanimous consent of all the other partners.[16] It is governed by similar rules to those governing stock companies.[17]

Promotion of Investment Stock Company. A promotion of investment stock company may not have less than two shareholders. No mandatory minimum capital stock is provided by law; however, minimum capital must be determined upon incorporation.

Partnerships

Limited-Liability Company. A limited-liability company must have at least than two partners and not more than fifty.[18] No mandatory minimum capital is provided by law; however, minimum capital must be determined upon incorporation. Capital is divided in equity participations, each of which must represent at least MXN 1 or a multiple of the amount.[19] They cannot be incorporated nor may their capital be increased through public subscription.[20]

Special Partnership. A special partnership may not have less than two partners. No mandatory minimum capital stock is provided by law; however, minimum capital must be determined upon incorporation. Partners may not engage in businesses similar to those of the partnership

---

16 General Law of Commercial Companies, Articles 35 and 211.
17 General Law of Commercial Companies, Article 208.
18 General Law of Commercial Companies, Articles 59 and 61.
19 General Law of Commercial Companies, Article 62.
20 General Law of Commercial Companies, Article 63.

without the unanimous consent of all the other partners.[21] It is governed by rules similar to those governing partnerships.

General Partnership. A general partnership may not have less than two partners. No mandatory minimum capital stock is provided by law; however, minimum capital must be determined upon incorporation. Partners may not engage in businesses similar to those of the partnership without the unanimous consent of all the other partners.[22]

Shares and Equity Quotas

The main differences between shares (which represent the capital of companies) and equity quotas (which represent the capital of partnerships) are the following:

(1) Shares are represented by negotiable nominal certificates,[23] while equity quotas may be represented by certificates but they may not be negotiable.

(2) Shares serve the purpose of accrediting and transferring the status and rights of shareholders,[24] while the status and rights of partners arise from their recordation in the special partners book of each partnership.[25] Notwithstanding the aforementioned, stock companies also are bound to keep a shares registry book in which all share transfers must be recorded in order for the company to acknowledge its holder as shareholder of the company.[26] Transfer of shares is usually performed through endorsement since they are considered as negotiable instruments.[27]

(3) Each share (of the same class) is equal in value and confers equal rights,[28] while equity quotas may be unequal as regards value and must always represent MXN 1 or a multiple of this amount.

(4) Each shareholder may hold one or more shares, while each partner may hold only one equity quota. If a partner makes a new contribution or takes over part, or all, of the interests of another partner, the value and its interest will be increased accordingly.

---

21 General Law of Commercial Companies, Articles 35 and 57.
22 General Law of Commercial Companies, Article 35.
23 General Law of Commercial Companies, Article 111.
24 General Law of Commercial Companies, Article 111.
25 General Law of Commercial Companies, Article 73.
26 General Law of Commercial Companies, Article 129.
27 General Law of Commercial Companies, Article 131.
28 General Law of Commercial Companies, Article 112.

Although the General Law of Commercial Companies provides that each share of the stock companies is equal in value and confers equal rights, by-laws may provide that:
(1) Certain shares will only confer voting rights in special meetings held to deal with specific matters;
(2) Certain shares will not grant any voting rights;
(3) Certain shares will grant only economic rights;
(4) Corporate rights of the shares will be limited to the voting right;
(5) Certain shares will grant veto right; and
(6) Affirmative votes of one or more shareholders will be required to take resolutions within the general shareholders' meeting.[29]

The General Law of Commercial Companies also allows the inclusion in the by-laws of the companies of restrictions to the transfer of the property or rights regarding shares of a specific class or series. When different classes of shares have been issued by a company, all resolutions that may affect the rights of any of such classes must be previously agreed by the holders of corresponding shares through a special shareholders' meeting, in which the voting quorum will be the same as that required to amend the by-laws of the company.[30] Promotion of investment stock companies are allowed to issue various classes of shares as described above.

Shareholder and Partner Liability

Shareholder and Partner Liability to Third Parties

Companies

Stock Company. A stock company is composed of two or more shareholders only responsible for the payment in full of their shares.[31] Upon incorporation, at least 20 per cent of the value of each share payable in cash must be paid while the value of each share, payable partially or totally in kind, must be fully paid.[32]

---

29 General Law of Commercial Companies, Articles 91 and 113.
30 General Law of Commercial Companies, Article 195.
31 General Law of Commercial Companies, Article 87.
32 General Law of Commercial Companies, Article 89.

Simplified Stock Company. A simplified stock company is composed of one or more shareholders who is and are only bound to pay their contributions.[33] Upon incorporation, shareholders must set the minimum capital stock which must be fully subscribed within a maximum term of one year after the company has been recorded in the Public Registry of Commerce.[34]

Special Partnership with Shares. A special partnership with shares is composed by one or more general or active partners who are personally, subsidiarily, unlimitedly, and jointly liable for all business obligations of the partnership and one or more limited partners whose only obligation consists in the payment of their respective contributions to the capital.[35] Any clauses contained in the by-laws of partnership which exclude mentioned liability have no legal effect towards third parties.

However, the partners may stipulate that, among themselves, the liability of one or more of them is limited to a certain sum.[36] Any person who causes or allows his name to appear in the name of this partnership will be subject to the same liability referred to above.[37]

Any person, non-related to the partnership or a limited partner who causes or allows his name to appear in the name of this partnership, will be subject to the same liability as the general or active partners (*socios comanditados*). The limited partners will be subject to the same liability if the words *Sociedad en Comandita* are not included in the name of the partnership.[38]

Partnerships

Limited-Liability Company. A limited-liability company is composed of two or more partners whose liability is limited to the amount of their contribution to the capital.[39] A person who is not related to the partnership and who causes or allows his name to appear in the name of the partnership will be subject to the same liability up to the highest of the contributions made by the partners.[40]

---

33 General Law of Commercial Companies, Article 260.
34 General Law of Commercial Companies, Article 265.
35 General Law of Commercial Companies, Article 207.
36 General Law of Commercial Companies, Articles 26 and 211.
37 General Law of Commercial Companies, Articles 28 and 211.
38 General Law of Commercial Companies, Articles 53 and 211.
39 General Law of Commercial Companies, Article 58.
40 General Law of Commercial Companies, Article 60.

The articles of association also may oblige the partners to make additional contributions in proportion to those they originally made.[41] Upon incorporation, the capital must be fully subscribed and at least fifty per cent of each equity participation must be paid.[42] The same rule applies to increases of capital stock subsequent to the incorporation of the partnership.

Special Partnership. A special partnership is composed of one or more general or active partners who are personally, subsidiarily, unlimitedly, and jointly liable for all business obligations of the partnership and one or more limited partners whose only obligation consists in the payment of their respective contributions to the capital.[43] Any clauses contained in the by-laws of the partnership which exclude the liability of the general or active partners have no legal effect towards third parties.

However, the partners may stipulate that, among themselves, the liability of one or more of them is limited to a certain sum.[44] Any person, non-related to the partnership or a limited partner who causes or allows his and her name to appear in the name of this partnership, will be subject to the same liability as the general or active partners. The limited partners will be subject to the same liability if the words *Sociedad en Comandita* are not included in the name of the partnership.[45]

General Partnership. All partners are personally, subsidiarily, unlimitedly, and jointly liable for the business obligations of the partnership.[46] Any clauses contained in the by-laws of partnership excluding such liability have no legal effect towards third parties; however, the partners may stipulate that, amongst themselves, the liability of one or more of them is limited to a certain sum.[47] Any person who causes or allows his and her name to appear in the name of this partnership will be subject to the same liability referred to above.[48]

The only forms of business enterprise available in Mexico that, as a general rule, afford all their investing participants (shareholders or partners) limited liability are the stock company, the capital stock

---

41 General Law of Commercial Companies, Article 70.
42 General Law of Commercial Companies, Article 64.
43 General Law of Commercial Companies, Article 51.
44 General Law of Commercial Companies, Articles 26 and 57.
45 General Law of Commercial Companies, Article 53.
46 General Law of Commercial Companies, Article 25.
47 General Law of Commercial Companies, Article 26.
48 General Law of Commercial Companies, Article 28.

promotion of investment company, the simplified stock company, and the limited liability company. New shareholders or partners of a previously incorporated company or partnership will be liable for all the obligations incurred prior to his and her and its admission.[49]

Shareholders or partners who withdrew or were excluded from a company or partnership will remain liable before third parties for unconcluded transactions at the time of his and her and its withdrawal or exclusion.[50] The limit of this liability will be the one who corresponds to the shareholders and partners of each kind of company.

Judicial resolutions issued against the company or partnership, condemning it to fulfill any obligation toward a third party, will be considered enforceable against its shareholders or partners when they were sued along with the company or partnership. In such case, the resolution will be executed first against the assets of the company or partnership and, if they were not enough to fulfill the obligation claimed through the judicial procedure, against the assets of the sued shareholders or partners.[51] If the obligation of the shareholders or partners was limited to the amount of their contributions, the resolution may only be executed against them up to the unpaid part of the amount.

Shareholders or partners whose contribution to the capital of the company or partnership consist in one or more credits will be liable for their existence and legality, as well as for the solvency of the debtor at the time when the contribution was made. If the aforementioned contribution consists of securities, the shareholder or partner must guarantee that they have not been subject to the publication provided by law for the case of loss of such securities.[52]

Liability among Shareholders and Partners

The General Law of Commercial Companies provides that shareholders of a stock company are authorized to enter into agreements with the other shareholders regarding:
(1) Drag-along rights (giving the right to the majority shareholder to include minority shareholders in the sale of its shares);
(2) Tag-along rights (giving the right to minority shareholders to sell their shares along with a majority shareholder);

---

49 General Law of Commercial Companies, Article 13.
50 General Law of Commercial Companies, Article 14.
51 General Law of Commercial Companies, Article 24.
52 General Law of Commercial Companies, Article 12.

(3) Rights and obligations related to the sale and purchase options regarding their shares;
(4) Disposal of the preferential right they have in proportion to the shares they own in the capital stock of the company;
(5) Voting rights in the shareholders' meeting;
(6) Sale of shares through public offering; and
(7) Other similar covenants.[53]

These agreements are not enforceable against the company unless a judicial resolution has been issued. Regarding simplified stock companies, all agreements entered into by and between the sole shareholder and the company must be recorded in the electronic publication system for commercial companies of the Ministry of Economy (*sistema electrónico de publicaciones de sociedades mercantiles*).[54]

Distributions

The by-laws and articles of incorporation and association of a company or partnership must include the way to distribute profits and losses among the shareholders and partners.[55] The following rules must be observed in the distribution of profits and losses:

(1) Profits and losses must be distributed in proportion to the nominal amount of the shares or the value of the corresponding equity quotas;[56]
(2) A working shareholder or partner (*accionista o socio industrial*) will be entitled to half of the profits and, if there is more than one working shareholder or partner, the half must be divided between them (working shareholders and partners do not participate in the losses of the corresponding company or partnership);[57]
(3) An agreement pursuant to which one or more shareholders or partners are excluded from the distribution of profits will not produce a legal effect;[58]
(4) Should there be loss of capital of the company or partnership, such capital must be reinstated or reduced before a distribution of profits is made;[59]

---

[53] General Law of Commercial Companies, Article 198.
[54] General Law of Commercial Companies, Article 264.
[55] General Law of Commercial Companies, Article 6.
[56] General Law of Commercial Companies, Article 16.
[57] General Law of Commercial Companies, Article 16.
[58] General Law of Commercial Companies, Article 17.
[59] General Law of Commercial Companies, Article 18.

(5) Profits may only be distributed after the financial statements of the company or partnership from which they arise have been approved by the general meeting of shareholders or partners;[60]
(6) Profits may only be distributed after losses suffered in one or more of the preceding fiscal years have been restored or the capital has been reduced;[61] and
(7) A minimum of five per cent of the net profits of the company or partnership must be annually set aside to form the reserve fund until it has reached the twenty per cent of the capital of the company or partnership,[62] and the reserve fund must be formed again if it has suffered any loss for any reason.

In case of non-fulfillment of the above obligation, the portion of the profits that was not set aside to form the reserve fund must be paid by the liable administrator(s) and manager(s).[63] This provision is not applicable to the simplified stock companies. Private creditors of a shareholder or partner are not entitled to enforce any right against him except regarding his profits pursuant to the corresponding financial statements; the amounts corresponding to the shareholder or partner when the company is liquidated; and any other reimbursement made in his favor. Private creditors of shareholders of companies may seize the shares of the debtor and sell them following the corresponding judicial procedure.

In general partnerships, special partnerships, and limited liability companies, the capital may not be distributed among the partners until after the partnership is dissolved and wound up.[64] In general partnerships and special partnerships, working partners, unless otherwise agreed, will be entitled to receive periodically the amounts required for their living. Said amounts and payment terms will be agreed by the majority of the partners or, if no such agreement is reached in regard thereto, by the judicial authority.[65]

In stock companies, an additional participation in the annual profits may be granted to the founders of the company. The participation may not exceed ten per cent of the annual profits and may not last more than

---

60 General Law of Commercial Companies, Article 19.
61 General Law of Commercial Companies, Article 19.
62 General Law of Commercial Companies, Article 20.
63 General Law of Commercial Companies, Article 21.
64 General Law of Commercial Companies, Articles 48, 57, and 86.
65 General Law of Commercial Companies, Article 49.

ten years following the incorporation of the company.[66] To evidence the granting of the aforementioned right, a founder bonus (*bono de fundador*) will be issued. The bonus will not be considered as capital of the company.[67]

In stock companies, if the company issued shares with limited voting rights, no profits may be paid in favor of ordinary shares until a profit of five per cent, or the higher percentage eventually agreed by the shareholders, has been previously paid in favor of the holders of limited voting rights shares.[68]

Shareholder and Partner Meetings

Companies

Stock Company. The general meeting of shareholders is the supreme authority of the company.[69] General meetings may be ordinary or extraordinary, depending on the matters dealt with.[70] They must be held at the company's principal place of business; otherwise, they will be null and void, except in case of *force majeure*.[71] However, by-laws may provide that resolutions taken outside a shareholders' meeting by unanimous consent of the shareholders representing all the shares with voting rights will have the same validity as if they had been adopted by a shareholders' meeting, provided that they are confirmed in writing.[72]

Ordinary general meetings must be held at least once a year, within four months following the termination of the business year, in order to approve the financial statements and to appoint or ratify the appointment of the directors and auditor(s).[73] Shareholders' meetings must be called by the sole administrator or board of directors or by the statutory auditor.[74] Shareholders who represent at least thirty-three per cent of the capital stock of the company may request in writing for a meeting to be called.

The request may be made by the holder of one share if no shareholders' meeting has been held through the past two years and when the

---

66 General Law of Commercial Companies, Article 105.
67 General Law of Commercial Companies, Articles 106 and 107.
68 General Law of Commercial Companies, Article 113.
69 General Law of Commercial Companies, Article 178.
70 General Law of Commercial Companies, Articles 180 and 182.
71 General Law of Commercial Companies, Article 179.
72 General Law of Commercial Companies, Article 178.
73 General Law of Commercial Companies, Article 181.
74 General Law of Commercial Companies, Article 183.

meetings held in the two years did not comply with the mandatory agenda for an annual meeting.[75] In order for an ordinary meeting to be considered as duly convened, at least half of the company's capital stock must be represented and its resolutions will be valid when taken by the majority of the votes present at the meeting.[76]

In a second call for ordinary meetings, resolutions will be valid when agreed by any percentage of the capital stock.[77] In order for an extraordinary meeting to be considered as duly convened, at least seventy-five per cent of the company's capital stock must be represented, and its resolutions will be valid when taken by the shareholders who represent at least half of the company's capital.[78] In a second call for extraordinary meetings, resolutions will be valid when taken by half of the capital stock of the company.[79] Administrators and statutory auditors may not vote in resolutions related to the approval of their reports.[80]

Shareholders who represent at least twenty-five per cent of the company's capital stock may challenge in court the resolutions taken through general meetings, provided that the lawsuit is filed within fifteen days following the closure of the meeting; the plaintiffs did not concur to the meeting or did not vote in the corresponding resolutions; and the lawsuit refers to the legal provision's violated clause of the governing instrument.[81] Shareholders' meetings must be recorded in a meeting minutes book. Extraordinary meetings must be notarized by a public notary or commercial public notary (*corredor público*) and recorded with the Public Registry of Commerce.[82]

Simplified Stock Company. All shareholders are entitled to participate in the resolutions of the company. All shares must be of equal value and will grant equal rights.[83] Resolutions must be taken by the majority of votes (including the amendment to the by-laws) and they may be taken through meetings held through electronic means if it was provided in the by-laws of the company.[84]

---

[75] General Law of Commercial Companies, Article 185.
[76] General Law of Commercial Companies, Article 189.
[77] General Law of Commercial Companies, Article 191. Notwithstanding the aforementioned, note that a different percentage may be agreed through the governing instrument of each company or partnership.
[78] General Law of Commercial Companies, Article 190.
[79] General Law of Commercial Companies, Article 191.
[80] General Law of Commercial Companies, Article 197.
[81] General Law of Commercial Companies, Article 201.
[82] General Law of Commercial Companies, Article 194.
[83] General Law of Commercial Companies, Article 268.
[84] General Law of Commercial Companies, Article 266.

Meetings must be called by the Administrator through a publication in the electronic publication system for commercial companies (*Sistema electrónico de publicaciones de sociedades mercantiles*) of the Ministry of Economy with an anticipation of five days. If the administrator fails to call the meeting, any shareholder may request to a judicial authority to make the respective call.[85] The shareholders will be entitled to modify the provisions included in the law for this kind of companies by transforming it to another kind of company before a public notary or commercial public notary.[86]

Partnerships

Limited-Liability Company. Resolutions are valid when approved by at least half of the capital stock, unless the governing instrument of the partnership requires a higher amount. If the voting quota is not reached in the first call of the meeting, a second call will be made and resolutions will be valid if taken with the majority of votes of the partners represented in the meeting.[87] All partners will be entitled to participate in the partners meeting with one vote for each MXN 1,000[88] unless special provisions regarding privileged equity quotas are contained in the by-laws of the partnership.[89]

Partners' meetings must be held at the domicile of the partnership at least once a year, on the date specified in the articles of association for the approval of the financial statements and to appoint or, as the case may be, ratify the appointment of the managers.[90] Partners' meetings must be called by the managers of the partnership or, if they do not make the corresponding call, by the statutory auditors, or, if they have not been designated, by the partners who represent more than seventy-five per cent of the capital of the partnership. Unless otherwise agreed, the calls will be made through certified letters with acknowledgment of receipt that must contain the agenda of the meeting and be addressed to each partner, with an anticipation of at least eight days from the meeting date.[91]

---

[85] General Law of Commercial Companies, Article 268.
[86] General Law of Commercial Companies, Article 269.
[87] General Law of Commercial Companies, Article 77.
[88] Usually, the governing instrument grants a vote for each MXN 1.
[89] General Law of Commercial Companies, Article 79.
[90] General Law of Commercial Companies, Article 80.
[91] General Law of Commercial Companies, Article 81.

The governing instrument of the partnership may provide the cases in which the partners' meeting will not be required. In such cases, a certified letter must be sent to the partners with the corresponding resolutions in order for them to cast their vote in writing. Notwithstanding the foregoing, in the above-mentioned case, partners representing more than seventy-five per cent of the capital of the partnership may request a meeting to be formally called.[92] To amend the governing instrument, the consent of the partners representing at least seventy-five per cent of the capital of the partnership will be required, unless the amendment is related to the object of the partnership or an increase of the obligations of the partners, in which case the consent of all the partners will be required.[93]

Special Partnership. Resolutions taken by the partners are valid when voted by the majority. Notwithstanding the foregoing, the by-laws of the partnership may provide that the majority will be calculated by the participation in the capital and not by number of partners; however, if one partner holds the majority of the interest, another vote will be required.[94]

General Partnership. Resolutions taken by the partners are valid when voted by the majority. Notwithstanding the foregoing, the by-laws of the partnership may provide that the majority will be calculated by the participation in the capital and not by number of partners, however, if one partner holds the majority of the interest, another vote will be required.[95]

To amend the by-laws, the unanimous consent of all the partners is required unless a different quorum is required by the by-laws of the partnership, in which case the minority partners will be entitled to withdraw from the partnership if they do not agree with the amendment.[96]

Shares and Equity Quotas Transfer Restrictions

Companies

Stock Company. In the by-laws of the company, restrictions for the transfer of shares or certain type of shares may be agreed.[97] It also may

---

[92] General Law of Commercial Companies, Article 82.
[93] General Law of Commercial Companies, Article 83.
[94] General Law of Commercial Companies, Articles 46 and 57.
[95] General Law of Commercial Companies, Article 46.
[96] General Law of Commercial Companies, Article 34.
[97] General Law of Commercial Companies, Article 91.

be agreed that the transfer of shares may only be performed with the authorization of the board of administration. The board may deny the corresponding authorization by designating a buyer for the shares at a market price.[98]

Special Partnership with Shares. The consent of all of the active or general partners and seventy-five percent of the limited partners is required.[99]

Partnerships

Limited-Liability Company. For the transfer of equity quotas and the admission of new partners, the consent of the partners representing the majority of the capital is required unless the by-laws provide a higher voting quota.[100]

If the admission of a new partner is authorized in the terms referred to above, all the other partners will be entitled to a preferential right to acquire the corresponding equity quota for the same consideration within a term of fifteen days following the date on which the authorization was granted. If more than one partner exercise this right, they will only be entitled to exercise it in the proportion of their participation in the capital of the partnership.[101]

Special Partnership. The consent of all of the partners is required. New partners may not be admitted without the consent of all the partners, unless the by-laws of the partnership provide that the consent of the majority shall suffice.[102]

If the admission of a new partner is authorized in the terms referred to above, all the other partners will be entitled to a preferential right to acquire the corresponding equity quota for the same consideration within a term of fifteen days following the date on which the authorization was granted. If more than one partner exercise this right, they will only be entitled to exercise it in the proportion of their participation in the capital of the partnership.[103]

---

98 General Law of Commercial Companies, Article 130.
99 General Law of Commercial Companies, Article 209.
100 General Law of Commercial Companies, Article 65.
101 General Law of Commercial Companies, Article 66.
102 General Law of Commercial Companies, Articles 31 and 57.
103 General Law of Commercial Companies, Articles 33 and 57.

General Partnership. All the other partners' consent is required. New partners may not be admitted without the consent of all the other partners, unless the by-laws of the partnership provide that the consent of the majority will suffice.[104]

If the admission of a new partner is authorized, all the other partners will be entitled to a preferential right to acquire the corresponding equity quota for the same consideration within a term of fifteen days following the date on which the authorization was granted. If more than one partner exercises this right, they will only be entitled to exercise it in the proportion of their participation in the capital of the partnership.[105]

Directors and Officers

In General

The articles of incorporation and association of a company or partnership must include the way in which the company or partnership will be managed and the roles of the administrator(s) and manager(s), as well as the designation of the administrator(s) and manager(s) and the persons who will be acting on behalf of the company or partnership.[106]

Representation of commercial companies is entrusted to their administrator(s) and manager(s), which will be entitled to perform all operations inherent to their corporate purpose, except as expressly provided by law or the by-laws and articles of incorporation and association.[107] The granting of powers of attorney in favor of administrators and managers and officers of companies and partnerships is usually performed through the incorporation meeting included in the by-laws and articles of incorporation and association.

The granting of powers of attorney in favor of administrator(s) and manager(s) must be notarized before a public notary or commercial public notary. Different rules related to administration and faculties of the administrators or managers as well as related to supervision apply to each type of company or partnership pursuant to the General Law of Commercial Companies.

---

104 General Law of Commercial Companies, Article 31.
105 General Law of Commercial Companies, Article 33.
106 General Law of Commercial Companies, Article 6.
107 General Law of Commercial Companies, Article 10.

Companies

Stock Company. The administration is entrusted to two or more directors (board of directors) or to a sole administrator, who need not be shareholders.[108] In case a board of directors has been appointed, and unless otherwise agreed, it will be considered as chairman of the board the first person appointed as member.[109]

The general shareholders' meeting, the board of directors, or the sole administrator are entitled to designate one or more general or special managers who need not be shareholders who will be entitled to exercise the faculties expressly granted in their favor.[110] Charges of administrator, officer, and manager are considered as personal designations and, therefore, they may not be performed through representatives.[111]

The board of directors or the sole administrator are entitled to delegate their powers of attorney or grant new ones within their own faculties.[112] The delegation and granting of powers of attorney do not restrict the faculties of the board of directors or the sole administrator and their removal does not imply the revoking of the powers of attorney previously granted or the delegations made.[113]

In order to consider a board of directors meeting as duly convened, at least half of its members must attend and its resolutions will be considered valid with the vote of the majority of the attendants. In case of a tie, the chairman of the board will have the casting vote.[114] The governing instrument of the company may provide that resolutions adopted without a meeting will be deemed valid if all the members of the board have confirmed its resolutions in writing.[115]

Directors have the liabilities inherent to their office and those arising from the obligations imposed by the law and the company's by-laws.[116] They are jointly liable with the company for the existence of the contributions made by the shareholders, for compliance with legal and statutory requirements in relation to dividends paid to the shareholders, for the existence and maintenance of the system of accounting, control,

---

[108] General Law of Commercial Companies, Article 142.
[109] General Law of Commercial Companies, Article 143.
[110] General Law of Commercial Companies, Articles 145 and 146.
[111] General Law of Commercial Companies, Article 147.
[112] General Law of Commercial Companies, Article 149.
[113] General Law of Commercial Companies, Article 150.
[114] The casting vote may be eliminated through the by-laws of the company or it may be granted in favor of another member of the board.
[115] General Law of Commercial Companies, Article 143.
[116] General Law of Commercial Companies, Article 157.

recording, filing, or reporting required by law, and for the faithful execution of the resolutions of the general meeting of shareholders.[117] Special liability is provided by law in the following cases:

(1) Directors who take part in resolutions and decisions regarding business transactions in which their interests are in conflict with those of the company are liable for the damage arising to the company as a result thereof;[118]
(2) Newly appointed directors who fail to report, in writing to the company's auditors, any irregularities incurred by their predecessors of which they are aware are jointly liable with such predecessors;[119]
(3) Directors who enter into any new business transaction on behalf of the company after the expiration of the term of the company's duration, or after a resolution to dissolve the company has been taken, are jointly liable for such transactions;[120]
(4) Directors who have authorized a purchase of shares of the company (save in those cases permitted by the law) are personally and jointly liable for any loss suffered by the company or its creditors;[121] and
(5) Directors who carry on the business of the company prior to the registration of its articles of incorporation in the Public Registry of Commerce are jointly liable without limit to third parties.[122]

The General Law of Commercial Companies allows the liability of the directors and officers of the company to be limited through its by-laws if this liability arises from acts executed by these persons or from resolutions adopted by them and they have not taken part in bad faith or illegal acts.[123] The liability of the directors may be enforced by the general shareholders' meeting[124] or by shareholders representing twenty-five per cent of the capital stock of the company.[125]

Directors of the company must keep confidential all company information that they know pursuant to their designation if such information is not considered public nor requested by any authority.

---

117 General Law of Commercial Companies, Article 158.
118 General Law of Commercial Companies, Article 156.
119 General Law of Commercial Companies, Article 160.
120 General Law of Commercial Companies, Article 233.
121 General Law of Commercial Companies, Article 138.
122 General Law of Commercial Companies, Article 02.
123 General Law of Commercial Companies, Article 91.
124 General Law of Commercial Companies, Article 161.
125 General Law of Commercial Companies, Article 163.

This confidentiality obligation is while directors are in charge and for one additional year following termination thereof.[126]

The board of directors or the sole administrator must provide to the statutory auditor(s) of the company a monthly report including at least a statement of the financial situation and a statement of results.[127] In addition, they must provide annually to the ordinary general meeting of shareholders a report which must include at least a report of the company on the fiscal year, as well as on the policies followed by the directors and on the principal projects existing; a report explaining the principal accounting policies and criteria used to prepare the financial information; a statement showing the financial situation of the company at the closing date of the fiscal year; a statement showing the financial results of the company during the fiscal year, duly explained and classified; a statement showing the changes in the financial situation during the fiscal year; a statement evidencing the changes in the capital of the company which took place during the fiscal year; and the notes which complement or clarify the information contained in the preceding statements.[128] Failure by the board of directors or sole administrator to provide the report will be grounds for the general shareholders' meeting to remove them.[129]

Supervision is entrusted to one or more auditors who need not be shareholders.[130] If, for any reason, no designation of a statutory auditor has been made, the board of directors or sole administrator must call within a term of three days for a general shareholders' meeting through which the designation must be made.[131] Pursuant to the General Law of Commercial Companies, the following individuals may not be designated as statutory auditors of a company:

(1) Persons who are incapacitated by law to engage in trade;
(2) Employees of the company, employees of companies in which they also own more than twenty-five per cent of the capital stock, or employees of companies in which they also own more than fifty per cent of the shares; and
(3) Direct blood relatives of the directors without limitation of degree, collateral relatives within the fourth degree, and relatives by affinity within the second degree.[132]

---

126 General Law of Commercial Companies, Article 157.
127 General Law of Commercial Companies, Article 166.
128 General Law of Commercial Companies, Article 172.
129 General Law of Commercial Companies, Article 176.
130 General Law of Commercial Companies, Article 164.
131 General Law of Commercial Companies, Article 168.
132 General Law of Commercial Companies, Article 165.

Statutory auditors are obliged to fulfill the following obligations:
(1) Request from the directors a monthly report, including at least a statement on the financial situation and a statement of results;
(2) Carry out an inspection of the operations, documentation, records, and other supporting evidence, to audit the operations required by law and in order to render the report mentioned in item 3, below;
(3) Render annually to the ordinary general meeting of shareholders a report regarding the veracity, sufficiency, and rationality of the information presented by the board of directors or the sole administrator to the meeting;[133]
(4) Include in the agenda for meetings of the board of directors and of the general shareholders' meetings the issues they may deem pertinent;
(5) Call for ordinary or extraordinary general shareholders' meetings when the directors fail to do so, or when they may deem it advisable;
(6) Attend all meetings of the board of directors to which they must be called, being entitled to express their opinions, but having no vote;
(7) Attend general shareholders' meetings, being entitled to express their opinions, but having no vote; and
(8) Exercise at any time an unlimited supervision over the business of the company.[134]

All shareholders individually are entitled to report in writing to the statutory auditor(s) any acts considered as irregular in relation to the administration of the company. Statutory auditor(s) must refer to the above-mentioned claims in the reports to be filed annually to the shareholders' meeting along with his and their suggestions.[135]

Simplified Stock Company. The administration is entrusted to an administrator who must be a shareholder of the company and who will represent the latter. The designation itself of the aforementioned administrator implies the granting of powers of attorney in that person's favor to execute all the acts and agreements required to pursue the corporate purpose of the company.[136]

---

133 General Law of Commercial Companies, Article 176. Failure by statutory auditor(s) to file the report will be grounds for removal by the general shareholders' meeting.
134 General Law of Commercial Companies, Article 166.
135 General Law of Commercial Companies, Article 167.
136 General Law of Commercial Companies, Article 267.

Special Partnership with Shares. Limited partners cannot take part in the administration or act as attorney-in-fact of the partnership.[137] Limited partners are liable before third parties for all obligations of the partnership in which they have intervened in violation of this restriction and if they customarily participated in the administration of the business of the partnership.[138] If the administrator is an active or general partner and the governing instrument of the partnership, provided his designation is irrevocable, he may only be judicially removed for misconduct, gross negligence, or inability.[139]

Stock Company Promoting Investment. The administration of these companies must be undertaken by a board of managers, not by a sole administrator.

Partnerships

Limited-Liability Company. The administration of the company is entrusted to one or more managers who may or may not be partners designated temporarily or for an undetermined term. If no appointment is made, all partners participate in the administration of the company.[140] Managers are liable for the appropriate use of the company's funds and, in general, for the correct administration of the company. They also are personally liable, jointly with the company, for the accuracy of the data contained in the partners' register of the company.[141]

Resolutions of the managers will be valid when taken with the vote of the majority of the members of the board; however, if the governing instrument of the partnership provides for unanimity, it will be required. Notwithstanding the aforementioned, if the majority of the managers deem that delay on acting will cause severe damage to the partnership, their resolution will be valid.[142]

Managers who had no knowledge of a resolution or who voted against the corresponding resolution will not be liable for it. Action against managers corresponds to the partners' meeting and to each partner individually, but they will not be entitled to exercise it if the partnership, with the vote of seventy-five per cent of the capital, released

---

137 General Law of Commercial Companies, Articles 54 and 211.
138 General Law of Commercial Companies, Articles 55 and 211.
139 General Law of Commercial Companies, Articles 39 and 211.
140 General Law of Commercial Companies, Articles 40 and 74.
141 General Law of Commercial Companies, Article 73.
142 General Law of Commercial Companies, Article 75.

the managers from liability. Creditors of the partnership also will be entitled to bring action against its managers, but it must be exercised after the partnership has been declared in bankruptcy.[143]

Managers' reports must be rendered each semester, unless it has been agreed otherwise by the partners.[144] A supervisory committee may be appointed if the articles of incorporation and association so provide, and may be composed of either partners or non-partners.[145]

Special Partnership. The administration of a partnership is entrusted to one or more managers who need not be partners.[146] Managers may be designated and removed by the majority of the partners.[147] Partners who voted against the designation of an elected manager who is not a partner will be entitled to withdraw from the partnership.[148] If the manager is a partner of the partnership and the governing instrument of the partnership, provided his and her designation as irrevocable, he and she may only be judicially removed for misconduct, gross negligence, or inability.[149]

If no designation is performed, all the general or active partners will be in charge of the administration.[150] Limited partners cannot undertake any part of the administration or act as attorney-in-fact of the partnership.[151] Limited partners are liable before third parties for all obligations of the partnership in which they have intervened in violation of this restriction and if they customarily participated in the administration of the business of the partnership.[152] Capital partners designated as manager may receive periodically a remuneration which will be charged as a general expense, if it is agreed by the majority of the partners.[153]

The manager will only be entitled to transfer and encumber the real estates of the partnership with the consent of the majority of the partners or in case the transfer is part of the corporate purpose of the partnership.[154] The manager will be entitled, under his and her sole liability, to grant powers of attorney for certain corporate business. To delegate

---

143 General Law of Commercial Companies, Article 76.
144 General Law of Commercial Companies, Articles 43 and 86.
145 General Law of Commercial Companies, Article 84.
146 General Law of Commercial Companies, Articles 36 and 57.
147 General Law of Commercial Companies, Articles 37 and 57.
148 General Law of Commercial Companies, Articles 38 and 57.
149 General Law of Commercial Companies, Articles 39 and 57.
150 General Law of Commercial Companies, Articles 40 and 57.
151 General Law of Commercial Companies, Article 54.
152 General Law of Commercial Companies, Article 55.
153 General Law of Commercial Companies, Articles 49 and 57.
154 General Law of Commercial Companies, Articles 41 and 57.

his and her charge, he and she will require the consent of the majority of the partners. Partners who voted against such delegation by a manager who is not a partner will be entitled to withdraw from the partnership.[155] All managers may act on behalf of the partnership, unless such authority is limited to one or more of them by the articles of partnership. In urgent cases when a failure to act might involve serious consequences for the partnership, one manager may take decisions by himself in the absence of the other manager(s).[156]

Managers' reports must be rendered each semester, unless it has been agreed otherwise by the partners.[157] Partners who take no part in the administration may appoint a supervisor to exercise supervisory functions over the manager and will be entitled to supervise the administration, reports, and papers of the partnership and perform the claims they deem convenient.[158]

General Partnership. The administration of the partnership is entrusted to one or more managers who need not be partners.[159] Managers may be designated and removed by the majority of the partners.[160] Partners who voted against the designation of an elected manager who is not a partner will be entitled to withdraw from the partnership.[161] If the manager is a partner of the partnership and the governing instrument of the partnership, provided his or her designation is irrevocable, he or she may only be judicially removed for misconduct, gross negligence, or inability.[162] If no designation is made, all the partners will be in charge of the administration.[163] Capital partners designated as managers may receive periodically a remuneration which will be charged as a general expense, if agreed by the majority of the partners.[164]

The manager will only be entitled to transfer and encumber the real estates of the partnership with the consent of the majority of the partners or in case the transfer is part of the corporate purpose of the partnership.[165] The manager will be entitled, under his and her sole liability, to

---

155 General Law of Commercial Companies, Articles 42 and 57.
156 General Law of Commercial Companies, Articles 45 and 57.
157 General Law of Commercial Companies, Articles 43 and 57.
158 General Law of Commercial Companies, Articles 47 and 57.
159 General Law of Commercial Companies, Article 36.
160 General Law of Commercial Companies, Article 37.
161 General Law of Commercial Companies, Article 38.
162 General Law of Commercial Companies, Article 39.
163 General Law of Commercial Companies, Article 40.
164 General Law of Commercial Companies, Article 49.
165 General Law of Commercial Companies, Article 41.

grant powers of attorney for certain corporate business. To delegate his or her charge he or she will require the consent of the majority of the partners. Partners who voted against such delegation by a manager who is not a partner will be entitled to withdraw from the partnership.[166] All managers may act on behalf of the partnership, unless such authority is limited to one or more of them by the articles of partnership. In urgent cases when a failure to act might involve serious consequences for the partnership, one manager may take decisions by himself or herself in the absence of the other manager(s).[167]

Managers' reports must be rendered each semester, unless it has been agreed otherwise by the partners.[168] Partners who take no part in the administration may appoint a supervisor to exercise supervisory functions over the managers and will be entitled to supervise the administration, reports, and papers of the partnership and perform the claims they deem convenient.[169]

Allocation of Powers of Attorney among Shareholders, Partners, and Directors

In General. In the case of the simplified stock company, the designation of the administrator implies the granting of powers of attorney in that person's favor to execute all the acts and agreements required to pursue the corporate purpose of the company; in all the other types of companies and partnerships, powers of attorney, in case shareholders and partners are willing to grant them, must be expressly granted in favor of the directors, managers, administrator, managers, and attorneys in fact.

Powers of attorney are freely determinable by the company's bylaws. The law does not provide for any division of power among the company's officers. Normally, full powers are given to the board of directors acting as a board. General or special powers of attorney may be granted by the board of directors or by the shareholders' or partners' meeting to a director or to any other individual or individuals as they deem convenient. The general or special attorneys-in-fact need not be directors, shareholders, partners, or officers of the company.

---

[166] General Law of Commercial Companies, Article 42.
[167] General Law of Commercial Companies, Article 45.
[168] General Law of Commercial Companies, Article 43.
[169] General Law of Commercial Companies, Article 47.

Power of Attorney for Lawsuits and Collections. This power of attorney is used to represent the company and partnership in litigations and in administrative procedures. Usually, this power of attorney also is granted to the legal counsels of the company and partnership in order for them to be able to represent the company in litigation in Mexico. This power of attorney also may be granted to foreigners without a Mexican visa; however, in certain types of litigations (criminal and labor matters), a Mexican attorney may be needed.

Power of Attorney for Administration Acts. This power of attorney is used to represent the company and partnership in all kind of contracts which do not imply the disposition of fixed assets or the issuance of negotiable instruments. This power of attorney may be granted to foreigners without a Mexican visa.

Power of Attorney for Lawsuits, Collections, and Administration Acts in Labor Matters. This power of attorney is used to represent the company and partnership in the execution of labor agreements, collective bargaining agreements, and litigations and usually is also granted to the legal counsels of the company and partnership. This power of attorney may be granted to foreigners without a Mexican visa. However, in certain types of litigation, a Mexican attorney may be needed.

Power of Attorney for Administration Acts in Tax, Social Security, and Customs Matters. This power of attorney is used to represent the company and partnership before the tax, social security, and custom authorities.

This power of attorney may be granted to foreigners without a Mexican visa. However, since the authorities require the attorney to have a valid Mexican tax ID, it is usually granted to the accountants.

Power of Attorney for Acts of Domain. This power of attorney allows the attorney in fact to dispose of the fixed assets of the company and partnership, including real properties. This power of attorney may be granted in favor of foreigners without a Mexican visa.

Power of Attorney to Subscribe and Grant Negotiable Instruments. This power of attorney is granted to subscribe negotiable instruments, to obtain loans, and to open and close bank accounts and appoint the persons who may sign into the bank accounts.

This power of attorney may be granted to foreigners without a Mexican visa. This is the only power of attorney that must be recorded with the Public Registry of Commerce.[170]

Access to Corporate Information

Corporate records are available for inspection, either in books or in 'folios' (the summary containing basic information concerning the business enterprise's public records covering the past twenty years). The Public Registry of Commerce provides the service of retrieving information from the records of business enterprises. There is no postal, telefax, telephone, courier, telex, or online index service available. The request must be made directly at the office of the Public Registry of Commerce where the business enterprise is incorporated.

There is no legal procedure for compelling disclosure of beneficial ownership by a nominee holding shares. Publicly quoted companies are required to publish consolidated and unconsolidated financial statements in a major newspaper, normally the *Official Gazette* and in the electronic system of the Ministry of Economy mentioned above after approval at the shareholders' meeting. Moreover, there are several acts that must be published through the electronic system established by the Ministry of Economy (known as the Electronic Publication System of Commercial Companies, *Sistema Electrónico de Publicaciones de Sociedades Mercantiles*)[171] that may be consulted by the general public.

The main acts that must be published pursuant to the General Law of Commercial Companies and the Agreement through which the Electronic Publication System is established and Provisions for its Operation (*Acuerdo mediante el cual se establece el Sistema Electrónico de Publicaciones de Sociedades Mercantiles y las disposiciones para su operación*)[172] are:

(1) Call to an incorporation general meeting of a stock company;[173]
(2) Call to general meetings;[174]
(3) Call to a meeting pursuant to an authority resolution;[175]

---

170 General Law of Negotiable Instruments and Credit Transactions, Article 9.
171 See http://www.psm.economia.gob.mx/PSM/.
172 *Official Gazette of the Federation*, 12 June 2015.
173 General Law of Commercial Companies, Article 99.
174 General Law of Commercial Companies, Article 186.
175 General Law of Commercial Companies, Articles 168, 184, and 185.

(4) Meeting resolutions regarding the increase of the corporate capital;[176]
(5) Foreign companies' operations balance sheet which must be published annually;[177]
(6) Financial statements, notes, and opinions of the statutory auditor if publication is required by the shareholders of the company;[178]
(7) Reduction of corporate fixed capital;[179]
(8) Merger resolutions, last balance sheet of each merging company, and basis for the payment of liabilities of the merged entities;[180]
(9) Spin-off resolutions;[181]
(10) Resolutions on the conversion of the company;[182]
(11) Notice for the payment of pending contributions to the corporate capital when the payment term or amount is not set forth in the share certificate;[183]
(12) Resolution of partial distribution of assets of the company subject to liquidation;[184]
(13) Liquidation balance sheet;[185] and
(14) Outcome of the draw to determine the shares to be redeemed.[186]

The publications also must be performed through any other means as it may be required by the company's by-laws and articles of incorporation and association or any additional special regulation. The information created, sent, received, or stored in the Electronic Publication System of Commercial Companies must be considered a data message[187] and, therefore, must have the same effects as those documents bearing a handwritten signature.

---

[176] General Law of Commercial Companies, Article 132.
[177] General Law of Commercial Companies, Article 251.
[178] General Law of Commercial Companies, Article 177.
[179] General Law of Commercial Companies, Article 9.
[180] General Law of Commercial Companies, Article 223.
[181] General Law of Commercial Companies, Article 228 *bis*.
[182] General Law of Commercial Companies, Article 228.
[183] General Law of Commercial Companies, Article 119.
[184] General Law of Commercial Companies, Article 243.
[185] General Law of Commercial Companies, Article 247.
[186] General Law of Commercial Companies, Article 136.
[187] Code of Commerce, Article 89.

Portugal

Luís Soares de Sousa and Diogo Horta Osório[1]
Cuatrecasas, Gonçalves Pereira
Lisbon, Portugal

Introduction

Pursuant to the Commercial Companies Code, private limited companies, public limited companies, general partnerships, and limited partnerships can be incorporated. As a rule, in private limited companies and public limited companies, shareholders are not liable for corporate debt. For this reason, these companies are commonly referred to as limited-liability companies.

Compared to private and public limited companies, a main aspect of general partnerships is the liability of shareholders for the company's debts. In fact, shareholders of a general partnership are fully liable for the company's debts, even though that liability is a subsidiary one. A general partnership should contain the name of the shareholders or, at least, the name of one shareholder, and the expression *e companhia*, meaning "and company". The personal link of the shareholders in general partnerships also explains the concern with loyalty duties and the strictness of non-competition rules.

Limited partnerships are mixed liability companies, which are composed of shareholders with limited liability (*comanditários*), who contribute capital, and shareholders with unlimited liability (*comanditados*), who contribute goods or services, assume the management of the company, and are liable for the company's debts. The corporate name of limited partnerships must contain the name of one *comanditado* and the suffix *em comandita* or *& comandita*.

Limited partnerships can be simple or by shares. In the first case, there is no representation of the share capital. In the second case, only the equity of the *comanditários* is represented by shares. While simple partnerships are based on the legal framework of general partnerships, the rules of public limited companies are, *mutatis mutandis*, applicable to share limited partnerships.

---

1 The authors acknowledge with thanks the assistance of Telma Carvalho, José Braga da Cruz, and Rita Caçador.

Due to the unlimited-liability regime, general partnerships and limited partnerships represent a residual minority of Portuguese corporations and, therefore, the most common types of companies in Portugal are private limited companies (Lda.) and public limited companies (S.A.). The analysis here will focus on private limited companies and public limited companies.

As noted above, shareholder liability, notably towards creditors, will depend on the type of company. As to private limited company and public limited company shareholders, the general rule is that the liability of the shareholder is limited to the nominal value of its shares and there is a joint liability for the payment of the agreed capital contributions.

The company and the shareholders have separate legal personalities and, therefore, the liability of a company may not be deemed the liability of its shareholders. As indicated below, the corporate veil can only be lifted by means of a judicial ruling or an arbitration award that, in exceptional and specific situations, may deem the shareholder personally liable.

Private Limited Companies and Public Limited Companies

Number of Shareholders and Minimum Capital

Private Limited Companies

Private limited companies can be held by two or more shareholders. If the company is held by a sole shareholder (or should it result from a transformation procedure where all shares are concentrated in a single member), the company will be subject to the specific legal regime of the single-member private limited companies.

Unless the company is converted into a single-member private limited company, private limited companies may be officially dissolved when, for a period exceeding one year, the number of shareholders is less than two.

The amount of the share capital is freely determined by the shareholders in the bylaws. The share capital is divided into shares (quotas)[2] with no physical representation. The nominal value of the shares can be different and the minimum amount required for a share is €1. The ownership of shares is registered with the Commercial Registry Department.

Initial capital contributions are part of the shareholder's obligation to invest in the company. In private limited companies, contributions consisting of services are not permitted. Initial capital contributions can be deferred up to five years as from the conclusion of the company's incorporation contract, provided certain conditions are met.

Public Limited Companies

Public limited companies can be held by five or more shareholders, except in case of total corporate control (*domínio total*) in which the company might be incorporated with a single member, which must be a legal entity or corporation. The share capital is divided into shares that are represented by share certificates (materialized shares) or registered in a specific account (book-entry shares). The shares also may be qualified as nominative shares or bearer shares. Each type of shares has its own transfer procedure and might or might not have nominal value. The same company may issue shares with or without a nominal value.

Public limited companies have a minimum share capital of €50,000. All the shares with nominal value issued by the same company must be issued with the same nominal value (at least €0.01). The value of the shares cannot be inferior to its nominal value. The purpose of this rule is the protection of the share capital and of the company's creditors. As in private limited companies, initial capital contributions consisting of services are not permitted. In case of initial cash capital contributions, the paying-in of 70 per cent of the shares' par value may be deferred. Whatever periods are set in the company's bylaws, the shareholder will only be in arrears after the company has made a demand for payment.

The liability of each shareholder is limited to the amount of the capital contributions respectively subscribed. Therefore, shareholders are not accountable towards the company's creditors, being only accountable towards the company for their initial capital contributions (which may be potentially incremented by the obligation to make ancillary capital contributions).

---

2 "Quotas" is the Portuguese designation for shares in private limited companies. "Quotaholder" is the Portuguese designation for shareholders in private limited companies. Throughout this chapter, references are only made to shares and shareholders.

Supplementary Capital Contributions and Shareholder Loans

Private Limited Companies

Source of Obligation. Supplementary capital contributions are cash contributions provided by the shareholders to a private limited company and are treated as quasi capital from an accounting standpoint. They are a flexible instrument to strengthen the company's capitalization, as opposed to increasing the company's share capital.

The bylaws may set out an obligation of capitalization by the shareholders, notably to contribute with supplementary capital contributions to the company's equity. The bylaws also must establish the maximum amount that the shareholders may be required to provide as supplementary capital contributions.

However, the effectiveness of such obligation always requires a previous shareholders' resolution calling upon the shareholders to provide supplementary capital contributions within the company bylaws' limits and setting the deadline for such supplementary capital contributions to be provided (the deadline cannot be less than thirty days counting as from the notification made to the shareholders for such purpose). On the other hand, shareholder loans are executed by way of agreement between the shareholder and the company and are not subject to a previous shareholders' resolution, unless the company's bylaws so require.

Object. Supplementary capital contributions must be provided in cash, and they cannot bear interest. However, shareholder loans may be remunerated or not, depending on what is agreed upon between the company and its shareholders, and may be provided in cash or any other fungible assets.

Legal Requirements for Repayment. Supplementary capital contributions may only be repaid if the amount of the company's equity does not become lower than the sum of the company's share capital and statutory reserves, and if such repayment is previously approved by a shareholders' resolution.

No similar requirements apply to the repayment of shareholder loans. In case of insolvency of the company, supplementary capital contributions may not be repaid and shareholder loans shall be deemed a subordinated credit that may only be repaid upon payment of all the insolvent company's debts.

Default. Failure to comply with the obligation to make supplementary capital contributions, when called, may entail the loss, total or partial, of the stake held by the defaulting shareholders in the company's share capital and, possibly, the shareholder's exclusion of the company. Shareholder loan default penalties must be set out in the agreement between the company and the shareholder, as the law does not provide any similar consequence for the non-compliance with the obligation to make shareholder loans.

Accounting Treatment. According to the Accounting Standards System (SNC), supplementary capital contributions are an element of equity capital/own funds whilst shareholder loans are an item of the liabilities. Therefore, supplementary capital contributions are a tool for the company's capitalization, whilst shareholder loans increase the company's debt.

Public Limited Companies

The supplementary capital contributions regime is not set forth for public limited companies. However, authors tend to accept its extension by analogy to public limited companies. In relation to shareholder loans, the legal regime is the same in private and public limited companies.

Allocation of Powers Between Shareholders and Directors

Private limited companies have a more "personal" nature and, as a rule, shareholders also are the directors of the company. The powers of the shareholders are broader in a private limited company and, in the by-laws, shareholders may choose to call certain competences that are directly related to the management of the company. Therefore, shareholders can limit the directors' powers and can even resolve on matters of their competence. Directors have a duty of obedience and loyalty towards shareholders.

Directors must be individuals with full legal capacity and can be appointed in the bylaws or by means of a shareholder resolution. Share-holders may remove or dismiss the directors at any moment, with or without cause. In public limited companies, the shareholders' competence to resolve on management matters is residual, i.e., the shareholders may only decide on the matters that are not assigned to the board of directors or that are specifically granted by the bylaws and the law. Unlike in private limited companies, shareholders do not have the power to limit the matters subject to the board of directors. The

board of directors has broader powers for the management of the company and may decide on any matter regarding the company's management, namely:
(1) Appointing its chairman (the bylaws can, however, establish that the general meeting appoints the chairman when appointing the board of directors);
(2) Substituting directors by a third person;
(3) Summoning general meetings;
(4) Issuing annual reports and the accounts for the financial year;
(5) Acquiring, disposing, and encumbering real estate;
(6) Providing securities by the company;
(7) Opening and closing premises or important parts of such premises;
(8) Making important extensions or reductions of corporate activity;
(9) Making important modifications to the company's organization;
(10) Establishing or terminating long-term and important cooperation with other companies;
(11) Changing headquarters and making capital increases, pursuant to the bylaws;
(12) Merging and demerging and pursuing company transformation projects; and
(13) Acting on any other matter that requires a board of directors' resolution.

Shareholder Meetings and Voting

In General

Shareholders must meet when required by law or the bylaws. The purpose of the meetings is to resolve and approve the most relevant company's issues.

The meetings must be convened either by any of the directors (in private limited companies) or by the chairman of the board of the general meeting (in public limited companies). If all shareholders agree to meet and vote (universal general meetings or *assembleias gerais universais*), no prior convening will be required.

Private Limited Companies

Apart from other matters set forth in the law or in the bylaws, shareholders make decisions on the following acts:
(1) Calling in and recovering supplementary contributions;

(2) Amortizing shares, acquiring, disposing of, and encumbering of own shares and consenting to division or transfer of shares;
(3) Dismissing shareholders;
(4) Dismissing directors and members of the supervisory board;
(5) Approving the annual report and accounts for the financial year, distributing profits, and apportioning losses;
(6) Waiving liability of directors or members of the supervisory board;
(7) Proposing legal action by the company against the management, shareholders, or members of the supervisory board, and dismissing and conducting such proceedings;
(8) Amending the bylaws; and
(9) Merging, dividing, converting, and dissolving the company and resuming activity of the dissolved company.

If the bylaws do not provide otherwise, the shareholders also make decisions on the following matters:
(1) Appointing members of the management;
(2) Appointing members of the supervisory body;
(3) Disposing of and encumbering real estate, and disposing of, encumbering, and leasing premises; and
(4) Subscribing or acquiring equity interests in other companies and their disposal or encumbrance.

Resolutions may be taken by a summoned general meeting, through a universal general meeting, through written vote, or through a unanimous written resolution. Furthermore, shareholders cannot be prevented from participating in general meetings, even if they are prohibited from voting. Shareholders may not vote, personally or through a representative, or in representation of a third party, when there is a conflict of interests with the company, in relation to the matter under decision. Such situations arise when the matter under decision regards:
(1) Release from an obligation or liability of the shareholder, either in his/her capacity as shareholder or as a director or member of the supervisory body;
(2) Litigation on the intent of the company against the shareholder or of the shareholder against the company, in any of the capacities referred to in the previous item, either before or after having resorted to the court;
(3) Loss by the shareholder of part of his share;
(4) Dismissal of the shareholder;

(5) Dismissal of the management or of a member of the supervisory body, with legal grounds; and
(6) Relations established or to be established, between the company and the shareholder, other than those provided for in the bylaws.

All matters regarding general meetings that are not specifically regulated in relation to private limited companies will be subject to the provisions set forth for public limited companies.

Public Limited Companies

Shareholders must decide on matters that are specially assigned to them by law or in the company's bylaws and that do not fall within the scope of the powers of other corporate bodies. Resolutions must be approved by a majority of votes (abstentions do not count), unless the law or the bylaws stipulate differently. The following matters must be approved by two-thirds of the votes cast, whether the shareholders are meeting for the first or the second time:
(1) Amendment of the bylaws;
(2) Mergers;
(3) Spin-offs;
(4) Conversions;
(5) Dissolution of the company; and
(6) Other matters for which the law requires a qualified majority.

Each share carries one vote, unless otherwise set out in the bylaws. The Commercial Companies Code forbids plural voting. Shareholders can only participate and vote if they are entitled to at least on vote. However, the bylaws can stipulate that shareholders with no voting rights may be present at the meeting and discuss the matters on the agenda. Pursuant to the Commercial Companies Code, the annual meeting for approval of the annual accounts is mandatory.

The purpose of this meeting is to discuss the annual report and accounts for the financial year; discuss the proposed application of the company's results; assess the management and supervision of the company in general and, although such matters may not appear on the agenda, proceed with the dismissal of directors, or grant them a vote of no confidence; and proceed with appointments that fall within the powers of the meeting. The board of directors or the executive board of directors must convene the general meeting referred to above and present to the shareholders the relevant proposals as well as any data required by law.

Rights in Proxy Voting

In public limited companies, the bylaws cannot prevent a shareholder from being represented at a general meeting. In this type of company, shareholders may be represented by any person with legal capacity. In private limited companies, representation is always valid if granted to the spouse, parent, descendent, or another shareholder.

The bylaws may expressly allow other representatives, except in case of resolutions taken by written vote (*deliberações por voto escrito*). In both types of companies, shareholders must be represented through a signed written document (proxy letter) addressed to the chairman of the general meeting.

Inspection of Shareholder Lists

The chairman of the general meeting must prepare a shareholder attendance list, which must be signed by all shareholders present, as well as all representatives present.

The attendance list must be kept in the records of the company and be available for inspection by any shareholder that holds at least one per cent of the share capital.

Access to Corporate Information

Private Limited Companies

In private limited companies, all shareholders have the right to receive information, despite the number of shares held. The bylaws can regulate the right to corporate information, as long as the right is not waived or unreasonably restricted.

Public Limited Companies

In public limited companies, a shareholder who holds at least one per cent of the company's share capital can have access to the following information, in the company's head office:
(1) The annual report and financial statements required by law, relating to the previous three financial years, including the opinions issued by the supervisory board, the audit committee, the general and supervisory council or the committee for financial matters, and any reports from the statutory auditor which are subject to publication, under the law;

(2) The notices of meetings, minutes and attendance lists of general and special meetings of shareholders, and meetings of bondholders carried out in the previous three years;
(3) The total value of remuneration paid to members of the corporate bodies in relation to each of the previous three years;
(4) The total amounts paid in relation to each of the previous three years to the ten employees of the company who received the highest remuneration (if the workforce exceeds 200) or the five employees of the company who received the highest remuneration, if the workforce is 200 or less; and
(5) The share registry document.

The information can be required in person or by a representative. Shareholders whose shares amount to ten per cent of the share capital may request, in writing, from the board of directors or executive board of directors, that information relating to corporate matters is also made available to them in writing.

Share Transfer Restrictions

Private Limited Companies

The transfer of shares must be done in writing and the company must consent to the transfer. Such consent shall be given through a written document (e.g., a shareholder resolution), with indication of the parties and the terms and conditions of the transfer.

Save for transfers between spouses, ascendants, descendants, or shareholders, the transfer of shares may not be effective towards the company until such consent is granted, except if the consent is excluded in the bylaws.

Public Limited Companies

The bylaws of a company cannot exclude the transferability of shares or limit it beyond the situations foreseen by law. The company's bylaws also may subject the transfer or the encumbrance of nominative shares to certain conditions.

The limitations may only be included in the bylaws with the consent of all shareholders whose shares are affected by such limitations. The limitations may relate only to the shares corresponding to a particular capital increase, provided that the resolution is passed simultaneously with such a capital increase.

Profit and Loss and Dividend Distribution

In the absence of a special provision or agreement, shareholders will share the company's profits and losses in proportion to the par value of their shares. A clause that excludes any shareholders from sharing in profits or that exempts them from sharing in any losses incurred by the company is null and void.

Likewise, clauses that establish that all the profits or losses belong to a single shareholder or to some shareholders are null and void. Unless otherwise provided in the bylaws, or a resolution adopted by a majority of three-quarters of the votes at a general meeting called for this purpose, one-half of the financial year's distributable profit must be distributed among the shareholders. In public limited companies, dividend payments are restricted as follows:

(1) At least five per cent of the annual profits must be attributed to the mandatory legal reserve and, if necessary, to refund that reserve, until that reserve reaches twenty per cent of the share capital value, before any dividend payment;

(2) Dividend payments are prohibited if the net assets of the company do not cover the par value of the share capital and the legal reserves; and

(3) Dividend payments are prohibited to the extent that annual profits are necessary to cover losses or pay any outstanding investigation and development expenses.

Moreover, dividends cannot be paid to shareholders if the equity of the company, including the net result of the year, as per the approved annual accounts, is less than the sum of the share capital and reserves (stipulated by law or in the bylaws) or becomes lower because of the distribution of dividends. Portuguese law authorizes the payment of interim dividends. Payment of interim dividends must be specifically authorized in the company bylaws.

If the company bylaws do not contain an express authorization for the payment of interim dividends, and are amended to insert such authorization, the first payment can only occur in the following fiscal year, not in the same fiscal year as the one in which such amendment was made to the bylaws. The company bylaws may authorize interim dividends to be paid once a year, in the second half of the year, provided that:

(1) The general meeting approves the advance distribution; and

(2) The resolution of the general meeting is preceded by an interim balance sheet, dated not more than 30 days before and certified by

a chartered accountant (*Revisor Oficial de Contas*) that evidences the existence of amounts available for the advance payment of dividends, in compliance with capital ratios maintenance and taking into account the verified results in the fiscal year to the date when the interim dividends will be paid.

Only one advance payment can be made in each fiscal year, and always in the second half of the year. The amounts to be attributed as advance payment may not exceed half of the distributable amounts. The rules apply to private limited companies. The only variation relates to the mandatory legal reserve, which cannot be less than €2,500.

Dissolution

A company must be dissolved pursuant to its bylaws and at the term set forth in the bylaws, upon resolution of the shareholders, upon the fulfilment of its legal purpose, if the corporate object becomes illegal, and in case of bankruptcy. For the immediate dissolution at the term set forth in the bylaws, or if the corporate object becomes illegal, shareholders may approve the company's dissolution by a simple majority of the votes cast.

In other cases, the resolution to proceed with the dissolution of the company must be passed by a majority of three-quarters of the votes corresponding to the share capital, unless the bylaws establish a higher majority or other requirements.

A company may be dissolved by administrative means when, for a period of more than one year, the number of shareholders was less than the minimum required by law, except where one of the shareholders is a corporation or an equivalent entity. Following liquidation, dissolution, and termination of the company, the former shareholders are liable for outstanding company liabilities up to the amount they received in the distribution of assets. Proceedings may be brought against the shareholders or the receivers, who will be considered legal representatives of the shareholders.

Liability of Shareholders

In General

In private limited companies and public limited companies, the limit of the shareholders' liability is normally determined by their capital contributions. Since only the company's assets guarantee the company's debts, the maximum loss a shareholder can suffer in such companies is the amount of capital contribution.

Apart from the capitalization obligations of the shareholders, notably ancillary contributions, supplementary capital contributions, and shareholder loans analyzed above, there are other cases that may widen the liabilities of a shareholder in private limited companies or public limited companies.

Since, under certain circumstances (see text, below), a shareholder may be jointly and severally liable with a director or a member of the supervisory board appointed by such shareholder towards the company or the remaining shareholders, reference to the general liability of directors and members of the supervisory board must be made.

Liability of Directors and Members of Supervisory Board

Directors are firstly liable to the company for any inaccuracy or inadequacy in the indications or declarations made in the incorporation of the company, i.e., those related to capital contributions, acquisition of assets by the company, special advantages, and compensation or reimbursement due for incorporation of the company.

The general rule regarding the liability of directors to the company is established by Article 72 of the Commercial Companies Code. According to Paragraph 1 of Article 72, directors are liable to the company for acts or omissions committed in disrespect of their duties established both in the law and in the company's bylaws, except if they prove that they acted without fault. For a company to initiate a lawsuit against its directors, a resolution of the general meeting must be approved by the votes of a simple majority of the shareholders present or represented in that general meeting. This lawsuit must be brought no later than six months following the resolution.

Without prejudice to their right to individually ask for damages, one or more shareholders who jointly own at least five per cent of the company's share capital, or at least two per cent of the company's share capital for a public limited company with shares admitted to trade on a regulated market, may bring a lawsuit against the directors asking for damages for the company when the company itself has not brought the lawsuit described in the preceding paragraph.

Directors also are liable to the company's creditors if they do not comply with the applicable legal provisions or the company's bylaws' rules that protect the company's creditors and, consequently, the assets of the company are no longer sufficient to pay the company's debts. In contrast to the regime of directors' liability to the company, there is no presumption of fault regarding the liability of the directors before the company's creditors, shareholders, and third parties. That is why, in order to receive compensation, proof of the director's fault, either in the form of negligence or wilful misconduct, must be submitted.

However, in all of the above referred cases, liability is excluded when the director proves that he has acted in compliance with the so-called business judgment rule. The director will not be liable for any damages if he proves that he acted on an informed basis, without personal interest and in accordance with rational business criteria. Likewise, liability is excluded in all of the above cases when the damage results from a resolution of the board of directors in which the director has not participated or has voted against.

In all the above cases, the liability of the members of the board of directors is joint and several among the directors, without prejudice to the right of recourse among them according to the level of fault of each of the directors and the damages caused by their respective actions or omissions. The preceding Paragraphs are applicable, *mutatis mutandis*, to the members of the supervisory board.

The liability of the members of the supervisory board is joint and several with the liability of the directors and only exists in case the damage suffered by the company, the creditors, the shareholders, or third parties would not have been suffered if the members of the supervisory board would have complied with their obligations.

Liability of Shareholders

In General

Shareholders may be liable to the company, other shareholders, or the company's creditors on several grounds. The liability of the shareholders may be divided into general liabilities, applicable to shareholders of all types of commercial companies, and specific liabilities, applicable to certain types of commercial companies or special relations established between them and their shareholders.

General Liability

In the General Chapter of the Commercial Companies Code, applicable to all types of commercial companies, there are three important rules regarding shareholders' liability:
(1) Liability for abusive resolutions;[3]
(2) Joint liability of the shareholders;[4] and
(3) Sole shareholder liability.[5]

Liability for Abusive Resolutions

According to Article 58 of the Commercial Companies Code, the following decisions are voidable:
(1) Those that violate the law, when not subject to nullity;
(2) Those that are likely to satisfy a shareholder's interest granting themselves or to third parties special benefits and that result in a loss for the company or for other shareholders or placing the company or other shareholders at risk, unless it is proven that the resolutions would have been adopted even without the contravening votes; and
(3) Those that were taken without the shareholder being provided with the minimum required information.

Pursuant to Article 58, Paragraph 3, of the Commercial Companies Code, shareholders who formed the majority in the approval of the resolutions referred to in item (2), above, will be jointly liable towards the company or towards the other shareholders for any losses caused to the company and the other shareholders.[6]

Nullity proceedings must be filed with the court within thirty days from the date on which the general meeting was adjourned, the third day subsequent to the sending of the minutes for postal voting, or the date on which the resolution came to the shareholder's attention, if the resolution adopted a matter that the meeting summoning did not refer to.

---

3 Commercial Companies Code, Article 58, Paragraph 3.
4 Commercial Companies Code, Article 83.
5 Commercial Companies Code, Article 84.
6 The Court of Appeal of Coimbra, on 25 September 2001 (*Colectânea de Jurisprudência*, 2001, IV, at p. 14), ruled that one can bring an action, at the same time, to affirm the nullity of an abusive resolution passed in a general meeting and claim compensation for damages caused by the shareholders who formed the majority in such resolution, according to the rules set forth in the Civil Procedure Code.

Joint Liability of Shareholders

Article 83 of the Commercial Companies Code sets forth three cases in which shareholders are jointly and severally liable with the directors for damages caused by the latter in the performance of their functions.[7] Article 83 establishes *culpa in eligendo* of the shareholder with the right to appoint a director or other statutory corporate members.

In this light, a shareholder who, alone or together with other shareholders that have entered into by and between a shareholder agreement with the shareholder, has the right to appoint a director in a private limited company without the favorable vote of the remaining shareholders will be jointly and severally liable with the appointed director. Such joint and several liability will apply when such director is liable to the company or the other shareholders and there was a fault by the shareholder in the appointment of the director. The rule also is applicable to collective entities that are appointed as directors in relation to the individuals that they appointed.

Moreover, a shareholder who by virtue of the number of votes has, alone or together with other shareholders that have entered into a shareholders' agreement with the shareholder, the power to appoint a director or a member of the supervisory board is jointly and severally liable with the appointed director or member of the supervisory board.

Once again, such liability will depend on the *culpa in eligendo* in the appointment of the director or the member of the supervisory board and the existence of liability of the appointed director or member of the supervisory board. In addition, liability depends on the fact that the resolution appointing such director or member of the supervisory board has been approved by the votes of the shareholder and by less than half of the votes of the remaining shareholders present or represented in that general meeting.

Finally, a shareholder who (by virtue of any contractual provision or the number of votes), alone or together with other shareholders, has entered into a shareholders' agreement with said shareholder, has the power to dismiss a director or a member of the supervisory board and, using the influence granted by such power, compels the director or member of the supervisory board to act or refuse to act in a certain way, is jointly and severally liable with such director or member of the

---

[7] The Court of Appeal of Lisbon, on 21 May 2010 (see http://www.dgsi.pt), ruled that Article 83 of the Commercial Companies Code should only be applicable when directors or other persons entrusted with control of the company's management and auditing breach their duties with fault.

supervisory board when the director or member of the supervisory board is liable for such actions or refusal to act.

Sole Shareholder Liability

In General. Under Article 84 of the General Chapter of the Commercial Companies Code, when a company reduced to a sole shareholder is declared insolvent, that shareholder will be unlimitedly liable for the company's debts incurred upon the date on which the shareholder became the company's sole shareholder. However, such liability will only be applicable upon evidence that the allocation of the company's assets to the company's debts rules were not complied with.[8]

The same provision applies to the period of time in which the shareholder was the sole shareholder of the company and subsequently other shareholders became shareholders of the company, and the company is declared insolvent upon the entrance of those new shareholders. This provision does not affect the applicability of Article 83 of the Commercial Companies Code and the regime of the affiliated companies (see text, below).

There is some controversy as to whether Article 84 of the Commercial Companies Code establishes a subsidiary or a joint and several liability and whether it is applicable to single-member private limited companies. Two main arguments are invoked to assert that Article 84 of the Commercial Companies Code establishes a joint and several liability, namely:

(1) It is the general regime for commercial obligations;[9] and
(2) If one considers this liability to be subsidiary, that would entail that the law would not penalize the single shareholder of general partnerships (*sociedades em nome colectivo*), since the subsidiary liability is already the type of liability applicable to its shareholders.

It has been argued that the purpose of this provision is to sanction the shareholder for the damages arising from the disregard of the assets separation rules and, as a consequence, it should only apply when it is

---

[8] The Supreme Court of Justice, on 26 June 2007 (*Colectânea de Jurisprudência – Supremo Tribunal de Justiça*, 2007, II, at pp. 131 *et seq.*), held that Article 84 of the Commercial Companies Code should be considered as a provision that disregards the corporate personality of companies reduced to only one shareholder, making the sole shareholder liable for the company's debts.

[9] Commercial Code, Article 100.

clear that the company's assets are not sufficient to pay the company's debts. Likewise, it has been argued that, since Article 84 of the Commercial Companies Code refers to companies reduced to only one shareholder, it cannot be applicable to companies that were originally incorporated with only one shareholder, such as the single-member private limited companies, or subsequently transformed into single-member private limited companies.

Since Article 84 of the Commercial Companies Code was part of the initial version of the Commercial Companies Code (approved by Decree-Law Number 262/86 of 2 September 1986) and single-member private limited companies were only admitted after that date, it also is claimed that Article 84 of the Commercial Companies Code should be understood under the options currently available and be applicable to single-member private limited companies. A majority of the legal community accepts that Article 84 of the Commercial Companies Code establishes a subsidiary liability and is applicable to the single-member private limited companies.

Specific Liabilities. There are additional and specific cases on which a shareholder may be held liable pursuant to the Commercial Companies Code. Some of those cases are established in the Commercial Companies Code, in the context of single-member private limited companies and affiliated companies, and others are developed by the jurisprudence of Portuguese courts.

To protect creditors of single-member private limited companies, Article 270-F of the Commercial Companies Code requires that all the contracts concluded between a sole shareholder and the company must pursue the company's corporate purpose, respect the legal form required for those contracts, and be made in writing. In addition, the documents that substantiate those contracts must be disclosed together with the management report and accounting documents and may be inspected by any interested party in the company's head office at any time.

In case of failure to comply with these obligations, the contract concluded between a sole shareholder and a company will be deemed null and void and the sole shareholder may be unlimitedly liable for the damages that may result from that contract to the company. It has been considered that the liability of the sole shareholder should not be limited to the contract entered into by and between the company and the sole shareholder and should include the debts incurred by the company after the date of such contract.

Once again, the Supreme Court of Justice has not ruled on this topic, but the majority of the Portuguese legal community accepts that the liability of the sole shareholder in these circumstances is restricted to the damages suffered by the company as a consequence of the contract.

Affiliated Companies

Articles 481 *et seq.* of the Commercial Companies Code regulates affiliated companies. The following relationships established between affiliated companies are regulated by Article 482 of the Commercial Companies Code:
(1) A company holds quotas or shares that represent ten per cent or more of another company's share capital;
(2) Two companies reciprocally hold quotas or shares that represent ten per cent or more of the other company's share capital;
(3) A company controls another company (a company controls another company when it exercises a dominant influence over the other company and said dominant influence is presumed when that company, directly or indirectly, holds the quotas or shares that represent the majority of the share capital or more than half of the voting rights of the other company, or has the possibility to appoint more than half of the members of the board of directors or of the supervisory board of the other company); and
(4) The companies are in a group relationship.

The Commercial Companies Code only sets forth specific liability rules of the shareholders for the cases of companies in a group relationship. There are three types of companies that are considered to be in a group relationship:
(1) A company (controlled company) whose quotas or shares are totally owned by another company (dominant company), either since its incorporation or subsequently (wholly owned subsidiary);
(2) Companies that enter into a contract subjecting themselves to a single and common direction (horizontal group agreement); and
(3) A company that enters into a contract with another company on whose terms one of those companies (controlled company) subjects its activity to the direction of the other company (subordination agreement).

The rules on shareholder liability are solely applicable to the companies described in item (3), above, and, by reference to Article 491 of the Commercial Companies Code, the companies described in item (1), above, *mutatis mutandis*. Under Article 501 of the Commercial Companies Code, the dominant company is responsible for the obligations incurred by the controlled company before or after the conclusion of the subordination agreement[10] and will remain responsible for those obligations until the termination of that subordination.[11]

Through Article 491 of the Commercial Companies Code, this provision also applies to a company that totally owns another company from the moment at which that company acquired the whole quotas or shares that represent the controlled company's share capital and will remain in force until the moment the dominant company loses control of ten per cent of the quotas or shares that represent the controlled company's share capital.[12] Such liability of the dominant company cannot be claimed sooner than 30 days from the date on which the obligation of the controlled company was due.

Since the dominant company can have a means of defence that the controlled company does not have against its creditors (the obligation of the controlled company was incurred after the registry and publication of the termination of the group relationship), Article 501 of the Commercial Companies Code provides that creditors of the controlled company cannot initiate enforcement proceedings against the dominant company based on an enforcement title that is only enforceable against the controlled company.

The liability of the dominant company for the debts of the controlled company is substantially broader than the liability established in Article 84 as it is not triggered by the insolvency declaration of the controlled company[13] and does not depend on a breach of the rules that impose the allocation of the company's assets to the company's debts.[14]

---

10 Court of Appeal of Lisbon, 6 April 1995 (see http://www.dgsi.pt).
11 The Supreme Court of Justice, on 31 May 2005, held (see http://www.dgsi.pt) that, even if a subordination agreement is terminated, the dominant company remains liable for the obligations incurred by the controlled company within the period set out in Article 501 of the Commercial Companies Code. Therefore, creditors of the controlled company have the right to demand the (former) dominant company to fulfil such obligations.
12 Supreme Court of Justice, 23 January 1996 (see http://www.dgsi.pt).
13 According to a decision by the Supreme Court of Justice on 31 May 2005 (see http://www.dgsi.pt), an ongoing insolvency proceedings concerning the controlled company does not prevent its creditors from demanding that the dominant company fulfil the obligations incurred by the controlled company within the period set out in Article 501 of the Commercial Companies Code, by virtue of Article 519, Paragraph 1, of the Civil Code.
14 The Supreme Court of Justice and the Court of Appeal of Lisbon, in their decisions of 31 May 2005 and 19 June 2008 (see http://www.dgsi.pt), held that, under Article 501 of the Commercial Companies Code, the dominant company will be held strictly liable for the controlled company obligations, whether it acted with or without fault regarding non-compliance with such obligations.

In addition, pursuant to Article 502 of the Commercial Companies Code, a controlled company has the right to require the dominant company to offset the annual losses that, for any reason, occur during the time the subordination agreement is in force, when said losses are not offset by the reserves made during that period. The liability may only be claimed after the termination of the subordination agreement, but it can be claimed while the subordination agreement is in force if the controlled company is declared insolvent.

In relation to a company whose quotas or shares are totally owned by another company, the reference to the period on which the subordination agreement is in force must be interpreted as the period from which the dominant company acquired the whole quotas or shares of the controlled company until the moment the dominant company loses control of ten per cent of the quotas or shares that represent the controlled company's share capital.[15]

Liability for losses must be exercised by the controlled company and not by its creditors. The creditors of the controlled company may only use their right of action by way of subrogation if the controlled company does not exercise this liability against the dominant company.

Piercing Corporate Veil

Piercing the corporate veil may be defined as a situation where an action pursued against a company ultimately leads to the disregard of the corporate personality and makes liable the shareholders of that company. In these cases, the shareholders lose the protection given by the existence of the company.

Apart from the specific liabilities above described, some decisions of Portuguese courts have disregarded the corporate personality and declared the shareholders liable for a company's debts. The decisions were mainly taken in cases of undercapitalization of the company and unclear delimitation of the boundaries between the company's activities and the shareholder's activities.[16]

---

15 Supreme Court of Justice, 31 May 2011 (see http://www.dgsi.pt).
16 The Supreme Court of Justice, in its decision of 26 June 2007 (*Colectânea de Jusrisprudência — Supremo Tribunal de Justiça*, 2007, II, at pp. 131 *et seq.*), accepted the doctrine of piercing the corporate veil and highlighted a set of situations that may lead to the application of this legal mechanism. Nevertheless, the Supreme Court did not pierce the corporate veil in the *sub judice* case. The decisions of the Court of Appeal of Lisbon on 29 April 2008 and 28 May 2008 (see http://www.dgsi.pt) are examples of the application of the referred doctrine to situations of intermingling of assets of the company and of the shareholders and the

However, the decisions have been rather haphazard and of limited impact. They applied general principles of civil law, i.e., the *bona fide* and abuse-of-right principles, and are incapable of providing solid and comprehensive guidelines to those who deal with this topic. As a consequence, the lifting of the incorporation veil is regarded as a last remedy and is only applied in cases where the *bona fide* and abuse-of-right principles are at stake and no other general principle is applicable.

Limitation Period

Shareholder liability cannot last forever and may only be exercised during a certain lapse of time. Article 175 of the Commercial Companies Code establishes that a company may only exercise its rights against a shareholder during a period of five years counted from the date on which the obligation of that shareholder became due, the term of the shareholder's fault, or the date on which the company's damage was suffered, depending on the circumstances.

Likewise, third parties may only exercise rights under Article 83 of the Commercial Companies Code against a shareholder during a period of five years counting as of the term of the shareholder's fault. The grounds on which the calculation of these limitation periods will be suspended or reinitiated are established in Articles 318 *et seq.* of the Civil Code.

(footnote 16 continued from previous page)
shareholders treat the company's assets as their own. Moreover, national courts have disregarded the corporate entity where there is siphoning of corporate funds or assets by the dominant shareholder(s), leading to the under-capitalization of the company (Court of Appeal of Oporto, 15 October 2001, *Colectânea de Jurisprudência*, 2001, IV, at p. 215).

United States

Michael J. Katz
Corporon & Katz, LLC
Greenwood Village, Colorado, United States

Introduction

The general status of a shareholder in a United States corporation, and his specific rights, duties, and liabilities, are statutorily defined in each of the fifty states.[1] Although the corporate law in each state has its roots in more than 300 years of common law, case law, and legislation, since 1950, the American Bar Association has worked through its Section of Business Law (formerly known as the "Committee on Corporation, Banking and Business Law") to draft a model code of corporate law for use in all states.[2] Although it is not universally accepted, the Act — known as the "Model Business Corporation Act" — has been adopted in whole or in substantial part by thirty states.[3]

The remaining states have promulgated their own statutes, or have adopted the General Corporation Law of the State of Delaware[4] (here identified as the "Delaware Code"). As it is well beyond the scope of this article to parse the statutory and case law of each state, we will concentrate on the applicable portions of the Model Business Corporation Act, and on its adoption and use in Colorado and similar Model Business Corporation Act states.

Basic Corporate Structure

United States corporations come in all sizes, from small privately-held entities with one to several dozen shareholders, to large private corporations

---

1 See Table 1 at the end of this chapter for a citation to the general corporate law statutes of the fifty states.
2 Model Business Corporation Act Annotated, Fourth Edition (2013), p. xii, published by the American Bar Association.
3 See Table 1 for a citation to the states that have adopted the Model Business Corporation Act.
4 8 Delaware Code (Delaware Code), Sections 101 *et seq.*

with shareholders that may number in the tens of thousands, and to publically-held corporations, the stock of which is traded on a recognized exchange.

Privately-held corporations may be identified statutorily as a "close corporation" or "closely-held corporation". Texas, for instance, defines a closely held corporation to be one that has fewer than thirty-five shareholders and that has stock that is not publicly traded.[5] Colorado, on the other hand, defines the same business entity as one that has three or fewer shareholders and that has stock that is not publically traded.[6] The Model Business Corporation Act does not contain references to "close corporations". Delaware, on the other hand, requires the close corporation to be privately held (meaning it is not publically traded), have thirty or fewer shareholders, and have an appropriate restrictive legend on its shares.

If the business-entity so qualifies, the applicable state statute may afford the corporation special rights or privileges. Thus, in Texas, shareholders of closely-held corporations are permitted to bring a "derivative" action[7] not in the name of the corporation (as is usually required), but in the name of the individual shareholder for his own benefit. In Colorado, the closely-held corporation is permitted to represent itself in a court proceeding (while corporations that fall outside of the definition must be represented by legal counsel), while Delaware law permits the entity to be managed directly by its shareholders and even allows it to be operated as though it were a partnership.

Single-person corporations are allowed in all states, meaning that a single shareholder will be allowed to wear the hat of the sole member of the Board and the only officer.[8] As shareholders often wear several hats in a closely-held corporation, they also expose themselves to the specter of unintended liability.

Similarly, privately-held corporations may be categorized for federal tax purposes as a "subchapter-c"[9] or a "subchapter-s"[10] corporation. The

---

5 Texas General Law (Texas Gen. Law), Section 21.563.
6 Colorado Revised Statute (CRS) 13-1-127(1)(a).
7 Texas General Law (Texas Gen. Law), Section 21.563.
8 *Industrial Com'n* vs. *Lavach*, 165 Colo. 433, 437, 439 P.2d 359, at p. 361 (1968): "[T]he fact stock is owned by a single shareholder is not grounds for disregarding the corporate entity." See also Model Business Corporation Act, Section 8.03: "(a) A board of directors must consist of one or more individuals . . ." and Model Business Corporation Act, Section 8.40: "(d) The same individual may simultaneously hold more than one officer in a corporation".
9 26 United States Code, Subchapter C.
10 26 United States Code, Subchapter S.

c-corporation may have any number of shareholders who may be natural persons and domestic and foreign business entities. All publicly-traded corporations are c-corporations. The revenue of this entity is "double taxed" in the sense that the corporation pays a tax on its revenue, and the shareholders pay tax on any dividends or distributions. The s-corporation is usually a closely-held corporation although, under the s-corporation rules, there may be as many as one hundred shareholders.

There may be only one class of stock, although some shareholders may have voting rights, while others do not. Each shareholder must be a natural person who is either a citizen or a permanent resident of the United States. It is considered a "pass-through" tax entity in that its revenue is taxed only one time at the shareholder's level. That is, the profits, losses and gains, if any, are passed directly to the shareholders who are then taxed at the shareholder's individual rate. The tax election by the corporation does not in any manner affect the basic rights or obligations of the shareholders under a state's corporate laws.

In both the Model Business Corporation Act and the Delaware Code, the main corporate participants are the incorporator,[11] the shareholder or shareholders,[12] the member or members of the board of directors (Board),[13] and one or more officers[14] each of which has specific rights and duties. The incorporator's sole purpose is to set up and then register the corporation with the state in which it is located. The shareholders own the equity interest of the corporation while the Board sets policy that is calculated to meet the "corporate purpose" and which policy is then carried out by the officers.

The "corporate purpose" is not to insure that shareholders realize as much gain on their investment as possible — although that certainly is one of the objectives — but is instead to advance the highest-level objective of the corporation. For instance, in the case of a microbrewery, its corporate purpose is identified as "making beer". If, in meeting the

---

11 Model Business Corporation Act, Section 2.01; Delaware Code, Section 101.
12 Reference to shareholders and the various rights granted to shareholders is found at the Model Business Corporation Act, Sections 7.01 *et seq*. The corresponding Delaware Code sections may be found at 8 Delaware Code (*Del. C.*), Sections 151–233.
13 Though, in the Model Business Corporation Act, a shareholders' agreement can eliminate even the necessity of a board of directors (See Model Business Corporation Act, Section 7.32; C.R.S 7-108-101), virtually all corporations large and small have a Board. See generally, Model Business Corporation Act, Section 8.01.
14 See generally, Model Business Corporation Act, Sections 8.01 *et seq*, C.R.S. 7-128-101 *et seq*., and 8 *Del. C.*, Sections 141 *et seq*.

corporate purpose, the corporation also increases the shareholders' equity value, the secondary goal has been met. Consider *Network Affiliates, Inc.* vs. *Schack*,[15] in which the court held that a corporation can act only within the scope of its corporate purpose and that acts outside the bounds of the corporate purpose are unenforceable. The corporate purpose is typically set forth in the bylaws,[16] although the incorporator may identify the purpose in the articles of incorporation.[17]

Once a corporation is registered with the state, the incorporator will call an initial meeting at which the Board is elected.[18] Once that election is completed, the incorporator's job is done and he will be dismissed from service. The Board will then consider and adopt bylaws,[19] and will discuss the initial capitalization of the corporation. The initial capitalization is where the shareholders come in.

A corporation is a hierarchical entity. The shareholders sit atop and have the general power to attend the annual meeting,[20] elect members of the Board, call special meetings of the Board,[21] offer direction to the Board through written proposals (usually done through the mechanism of calling a special meeting), and view the corporate books, including the financial records and the shareholder list.[22]

In turn, the board has the general power to operate the business from day-to-day either by itself — meaning that a Board member has the power to bind the corporation — or most often through officers. As previously noted, the law allows one person to participate at one level or at all three. Most often, large corporations operate with clear and autonomous separation: although a shareholder may sit on the Board and may even have a position as an officer, this person will not usually have control of the voting power of the shareholders and will not have the ability to elect the majority of Board members.

---

15 *Network Affiliates, Inc.* vs. *Schack*, 682 P.2d 1244 (Colo. App. 1984).
16 Bylaws set forth the structure for the internal governance of a corporation. They are, in essence, the road map that the corporation follows in order to carry on its business from day to day.
17 Model Business Corporation Act, Section 2.02.
18 Model Business Corporation Act, Section 2.01; C.R.S. 7-102-105 and 7-102-106.
19 Model Business Corporation Act, Section 2.06 "Official Comment".
20 An annual meeting is a mandatory corporate formality. See Model Business Corporation Act, Section 7.01; Delaware Code, Section 211(b).
21 A "special meeting" is any meeting other than the annual meeting. Model Business Corporation Act, Section 7.02 "Official Comment", at pp. 7–15.
22 Model Business Corporation Act, Section 16.02; Delaware Code, Section 220.

Shareholder Veil of Protection

Depending upon the size of the corporation and whether it is a subchapters-c or subchapter-s, the classes of shares of stock may be many in number and may include one or more classes that have the right to vote; one or more classes of non-voting shares; as well as shares that have preferential rights to dividends. Regardless of the separation of shareholders into various classes and regardless of the number of shareholders (from one to 10,000 or more), all have one thing in common: shareholders who do not otherwise personally guarantee a corporation's debt or duties are free from personal liability for the corporation's financial or other obligations.[23]

The protection afforded the shareholders is sometimes called the "corporate veil"[24] in that it covers the shareholders personal assets from the corporate liabilities and debt. Both the Model Business Corporation Act and the Delaware Code codify this concept. In the Model Business Corporation Act, Section 6.22(a) states:

> "A purchaser from a corporation of its own shares is not liable to the corporation or its creditors with respect to the shares except to pay the consideration for which the shares were authorized to be issued (Section 6.21) or specified in the subscription agreement (Section 6.20). Compare this with Delaware law at Delaware Code, Section 102(b)(6) that states: ". . . the stockholders of a corporation may not be personally liable for the payment of the corporation's debts except as they may be liable by reason of their own conduct or acts."

The Supreme Court of Colorado held as early as 1880 that, once a shareholder has paid in full for his shares of stock: ". . . they are not personally liable, either to creditors of the incorporation or to other stockholders".[25] The Supreme Court of Hawaii, in *dictum*, in *Roberts*

---

[23] For a history of the limitation of liability of shareholders, review Model Business Corporation Act, Section 6.22: "Historical Background".

[24] *Black's Law Dictionary* (9th Edition), at p. 390, defines the corporate veil as: "The legal assumption that the acts of a corporation are not the actions of its shareholders, so that the shareholders are exempt from liability for the corporation's actions".

[25] *Smith et al.* vs. *Londoner*, 5 Colo 365 (Colo. 1880). 1 Fletcher, *Cyclopedia of the Law of Private Corporations*, Section 41.20, at p. 596 (perm. ed., 1999).

Hawaii School of Business, Inc. vs. *Laupahoehoe Transportation Company, Inc.*,[26] stated: "The common purpose of statutes providing limited shareholder liability is to offer a valuable incentive to business investment". This then forms the foundation upon which a shareholder's standing in the corporation is built. Absent the affirmative act of guaranteeing a corporation's debt or obligations, absent anything in the articles of incorporation or bylaws to the contrary (meaning that the corporation may, if it wishes, require the shareholders to be personally liable for its debt and obligations), and absent the shareholder's own acts, the shareholder is shielded from liability.

Corporate Formalities

The key to maintaining the corporate veil of protection for its shareholders is for the corporation to adhere strictly to the so-called "corporate formalities".[27] The minimum corporate formalities that must be followed include:

(1) Properly incorporating;[28]
(2) Holding an organizational meeting;[29]
(3) Drafting and adopting bylaws;[30]
(4) Holding the annual meeting;[31]
(5) Holding special meetings when the Board is making decisions that fall outside the mere day-to-day operational judgment calls;[32]
(6) Transcribing the minutes of all shareholder and Board meetings;[33]

---

26 *Roberts Hawaii School of Business, Inc.* vs. *Laupahoehoe Transportation Company, Inc.*, 982 P. 2d 853 (Hawaii 1999).
27 "Observing Corporate Formalities", see https://www.lexisnexis.com/legalnews room/lexis-hub/b/commentary/archive/2008/05/23/observing-corporate-formalities.aspx and http://www.legalmatch.com/law-library/article/corporate-formalities-checklist.html.
28 Merely identifying a business as the "XYZ Corporation" will offer no protection from personal liability if not incorporated under the law of the state in which the business is operating.
29 An organizational meeting is the very first meeting at which directors are elected. Although the law does not specifically call for an organizational meeting, having one and having minutes of the meeting demonstrate the corporation's adherence to the corporate structure.
30 Model Business Corporation Act, Section 2.06; Delaware Code, Section 109.
31 Model Business Corporation Act, Section 2.06; Delaware Code, Section 109, Note 20.
32 This would include the decision to materially vary from corporate purpose; to sell material assets of the corporation outside the normal course of business; and to change directors.
33 Model Business Corporation Act, Section 16.01(a).

(7) Maintaining proper financial records;[34] and
(8) Signing documents, contracts, purchase orders, and other binding agreements in the corporate name.[35]

The failure to substantially follow the corporate formalities is the reason that shareholders, officers, and directors may end up being exposed to personal liability.

Shareholder General Status

In General

Corporations large and small are equally treated under the Model Business Corporation Act and under the statutes of most states, meaning that, absent special rights given to specifically-identified corporation,[36] shareholders of small corporations and of large corporations are treated equally. As a result, the Model Business Corporation Act, the Delaware Code, and most states offer shareholders the following rights and distinctions.

Classes of Stock

The Model Business Corporation Act and the law in all fifty states[37] permit a corporation to issue any number of "classes" or "series" of stock.[38] The classes of stock may be differentiated by almost any attribute that is inherent in the ownership of stock.

For instance, classes can be separated into voting and non-voting shares. In such a case, the class that has voting rights can, and does, impose its will on all other classes through the election of Board

---

34 Model Business Corporation Act, Section 16.01(b).
35 This means that all documents that bind the corporation in any manner should be signed: "XYZ Corporation, by Jane Doe, President". The officer authorized to sign on behalf of the corporation will be set by the Board in the bylaws. Further, members of the Board may be given the power to sign on behalf of the corporation.
36 As previously noted, the Delaware Code and other state statutes have special provisions for closely-held corporations.
37 Model Business Corporation Act, Section 6.02 "Statutory Comparison".
38 The Model Business Corporation Act, Section 6.02, allows that, if the articles of incorporation so permit, the Board may without the permission of the shareholders: "... classify any unissued shares into one or more classes or into one or more series within a class".

members and through the use of its vote in general. The non-voting shares on the other hand may receive preferential treatment when it comes to dividends or when the corporation is sold or liquidated and final distributions are made.

Voting classes also can be given unequal voting rights by, for instance, allowing one share of stock in a certain class to count for five votes instead of the usual one vote. Typically, classes of stock that have enhanced rights to dividends or distributions at the time of liquidation are called "preferred" since they are usually given first right to the money.[39] A "series" of stock typically refers to a particular offering of a preferred class. The Board could decide that it will offer preferred shares (for instance, called "Class B Preferred Shares") as a way of raising capital.

It can then decide that it wants to raise the money in five different tranches and therefore identifies the offerings as "Class B Preferred Series One", "Class B Preferred Series Two", and so forth.[40] Once a series has been sold, the Board can then decide at a later date whether to offer the second series. Although this sounds like the realm in which publically-traded corporations operate, in fact, large private corporations use the same structure.

Share Certificates

Although somewhat counterintuitive, under the Model Business Corporation Act,[41] the Delaware Code,[42] and in virtually all states,[43] the corporation may issue stock without the delivery of physical certificates. Most shareholders, however, want the piece of paper as it is the physical embodiment of the owner's rights[44] and is the vehicle by which the shareholder and any transferee can be informed of restrictions affecting transfers.

---

[39] "A preferred stock is a class of ownership in a corporation that has a higher claim on its assets and earnings than [other classes]". See http://www.investopedia.com/terms/p/referredstock.asp?ad=dirN&qo=investopediaSiteSearch&qsrc=0&o=40186.

[40] Given the liberal construction of the Model Business Corporation Act, however, there is nothing preventing general classes of stock being called "series" of stock. Model Business Corporation Act, Section 6.02(a)(1–3).

[41] Model Business Corporation Act, Sections 6.25 and 6.26.

[42] Delaware Code, Section 158.

[43] Model Business Corporation Act, Section 6.26 "Statutory Comparison".

[44] "A certificate for shares certifies that one is a holder of a certain number of shares of stock . . . [.] [I]t is a convenient instrument for transfer of title". *Ballantine on Corporations* (rev. ed., 1946), at p. 466. See https://en.wikipedia.org/wiki/Stock_certificate.

Virtually all corporations issue certificates of stock. If issued, a certificate must on its face and at a minimum identify the corporation and the state in which it was incorporated; state the name of the owner of the shares; and state the number of shares and the class and/or series to which it belongs.[45]

Shareholder Control of Board of Directors

As previously noted, shareholders under the law of all fifty states have the power to elect the members of the Board.[46] In turn, the Board sitting as the autonomous head of the corporation sets the agenda for both the large-picture corporate purpose and the day-to-day operation of its business.[47]

Although this makes perfect sense, the fact is that shareholders owning less than a majority of the shares (called "minority shareholders") and who have not otherwise coalesced into a "voting block" or "voting group" rarely get to impact the election of Board members or any other matter that may come before the shareholders for a vote.

A voting block is the aggregation of shareholders around a specific goal where each shareholder agrees to vote on the issue in an agreed fashion.[48] This lack of ability to influence Board elections may be mitigated if the corporation allows for "cumulative voting".

Cumulative voting is "[a] system in which each voter may cast more than one vote for the same candidate. Cumulative voting helps a minority elect at least one representative".[49] The Model Business Corporation Act at Section 7.28(c) sets forth the mechanics of this calculation: each share entitled to vote for Board members may take the number of votes that he has and may then multiply that by the number of directors to be elected. The product of the calculation is then available to the shareholder to cast for one or more candidates.

---

45 Model Business Corporation Act, Sections 6.25(b) and 6.25(c).
46 This is true once the incorporator has elected the Board at the initial meeting, or the Board is otherwise formed through the articles of incorporation.
47 Indeed, from the perspective of a large corporation, allowing the shareholders instead of the Board to actively manage the business would create an impossible jumble of conflicting corporate decisions.
48 Model Business Corporation Act, Section 7.26. See www.investorwords.com/15241/block_voting.html for a general definition of a voting block. See also *Unitrin, Inc* vs. *Roberts et al*, 651 A.2d 1361, 1379 (Del. 1995), as to how a voting block may be used.
49 *Black's Law Dictionary* (9th Ed.), at p. 1713. Model Business Corporation Act, Section 7.28; see https://www.sec.gov/answers/cumulativevote.htm.

For instance, if a shareholder has one vote per share and owns 1,000 shares, he has 1,000 votes. If three directorships are to be filled, the shareholder will multiply the number of votes by three to reach a product of 3,000. The shareholder now has that number of votes that can be cast for one candidate, or that can be divided between two or more candidates. Cumulative voting, if allowed, must be granted under the articles of incorporation.[50] It is, however, rare to see cumulative voting allowed in any organization.

Shareholder Meetings, Quorum, and Proxies

The Model Business Corporation Act,[51] the Delaware Code,[52] and the statutes of all fifty states[53] require there to be an annual meeting, the purpose of which is to elect directors. In lieu of an actual meeting, however, the Model Business Corporation Act and the Delaware Code allow for such election by written consent.[54] This alternative to a live meeting under the Model Business Corporation Act, however, requires that all shareholders entitled to vote give specific written consent to this action:[55]

> "[The Model Business Corporation Act] permits shareholders to take action by unanimous written consent and is applicable to all corporations. As a practical matter, unanimous written consent is obtainable only for matters on which there are relatively few shareholders entitled to vote . . . ."[56]

Thus, in large corporations, physical annual meetings are held (usually at the headquarters of the corporation) at which directors are chosen. It also is usual for such meetings to have other matters on the agenda, including the ratification of the actions of the Board for the previous year, and approval of the selection of accountants.

Consider also that most states grant shareholders the right to call a special meeting for any purpose so long as the statutory minimum

---

[50] Model Business Corporation Act, Section 7.28(a).
[51] Model Business Corporation Act, Section 7.01.
[52] Delaware Code, Section 211.
[53] Model Business Corporation Act, Section 7.01 "Statutory Comparison".
[54] Model Business Corporation Act, Section 7.01(a). Delaware Code, Section 211(b).
[55] Model Business Corporation Act, Section 7.01(a). The Delaware Act allows such action and further allows it to take place even in the absence of unanimous consent. Delaware Code, Section 211(b).
[56] Model Business Corporation Act, Section 7.04, "Official Comment".

number of votes first affirm the necessity of the meeting. Under the Model Business Corporation Act, the minimum number of voting shares necessary to call a special meeting is ten per cent of the shares authorized to vote on a matter. In a large corporation where ownership is divided among hundreds or thousands of shareholders, it would mean that the initiating shareholder must contact all other shareholders in writing (which may be an expensive process in itself) and discuss the purpose of the special meeting.

Next, the minimum number of shareholders holding sufficient votes must reach a consensus, must reduce this consensus to writing, and must then prove to the corporation that they hold at least the minimum percentage able to call the meeting in the first place. Finally, if the meeting is called, a majority of votes must be cast in favor of the matter before it becomes a directive to the Board. In practice, and except for closely-held corporations which may have some success in this regard, gaining the necessary consensus under this structure is almost impossible.

At any meeting of the shareholders, a quorum[57] of the shares entitled to vote on a matter must be present in order to carry on business.[58] If, for instance, there are a thousand votes represented by the 1,000 outstanding shares of the single class of stock entitled to vote, in order for business at an annual or special meeting to go forward, at least 501 votes must be present. Assuming that this quorum is present, and assuming that the matter before the meeting requires only a majority of the votes present in order to carry the proposal, 251 votes would be needed to approve the matter being considered. The "majority rules" concept changes somewhat for the annual meeting where the Board members are chosen by ". . . a plurality of the votes cast by the shares entitled to vote in the election . . . ".[59] When, for instance, two Board members are to be elected, the two candidates that garner the highest number of votes will be selected even hough each may have received only a fraction of the votes cast.

The word "proxy" has no fixed definition. *Black's Law Dictionary* allows for three separate uses: the first refers to one who is authorized to

---

[57] A quorum represents the minimum number of votes (usually a majority of the outstanding votes entitled to vote on a matter) entitled to vote on a matter before a meeting.
[58] Model Business Corporation Act, Section 7.25.
[59] Model Business Corporation Act, Section 7.28(a). Even the plurality rule can be changed by the articles. See Model Business Corporation Act, Section 7.28(a) and the "Official Comment" for the same Section.

act as a substitute for another; the next refers to the mere act of granting a person the right to stand in for another; and the third refers to the identity of the document that is used to grant such rights to a person.[60] The Model Business Corporation Act acknowledges this by specifically adopting the very first definition.[61]

Thus, in a corporate setting and under the Model Business Corporation Act, the proxy is a person that is nominated by the shareholder to stand in his place not only to vote (although the proxy may be limited to only this act), but also for any other purpose.[62] The identity of, and the limitations placed on, the proxy may be delivered by any means to the corporation in order to be effective.[63] Indeed, an email to the corporation that simply identifies a person as the shareholder's proxy is effective so long as the date of the transmission can be determined. The Model Business Corporation Act also places a time limit on the proxy of eleven months "unless a longer period is expressly provided in the appointment form".[64]

The granting of a proxy is essentially the nomination of an agent.[65] As is usual in such arrangements, the "principal" (the shareholder) will direct the agent (the proxy) on how to vote or take action on the shareholder's behalf. As also is usual in the principal-agent relationship, the proxy election is revocable at any time by the shareholder unless the transmission to the corporation identifies the proxy's election as being irrevocable and such election is coupled "with an interest".[66] Coupling the proxy relationship with an interest is an agency concept that gives the proxy the absolute right to maintain the proxy status until the interest has been satisfied.

For instance, a shareholder can use his stock as collateral for a loan. In order to perfect the lender's rights to the shares, the shareholder will grant the lender a security interest in the shares and will give the lender the right to act as the shareholder's proxy until the loan is paid back. In that case — and as is the case in most other matters where the proxy is coupled with an interest — the proxy is permitted to vote and act in the stead of the shareholder in any manner the proxy deems appropriate.

---

60 *Black's Law Dictionary*, (9th Ed.), at p. 1346.
61 Model Business Corporation Act, Section 7.22. See also the "Official Comment" for this Section.
62 Model Business Corporation Act, Section 7.22(b).
63 Model Business Corporation Act, Section 7.22(c).
64 Model Business Corporation Act, Section 7.22(c).
65 "The appointment of a proxy is essentially the appointment of an agent ...". Model Business Corporation Act, Section 7.22 "Duration of Proxy".
66 Model Business Corporation Act, Section 7.22(c).

The Model Business Corporation Act offers several non-exclusive examples of such interests[67] while noting also that other arrangements may be made between the shareholder and the proxy that would allow the proxy election to be irrevocable.[68]

Where the proxy is coupled with an interest, the satisfaction of the underlying interest (e.g., repayment in full of the loan) usually extinguishes the proxy. The death or incapacity of the shareholder serves to terminate the proxy's appointment once notice of the same is delivered to the corporation.[69] Until delivery of such notice, the proxy is permitted to act.

Corporate Records and Shareholder Access

Regardless of the size of the corporation, all fifty states grant shareholders the right to review and copy some or all of the "corporate records".[70] "Corporate Records" are identified in the Model Business Corporation Act, Section 16.01 as being:

(1) Articles of incorporation, as amended;
(2) Bylaws, as amended;
(3) All resolutions of board meetings relating to the creation of classes of stock;
(4) All minutes of the shareholders for the last three years;
(5) Accounting and financial records;
(6) Shareholder lists;
(7) All written communication between the corporation and the shareholders for the past three years;
(8) Name and contact information of each Board member and officer; and
(9) Annual report[71] of the corporation that is delivered to the secretary of state.[72]

---

67 Model Business Corporation Act, Section 7.22(d).
68 Model Business Corporation Act, Section 7.22 "Irrevocable Proxies".
69 Model Business Corporation Act, Section 7.22(e).
70 Model Business Corporation Act, Section 16.02 "Historical Background" and "Statutory Comparison".
71 The annual report is usually a short report that acknowledges the continuation of the corporation and that also may require the names and address of all directors, officers, and even shareholders. As each state may be different, the reader should consult the law of the state in which he is interested.
72 Model Business Corporation Act, Section 16.01(a), (b), (c), and (e).

Business records are most often kept at the "principal offices"[73] of the corporation.[74] Some states allow the records to be kept at the "registered office" (which may be the location of the registered agent, who in turn may be an unrelated third-party corporation), or at the offices of the transfer agent if the corporation is large enough and has enough share-transfer transactions to warrant the use of a transfer agent.[75]

This basic shareholder's right arose from the common law[76] that recognized that a shareholder's financial stake in the corporation should allow for some form of shareholder oversight.[77] In states that follow the Model Business Corporation Act, Section 16.02(a) states that a shareholder that provides the corporation at least five business days' prior written notice may inspect the above-described Corporate Records during normal business hours.

The right to review the above-described documents is inalienable under the Model Business Corporation Act (and in most states) and cannot be abrogated by the articles of incorporation, the bylaws, or any act of the Board or an officer.[78] However, once a shareholder seeks a record that falls outside the list of documents stated above,[79] the Model Business Corporation Act requires the shareholder to have a good faith reason to review the documents to insure that such review is in furtherance of a "proper purpose".[80]

The phrase "proper purpose" is subject to interpretation. For instance, a shareholder may deem it to be a "proper purpose" to look at the financial records on a yearly basis, while the corporation would claim that the mere inspection, with no other purpose in mind, is an

---

[73] The "principal office" is the location of the executive offices, the address of which must be identified at least yearly in any annual report or at the annual meeting. Model Business Corporation Act, Section 1.40.

[74] Model Business Corporation Act, Section 16.01(e).

[75] Model Business Corporation Act, Section 16.01 "Where Records Are Kept".

[76] See *Parsons* vs. *Jefferson Pilot Corp.*, 426 S.E.2d 685 (N.C. 1993), where the court tapped into the common law to expand the availability of corporate records beyond what was allowed by statute.

[77] "A shareholder's right to inspect corporate books and records stems basically from the need to obtain information to protect the shareholder's economic interest in the corporation." Model Business Corporation Act, Section 16.02 "Historical Background".

[78] Model Business Corporation Act, Section 16.02(e).

[79] Documents such as financial records, minutes of meetings of the Board outside of those that dealt with the creation of classes of stock, and additional information about shareholders are examples of documents that are not automatically available to a shareholder.

[80] Model Business Corporation Act, Section 16.02(c) and (d).

"improper" purpose. The Model Business Corporation Act defines the phrase to mean ". . . a purpose that is reasonably relevant to the demanding shareholder's interest as a shareholder",[81] and as such does not provide much guidance on the matter. As a result, one must look to case law for a better definition.

In the matter of *Security First Corp.* vs. *U.S. Die Casting and Development Company*,[82] the court opined that prior to handing over documents requested by a shareholder, the shareholder must prove, by a preponderance of the evidence,[83] that there is a credible basis for believing that the disclosure will uncover corporate wrongdoing. In *Weigel* vs. *O'Connor*,[84] the court (citing *Sawers* vs. *American Phenolic Corporation*)[85] found that the statutory language "for any proper purpose"[86] means that the shareholder must have an "honest motive" to seek the documents and must act in "good faith". The court then went on to say:

"A proper purpose is one which seeks to protect the interest of the corporation as well as the interests of the shareholder seeking the information."

Finally, in *Grossman* vs. *Cleveland*,[87] the court determined that a similar phrase — "specific purpose" — found in the Ohio statute must be liberally construed in favor of the shareholder's right to review. Courts have thus allowed access to:

(1) Financial records to allow a shareholder to value his shares;[88]
(2) Shareholder records (which disclosed the price paid by other shareholders for shares of stock), so a dissenting shareholder could determine what his stock was worth on the open market;[89]

---

[81] Model Business Corporation Act, Section 16.02(d).
[82] *Security First Corp.* vs. *U.S. Die Casting and Development Company*, 687 A.2d 563 (Del. 1997).
[83] As stated in *Black's Law Dictionary* (9th Ed.), the preponderance of the evidence: "... though not sufficient to free the mind wholly for all reasonable doubt, is still sufficient to incline a fair and impartial move to one side of the issue rather than the other." *Black's Law Dictionary* (9th Ed.), at p. 1301.
[84] *Weigel* vs. *O'Connor*, 373 N.E. 2d, 421 (IL Ct. App. 1978).
[85] *Sawers* vs. *American Phenolic Corporation*, 89 N.E.2d 347 (IL 1950).
[86] The statute is found at 805 ILCS 5/7.75
[87] *Grossman* vs. *Cleveland, Cartage Co.*, 93 So.2d 154 (OH 1959).
[88] *Friedman* vs. *Altoona Pipe and Steel Supply Co.*, 460 F.2d 1212 (3d Cir. 1972).
[89] *E.I.F.C., Inc.* vs. *Atnip*, 454 S.W.2d 351 (KY. App. 1970).

(3) Shareholder records to allow a labor union shareholder to contact other shareholders for the purpose of disclosing the resolution of a labor matter;[90] and
(4) For the purpose of determining possible board mismanagement.[91]

On the other hand, courts have refused a shareholder's demand where:
(1) The shareholder's only purpose for reviewing shareholder records was to determine who might be interested in selling his shares;[92]
(2) The sole purpose of the shareholder's purchase of shares was to gain access to the corporation's books and records;[93] and
(3) The sole purpose of the stock broker's purchase of shares was to obtain access to the shareholders list with the hope of soliciting purchases or sales in exchange for the brokerage fees.[94]

Distributions to Shareholders

A "distribution" is the voluntary delivery to a shareholder of money (a "cash dividend"), additional shares of stock (a "share dividend" pursuant to the Model Business Corporation Act, Section 6.23), through a buy-back of the shareholder's stock in exchange for the then-current market value of the stock, the delivery of a corporate promissory note or other negotiable or non-negotiable instrument, or even the delivery of corporate assets (an "asset dividend" or "property dividend").[95]

No corporation is required to issue a dividend and is not required to issue a distribution[96] until it is sold, or is wound up and liquidated, although, under Section 1368 of the Internal Revenue Code, the sub-chapter s corporation must account at the end of the year for its profits, losses, income, and expenses and must pass-through the results of the same to the shareholders who in turn pay any tax at their individual rate.

Most often, a large corporation will, if at all, issue a cash dividend from its profits first to any shareholders that hold a distribution

---

[90] *Food and Allied Service Trade Depart., AFL-CIO* vs. *Wal-Mar Stores, Inc*, 1992 WL 11285 (Del. Ch. 20 May 1992).
[91] *Miles* vs. *Bank of Heflin*, 328 So.3d 281 (Ala. 1976).
[92] *Shabshelowitz* vs. *Fall River Gas Co.*, 588 N.E.2d 630 (Mass. 1992).
[93] *In State ex rel. Pillsbury* vs. *Honeywell, Inc*, 191 N.W.2d 406 (Minn. 1971).
[94] *White* vs. *Jacobsen Manufacturing Co.*, 293 F.Supp 1358 (E.D. Wis. 1968).
[95] See https://en.wikipedia.org/wiki/Dividend. This site contains additional references and citations.
[96] Model Business Corporation Act, Section 6.40(a).

preference, and then to all remaining shareholders. So long as the distribution does not violate liquidity restrictions identified in the next paragraph, the distributions can be made at any time and in any amount.

Although shareholders of publically-traded corporations believe that they have a "right" to a cash dividend or a stock dividend (in the form of a stock split), the fact is that most corporations, large or small, private or public, do not issue dividends. Instead, they offer the shareholders the right to realize profit at the time the shareholder sells his stock, at the time that the corporation is sold, or at the time it is wound up and dissolved.[97]

The Model Business Corporation Act is liberal in the scope of power it grants the board to issue distributions. In *Judah* vs. *Delaware Trust*,[98] for instance, the court allowed that the issuance of a dividend in foreign currency (as permitted by the articles of incorporation) did not require the corporation — which had significant liquid United States assets — to reissue the dividends after the foreign currency became worthless.

The Model Act, however, makes it clear that the Board cannot declare a distribution if the effect of the same would result in the corporation being unable to pay its debts as they become due or result in the remaining assets of the corporation being insufficient to pay for the sum of all of its short and long-term liabilities plus any amount that would be needed for preferred shareholders.[99]

The board must act in good-faith[100] when making the decision to approve a distribution by first consulting its financial books and records that must have been prepared using generally accepted accounting principles,[101] and by then making the final decision whether to declare the distribution since, typically, once a dividend is declared, it cannot be unilaterally revoked by the Board.[102]

---

[97] There also is a tax advantage to receiving a liquidation distribution over a dividend. In the former case, the profit is taxed at the United States capital gains rate that now is twenty per cent (which is measured by the amount distributed less the amount paid for the stock), whereas a dividend is taxed as the shareholder's personal rate that could be as high as forty per cent.
[98] *Judah* vs. *Delaware Trust*, 378 A.2d 624 (Del. 1977).
[99] Model Business Corporation Act, Section 6.40(c).
[100] Model Business Corporation Act, Section 8.30. See also, Campbell, Jr., "A Positive Analysis of the Common Law of Corporate Fiduciary Duties", 84 Ken. L.J. 455 (1995–96).
[101] Model Business Corporation Act, Section 6.40 "Generally Accepted Accounting Principles".
[102] *McLaren* vs. *Crescent Planing Mill Co.*, 93 S.W. (MO 1906).

Restrictions of Share Transfer

Privately-held (and many publicly-traded) corporations place restrictions on the ability of a shareholder to sell his shares. The Model Business Corporation Act acknowledges the right of the corporation to restrict what otherwise is a shareholder's right to sell personal property[103] at Section 6.27(a):

> "The articles of incorporation, bylaws, an agreement among shareholders, or an agreement between shareholders and the corporation may impose restrictions on the transfer or registration of transfer of shares of the corporation."

Although the restrictive language may, by law, be found in the articles of incorporation or bylaws, it is more usual for either document to simply state that the shareholder's right to transfer will be restricted in accordance with a "Shareholders' Agreement" or a "buy-sell" agreement. In this way, the articles or bylaws will not be burdened with language that most often covers dozens of pages. Indeed, if the restrictive language is inserted into the articles, the only way that the limitations can be amended would be by filing an amendment to the articles, which in turn would require administrative action at the state level and would cost at least the filing fees.

In a privately-held corporation the transfer restrictions usually call out and control situations in which a shareholder may seek to voluntarily sell shares, or in which a shareholder has his shares divested involuntarily. For instance, under the Model Business Corporation Act, Section 6.27 (c) and (d), the state is allowed to control the shareholder's right to:

(1) Sell shares to another shareholder;
(2) Sell shares to an unrelated third party;
(3) Sell to a spouse or domestic partner;
(4) Transfer the shares of a deceased shareholder by bequest or under operation of law if no will is present;
(5) Transfer shares because of retirement as an employee or because of termination of employment;
(6) Voluntarily withdraw from the corporation with the intent of then transferring the shares;

---

103 Consider the discussion under the "Official Comment" paragraph of Section 6.27, wherein it is acknowledged that even today some jurisdictions will strictly construe the Shareholders' Agreement since it violates the common law right of a person to freely sell his personality.

(7) Take any action with the shares the result of which would be to negatively affect the corporation's tax status;
(8) Cause or permit the shares to be used as collateral for a loan, or be the subject of other collection efforts or liens; or
(9) Have the shares transferred to a trustee in a bankruptcy or insolvency action.[104]

Piercing Corporate Veil

Attention to the corporate formalities by the corporation's management is the keystone to protecting the shareholder's shield against personal liability.[105] Large privately-held corporations and publicly-traded entities tend to have in place meaningful checks and balances that insure that the corporate formalities are followed.

Although the Board members and officers may be the owners of a majority of the outstanding shares in such entities, they are well aware of the separation that must be maintained between the corporation and the shareholders.

In closely-held corporations, however, the line between an independent management team of neutral board members, and a Board that instead improperly mixes the role of the board with that of the shareholders, becomes so blurred that inattention to the corporate formalities quickly follows. This failure in turn allows creditors and parties injured by the acts of the corporation to attack the shareholders, directors, and officers as being the mere "alter ego" of the corporation, which action, if successful, permits the injured party to collect a judgment from the assets of the corporation, shareholders, officers, and directors.

Although there is no bright-line test for determining whether the veil may be avoided, many states have adopted the same or similar elements that must be present in order for the cause of action to apply. In Colorado, for instance, it has been stated that:

> "Courts consider a variety of factors in determining status as an alter ego, including whether: (1) the corporation is operated as a distinct business entity; (2) funds and assets are commingled;

---

[104] Model Business Corporation Act, Section 6.27, "Restrictions on Transfer of Shares and Other Securities".
[105] Consider *Dietel* vs. *Day*, 492 P.2d 455 (AZ 1972), where the court agreed that a legitimate purpose of a corporation is to avoid personal liability.

(3) adequate corporate records are maintained; (4) the nature and form of the entity's ownership and control facilitate misuse by an insider; (5) the business is thinly capitalized; (6) the corporation is used as a 'mere shell'; (7) legal formalities are disregarded; and (8) corporate funds or assets are used for non-corporate purposes."[106]

Minnesota courts have found that:

"Several factors are relevant to the inquiry, including: insufficient capitalization for purposes of corporate undertaking, failure to observe corporate formalities, nonpayment of dividends, insolvency of debtor corporation at time of transaction in question, siphoning of funds by dominant shareholder, nonfunctioning of other officers and directors, absence of corporate records, and existence of corporation as merely facade for individual dealings."[107]

Illinois, on the other hand, has a more simple method:

"Illinois courts will pierce the corporate veil where: (1) there is such a unity of interest and ownership that the separate personalities of the corporation and the parties who compose it no longer exist, and (2) circumstances are such that adherence to the fiction of a separate corporation would promote injustice or inequitable circumstances."[108]

Notwithstanding the lack of a bright-line rule, the courts seem able to join various elements together to reach an equitable decision. In *NEC Electronics* vs. *Hurt*,[109] for instance, the defendant Porter Hurt was the sole shareholder and chief executive officer of PH Corporation, a California-registered corporation. Hurt "borrowed" from the corporation for his own use $2,800,000, but did not bother to create minutes of a special meeting and did not evidence the loan through use of any debt instrument. Next, he had the corporation directly pay for a yacht owned only by him, and had the corporation lease a vehicle for his wife's sole use. Finally, he used his personal funds to pay for corporate obligations without properly accounting for the funds as a capital contribution or loan.

---

106 *McCallum Family L.L.C.* vs. *Winger*, 221 P.3d 69, 74 (Colo. 2009).
107 *Victoria Elevator Co.* vs. *Meriden Grain Co*, 283 N.W.2d 512, 512 (Minn. 1979).
108 *Tower Investors, LLC* vs. *111 East Chestnut Consultants, Inc.*, 864 N.E.2d 927, 1033-1044 (IL 2007).
109 *NEC Electronics* vs. *Hurt*, 208 Cal. App. 3d 772 (CA Ct. of Appeals 1989).

In April 1985, PH declared itself to be insolvent and tried to compromise claims of its creditors. From this arose a claim that Mr. Hurt should be held personally liable to the creditors who claimed him to be the mere alter ego of the corporation. The court agreed and stated that there are two general reasons for piercing the corporate veil in an alter ego action:

> "First, there must be 'such unity of interest and ownership that the separate personalities of the corporation and the individual no longer exist' (citation omitted). Second, it must be demonstrated that 'if the acts are treated as those of the corporation alone, an inequitable result will follow' (citation omitted)".[110]

The court went on to note:

> "When considering the application of the alter ego doctrine to a particular situation, it must be remembered that it is an equitable doctrine and, although courts have justified its application through consideration of many factors, their basic motivation is to assure a just and equitable result (citation omitted)."

Thus, it was not the fact that he was the sole shareholder and chief executive officer of the corporation that allowed the successful attack on his personal assets, but instead, it was his complete disregard for the corporate formalities that exposed him to personal liability.

In *The Boatmen's National Bank of St. Lewis* vs. *Smith*,[111] the federal court found that the alter ego doctrine could be used "in reverse" in the sense that the assets of one corporation not otherwise a party to a loan could be used to satisfy the debts of a shareholder. Here, Smith, who claimed to have insufficient personal assets to cover a debt, owned several corporations: (i) M-T Acquisition Corporation ("M-T", against which a judgment was granted along with Smith); and, (ii) RFS Enterprises, Inc ("RFS", who was not named in the suit). The M-T creditor sought to take the assets of RFS to satisfy the Smith personal liability. In both entities, Smith was the sole shareholder, officer, and director.

Smith argued that while a creditor can in some cases pierce the veil to attack the shareholder of the debtor-corporation, the same creditor

---

110 *NEC Electronics* vs. *Hurt*, 208 Cal. App. 3d 772, 777 (CA Ct. of Appeals 1989).
111 *The Boatmen's National Bank of St. Lewis* vs. *Smith*, 706 F. Supp. 30 (Northern District IL 1989).

cannot then go after the assets of another corporation owned by the shareholder when that corporation was not a party to the debt. The court first affirmed that while Illinois had no case law that supported the reverse-piercing theory, other jurisdictions did.[112] The *Boatman's* court then stated:

> "Generally, before the separate corporate identity of one corporation will be disregarded and treated as the alter ego of another, it must be shown that it is so controlled and its affairs so conducted that it is a mere instrumentality of another, and it must further appear that observance of the fiction of separate existence would, under the circumstances, sanction a fraud or promote injustice."

Finally, the court analyzed Smith's interaction with both of his corporations and found that, like the *NEC Electronics* defendant,[113] Smith ignored the corporate formalities by allowing RFS to fund Smith's lifestyle, citing the fact that Smith did not even maintain a personal bank account. According to Smith, "loans" were made to his wife and him from the corporation, yet no documentation of the debt was ever created. Under these circumstances, the court found that Smith's creditor could pierce the RFS veil and could attach its assets (and those of its shareholder, Smith) to satisfy the M-T debt.

However, the mere ownership of all outstanding shares by the officers and directors of the corporation is not sufficient in and of itself to allow for this equitable remedy.[114] Instead, one also must show that, as above, the corporation was a mere "instrumentality" of the shareholders that was used to defraud the injured party, or was used in such a way that allowing the corporate veil to prevail would expose the plaintiff to an equitably unfair and unjust loss. As can be imagined, the latter requirement is open to the most interpretation.[115]

---

[112] *Dahl* vs. *Gardner*, 583 F.Supp. 1262, 1268 (D. Utah 1984) (". . . the equitable alter ego doctrine may be applied in the 'reverse' sense to disregard the corporation to reach corporate assets for the obligations on an individual").

[113] *NEC Electronics* vs. *Hurt*, 208 Cal. App. 3d 772 (CA Ct. of Appeals 1989).

[114] *White* vs. *Winchester Land Development Corp.*, 584 S.W.2d 56 (Ct. App. KY 1979): "[The] mere ownership and control of a corporation by the person sought to be held liable is not alone a sufficient basis for denial of entity treatment".

[115] In these cases, the burden of proof is with the plaintiff who must prove that it is more likely than not that the defendant performed some act that would allow the plaintiff to pierce the veil. See Colorado Revised Statute 13-25-127(1).

Ultra Vires Acts

The Latin term *ultra vires* means "unauthorized; beyond the scope of power allowed or granted by a corporate charter or by law".[116] In the past, this common law doctrine allowed a shareholder, creditor, competitor, or governmental entity to void the enforcement of an unauthorized corporate act through the claim that the corporation failed to follow the purpose it stated in its Articles of Incorporation.

In *Blue Cross and Blue Shield of Alabama* vs. *Protective Life Insurance Company*,[117] for instance, the court found that a corporation whose articles of incorporation stated that it was formed for the purpose of maintaining a health care system could not then acquire a subsidiary whose purpose was to market life insurance plans. This cause of action, however, has fallen into disfavor; not so much because corporations are now operating as good corporate citizens, but because of the adoption of statutory language akin to that found in Section 3.04 of the Model Business Corporation Act that states:

> "Except as provided in subsection (b) [of this Section 3.04], the validity of corporate action may not be challenged on the ground that the corporation lacks or lacked power to act."

Subsection (b) enumerates the exceptions to the rule:
(1) A shareholder may sue the corporation to enjoin a particular act;
(2) The corporation may sue an incumbent or former director, officer, employee, or agent of the corporation; and
(3) The state may bring an action under Section 14.30 of the Model Business Corporation Act which allows for the judicial dissolution of a corporation.

In *Dingus* vs. *Fada Serv. Co.*,[118] the court found:

> "In times past, corporations were formed with more limited purposes (or objects) and powers, and these [were] more strictly construed [by the courts]. Any corporate act beyond such capacity was deemed *ultra vires*, void, illegal, and a nullity."

---

116 *Black's Law Dictionary* (9th Ed), at p. 1662.
117 *Blue Cross and Blue Shield of Alabama* vs. *Protective Life Insurance Company*, 527 So. 2d 125 (Ala. Civ. App. 1987).
118 *Dingus* vs. *Fada Serv. Co*, 856 S.W.2d 45 (Ky. Ct. App. 1994).

The court then stated:

> "By the more modern approach, an *ultra vires* act if not a public wrong is not illegal. The question is not one of 'capacity' but of powers."

Finally, citing the Kentucky statute[119] that closely mirrors Section 3.04 of the Model Business Corporation Act, the Court states that:

> "[T]he doctrine of ultra vires has lost its favor with courts. Clear distinction must be made between conduct which is illegal, tainted by fraud, prohibited by statute and contrary to public policy; and conduct alleged to be ultra vires or beyond the expressed or implied powers of a corporation."[120]

Although an action by a third party claiming that a corporate act was *ultra vires* may not go far, all jurisdictions have adopted by statute some form of Section 3.04 of the Model Business Corporation Act,[121] which still allows for shareholder suits that seek damages because of an *ultra vires* act of a corporation.[122]

Shareholder Suits and Derivative Actions

In General

Each state still permits an aggrieved shareholder to sue the corporation for an *ultra vires* act. Most often, such matters are brought by a shareholder in a "derivative action". A shareholder derivative action is an: " . . . action or proceeding brought to enforce a secondary right on the part of one or more shareholders of a business corporation against any present or former officer or director of the corporation because the corporation refuses to enforce rights that may properly be asserted by it".[123] In *Etzler*, the court agreed that:

> "Financial irregularities, waste of corporate assets, alleged ultra vires acts by ostensible directors, and self-dealing are well-recognized grounds for seeking relief in a shareholder derivative action."

---

119 KRS 271B.3-040.
120 *Field* vs. *Haupert,* 647 P.2d 952 (Or. App 1982).
121 Model Business Corporation Act, Section 3.04 "Statutory Comparison".
122 Model Business Corporation Act, Section 3.04 "When Lack of Power May Be Asserted".
123 *Etzler* vs. *Etzler,* 134 A.3d 495, 502 (Penn. 2015).

The Model Business Corporation Act delves deeply into the derivative-action waters with a fully revised subchapter entitled "Derivative Proceedings".[124] In this chapter, the drafters are trying to balance a shareholder's right to protect the corporate purpose and to correct negligent or intentional actions of the Board with protection for the corporation against frivolous shareholder actions. As stated in the introduction to this subchapter:

> "Subchapter D deals with the requirements applicable to shareholder derivative suits. A great deal of controversy has surrounded the derivative suit, and widely different perceptions as to the value and efficacy of this litigation continue to exist. On the one hand, the derivative suit has historically been the principal method of challenging allegedly illegal action by management. On the other hand, it has long been recognized that the derivative suit may be instituted more with a view to obtaining a settlement resulting in fees to the plaintiff's attorney than to righting a wrong to the corporation (the so-called 'strike suit')."[125]

The various states have dealt with a shareholder's right to a derivative action in different ways and there is no consistent thread that may be drawn through all of them. For instance, Colorado has two short statutes that deal with "Actions by Shareholders",[126] while Connecticut has adopted much of the language of Subchapter D.[127] Although a shareholder must look to his specific state law to determine what needs be done in order to prosecute a derivative action, there are some generalities that are always considered.

Standing

"Standing" refers to the power of a person or entity to enforce a duty or right.[128] The Model Business Corporation Act provides that only a shareholder who owned stock at the time of the alleged act or omission may bring an action and, even if the shareholder meets the first element,

---

124 Model Business Corporation Act, Subchapter D, Sections 7.40 to 7.47.
125 A strike suit is defined by *Black's Law Dictionary* (9th Ed), at p. 1572 as: "A suit (especially a derivative action) often based on no valid claim, brought either for nuisance value or as leverage to obtain a favorable settlement."
126 C.R.S 7-107-401 and C.R.S. 7-107-402. In this case, the state did not adopt the Model Business Corporation Act's language.
127 Con. Gen Stat. Section 33-720 through 727.
128 *Black's Law Dictionary* (9th Ed.), at p. 1536.

he must: ". . . fairly and adequately represent [ ] the interests of the corporation in enforcing the right of the corporation".[129]

The Oregon appellate court in *Metal Tech Corp.* vs. *Metal Teckniques*[130] adopted this limitation even in the absence of specific statutory by stating:

> "Although there are no statutory rules in Oregon governing standing in derivative litigation, we hold that general principles of standing require that, in order to bring a derivative suit, a shareholder must own stock at the time of the alleged wrong and retain ownership for the duration of the litigation."

The same result was reached in the matter of *Green* vs. *Bradley Construction, Inc.*[131] Similarly, the court, in *Schoon* vs. *Smith*,[132] found that a "mere" director who owned no stock was prohibited from bringing a derivative action even although he had the best interests of the corporation in mind.

In *Adiel* vs. *Electronic Financial Systems, Inc.*,[133] the court interpreted the second element described above and denied a shareholder the right to bring a derivative action. In that case, the shareholder in question owned a separate business entity that he wanted the corporation to buy. The Board refused and the shareholder countered by suing through derivative action claiming that it would be in the best interest of the corporation to purchase his business.

Instead, the court found that the plaintiff's motivation was "inimical" to the interests of the shareholders and thus gave him no standing to bring the action, even though he was a shareholder during the requisite period of time. Similarly, a shareholder cannot maintain a derivative action when he has named the remaining shareholders as defendants (since by definition he cannot be said to represent their best interests) or when the remaining shareholders affirm that the plaintiff does not represent their interests.[134]

---

129 Model Business Corporation Act, Section 7.41.
130 *Metal Tech Corp.* vs. *Metal Teckniques*, [sic] *Co.*, 703 P.2d 237, 302 (Or. App. 1985).
131 *Green* vs. *Bradley Construction, Inc.*, 431 So.2d 1226 (Ala. 1983).
132 *Schoon* vs. *Smith*, 953 A.2d 196 (Del. 2008).
133 *Adiel* vs. *Electronic Financial Systems, Inc.*, 513 So.2d 1347 (Fla Dist. Ct. App. 1987).
134 *Eye Site, Inc* vs. *Blackburn*, 750 S.W.2d 274 (Tex. Ct. App. 1988).

Written Demand Prior to Starting Suit

Section 7.42 of the Model Business Corporation Act requires the complaining shareholder to:
(1) Deliver written notice to the corporation asking that the matter in question be acted upon; and
(2) Refrain from filing during a period that is the earlier of 90 days from the date that the notice was delivered; the date that the corporation rejects the demand; or a sooner date if failure to file an action would cause irreparable harm to the corporation.

The requirement that prior notice be given has been recognized for over a century as a prerequisite to bringing the derivative action.[135] Although no "magic" written notice or period of time has ever been agreed upon, case law indicates that some written notice and some period of time to permit the corporation to act or reject is reasonable and necessary.[136]

It is often the case, however, that a shareholder-plaintiff will seek to avoid the written notice requirement and instead directly file an action without notice. In *Lewis* vs. *Graves*,[137] for instance, a shareholder brought an action against a corporation without first providing notice. The shareholder believed such an act to be futile since he would be giving notice to the very directors that took the action about which he complained.

The court cited Federal Rule of Civil Procedure 23.1, which requires notice be given, and then found that, even if notice was not required, the cited Federal Rule of Civil Procedure would still require the plaintiff to plead with particularity why giving of notice would be futile. In this case, and even though the Board affirmed the very act that was cited in the litigation as being *ultra vires*, the court found that the plaintiff's failure to give notice destroyed the opportunity for the "... derivative corporation itself [. . .] to take over a suit which was brought on its behalf in the first place, and thus to allow the directors the chance to occupy their normal status as conductors of the corporation affairs". In the matter of *Gomez* vs. *American Century Companies, Inc.*,[138] the court, applying the law of Maryland, affirmed that notice was a required prerequisite even in a case where federal law was relied upon.

---

[135] *Hawes* vs. *Oakland*, 104 U.S. 450 (U.S. Supreme Court 1882), in which the court stated that a derivative plaintiff must "... show to the satisfaction of the court that he has exhausted all the means within his reach to obtain, within the corporation itself, the redress of his grievances...".
[136] *Mozes [sic]* vs. *Welch*, 638 F. Supp. 2015 (D. Conn. 1986), where the court found that a corporation's eight-month delay in responding to a written notice was reasonable.
[137] *Lewis* vs. *Graves*, 701 F.2d 245 (2d Cir. 1983).
[138] *Gomez* vs. *American Century Companies, Inc.*, 710 F.3d 811 (8th Cir. 2013).

Although written notice may be required, there is no obligation on the part of the corporation to respond to the shareholder,[139] although in some cases, the Board's refusal to act may trigger the court's inquiry whether such decision was made in good faith and in a disinterested manner.[140] If, however, the corporation instead, and in accordance with the Model Business Corporation Act, Section 7.43, "commences an inquiry into the allegations made in the demand or complaint",[141] the court has the option to stay any proceedings to allow the corporation time to first investigate and then to properly respond. Twenty-four states have adopted this language.[142]

This is a logical option given the purpose of the notice provision which is to give the corporation time to decide on what action to take and to use its "business judgment"[143] when making a decision. The Model Business Corporation Act, Section 7.44, continues to evidence the corporation's right to take action on its own by stating that the court "shall" dismiss a derivative action if after "a good faith" inquiry:

(1) A majority vote of "qualified directors" present at a meeting determines that the matter should be dismissed;[144]

(2) A majority vote of a committee consisting of two or more qualified directors appointed by the Board decide that the matter should be dismissed;[145] or

(3) If, upon motion by the corporation, the court appoints "a panel of one or more individuals to make a determination whether maintenance of the derivative proceeding is in the best interests of the corporation".[146]

The Model Business Corporation Act defines a "qualified director" as being one who at the time of the action: ". . . does not have (i) a material interest in the outcome of the proceeding, or (ii) a material relationship

---

[139] *Lewis* vs. *Graves*, 701 F.2d 245 (2d Cir. 1983) and Model Business Corporation Act, Section 7.42 "Response by the Corporation".

[140] *In re PSE&G Shareholder Litigation*, 718 A.2d 254 (N.J. Super. Ct., Ch. Div. 1998). See also, "Judicial Schizophrenia in Corporate Law: Confusing the Standard of Care with the Business Judgment Rule", 24 Alaska L. Rev. 23.

[141] Model Business Corporation Act, Section 7.43.

[142] Model Business Corporation Act, Section 7.43 "Statutes".

[143] The substance of the "business judgment rule" is that the matter decided must have first been considered in good faith and may not have been arbitrarily decided. *Rhue* vs. *Cheyenne Homes, Inc.*, 449 P.2d 361 (Colo. 1969).

[144] Model Business Corporation Act, Section 7.44 (b)(1).

[145] Model Business Corporation Act, Section 7.44 (b)(2).

[146] Model Business Corporation Act, Section 7.44 (e).

with a person who has such an interest".[147] It should be noted, however, that few states have adopted the Model Business Corporation Act's qualified director directive, thus leaving the door open for litigation to determine the very issue of whether the directors are disinterested.

At first blush, it seems that allowing the directors to determine the fate of the shareholder's action is much like allowing the fox to guard the hen house. Indeed, the addition of the "good faith" inquiry obligation under the Model Business Corporation Act, Section 7.44, opens up the factual minefield that exists when the term is used in a statute. In the matter of *In re PSE&G Shareholder Litigation*,[148] for instance, the court was asked to determine whether the Board's refusal to proceed with derivative litigation was done in good faith and was thus protected by the business judgment rule. The court found that:

> "The rationale behind the business judgment rule is to encourage qualified men and women to serve as directors and to motivate them to be willing to take entrepreneurial risks. The duties of directors consist principally of establishing corporate policy, weighing major business decisions and overseeing management."[149]

Where, however, the corporation can demonstrate that the decision not to pursue a derivative action was made by a committee of disinterested and independent Board members who were not named as litigants, the court will affirm the dismissal. In *Auerbach vs. Bennett*,[150] the court found that, even although the derivative litigation was brought against members of the Board and the auditor who authorized illegal overseas payments, the fact is that the decision to force dismissal was an independent committee's decision which in turn fell within the embrace of the business judgment rule since the issues at hand concerned legal, ethical accounting procedures and other matters.[151]

---

147 Model Business Corporation Act, Section 1.43 (a)(1).
148 *In re PSE&G Shareholder Litigation*, 718 A.2d 254 (N.J. Super. Ct., Ch. Div. 1998). This case also has an excellent discussion of business-judgment-rule judicial decisions made in several different jurisdictions. *PSE&G Shareholder Litigation*, 718 A.2d 254 328 (N.J. Super. Ct., Ch. Div. 1998).
149 The Board has the burden of proof in a derivative matter to affirm that the Board dismissed the matter at hand only after using good faith and unbiased logic. *In re PSE&G Shareholder Litigation*, 718 A.2d 254, 335 (N.J. Super. Ct., Ch. Div. 1998).
150 *Auerbach* vs. *Bennett*, 393 N.E.2d 994 (NY 1979).
151 In *Greenfield* vs. *Hamilton Oil Corp.*, 760 P.2d 664 (Colo. Ct. App. 1988), the court determines an independent committee must be given more power than the mere right to make a recommendation to the Board. Instead, its decision must be followed if the corporation is to survive an abuse-of-business-judgment claim.

The Model Business Corporation Act[152] and twenty-four states[153] require that any decision to discontinue or settle a derivative action must first be approved by the court. As noted in the *Official Comment* to the Model Business Corporation Act, Section 7.45:

> "This requirement seems a natural consequence of the proposition that a derivative suit is brought for the benefit of all shareholders and avoids many of the evils of the strike suit by preventing the individual shareholder-plaintiff from settling privately with the defendants."

Conclusion

Shareholders in a large corporation have relatively little power to control the direction of the corporation, while shareholders in closely-held corporations have significant power in this regard. Regardless of the size of the corporation, all shareholders share the right to an annual meeting, the right to call special meetings, the right to review books and records, and the right to bring a derivative action to protect the corporation's integrity and purpose.

---

[152] Model Business Corporation Act, Section 7.45.
[153] Model Business Corporation Act, Section 7.45 "Statutes".

CITATIONS TO STATE/TERRITORY CORPORATION LAWS

State	Citation	Model Business Corporation Act Adoption
Alabama	Ala. Code Sections 10-2B-1.01	X
Alaska	Alaska Stat. Sections 10.06.995	
Arizona	Ariz. Rev. State Sections 10-120	X
Arkansas	Ark. Code 4-27-101 et seq.	X
California	Cal. Corp. Code Sections 100 et seq.	
Colorado	Colo Rev. Stat. 7-90-101 et seq.	
Connecticut	Conn. Gen. Stat. Sections 33-660	X
Delaware	Del. Code Tit. 8 Sections 101 et seq.	
District of Columbia	D. C. Code Sections 29-101.01 et seq.	X
Florida	Fla. Stat Sections 607.0101	X
Georgia	Ga. Code Sections 14-2-101	X
Guam	18 Guam Code Ann. Sections 28101 et seq.	X
Hawaii	Haw. Rev Stat Sections 414-1	X
Idaho	Idaho Code Sections 30-1-101, 805	X

State	Citation	Model Business Corporation Act Adoption
Illinois	Ill Comp. Stat. Sections 5/1.01	
Indiana	Ind. Code Sections 23-1-17-1	X
Iowa	Iowa Code Sections 490.1.1	X
Kansas	Kan. Stat. Sections 17-7404	
Kentucky	Ky. Rev. Stat. Sections 271B.1-010	X
Louisiana	La. Rev. Stat. Sections 12:178	
Maine	Me. Rev. Stat. Tit. 13-C, Sections 101	X
Maryland	Md. Cod Corps. & Ass'ns Sections 1-103	
Massachusetts	Mass. Gen Laws 156D, Sections 1.01	X
Michigan	Mich. Comp. Law Sections 450.1101	
Minnesota	Minn. Stat. Sections 302A.001	
Mississippi	Miss. Code Sections 79-4-1.01	X
Missouri	Mo. Rev. Stat. Sections 351.010	
Montana	Mont. Code Ann Sections 35-1-112	X
Nebraska	Neb. Rev. Stat Sections 21-2001	X

State	Citation	Model Business Corporation Act Adoption
Nevada	Nev. Rev. Stat. Sections 78.010	
New Hampshire	N.H. Rev. Stat Sections 293-A:1.01	X
New Jersey	N.J. Stat Sections 14A: 1-1	
New Mexico	N.M. Stat Sections 53-11-1	
New York	N. Y. Bus Corp. Law Sections 101	
North Carolina	N.C. Gen. Stat Sections 55-1-01	X
North Dakota	N.D. Cent. Code Sections 10-19.1-01	
Ohio*	Ohio Rev. Code Sections 1701.01	
Oklahoma	18 Okl. Stat Chptrs. 1-32; Chpt 22 - General Corporation Act	
Oregon	ORS 60.101 *et seq.*	X
Pennsylvania	15 Penn. Consol. Stat. 101 *et seq.*	
Rhode Island	R.I. Gen. Laws Sections 7-1.2-101 *et seq.*	X
South Carolina	S.C Code Ann. Sections 33-1-101 *et seq.*	X
South Dakota	SDCL 47-1A-101 *et seq.*	X

State	Citation	Model Business Corporation Act Adoption
Tennessee	T.C.A Sections 48-101-101 *et seq.*	X
Texas	Tex. Bus. & Com Code Sections 1.101 *et seq.*	
Utah	Utah Code Sections 16-10a-101 *et seq.*	X
Vermont	11 V.S.A Sections 1- 568	X
Virginia	Va. Code Ann. Sections 13.1-301 *et seq.*	X
Washington	Wash. Rev. Code Sections 23B.01.010 *et seq.*	X
West Virginia	W. VA. Code Sections 31D-1-101 *et seq.*	X
Wisconsin	Wis. Stat. Sections 180.0101 *et seq.*	X
Wyoming	W. S. Sections 17-16-101 *et seq.*	X

Index

A

Access to Corporate Information
    AG 133
    Central Depository and Clearing Company 115
    Companies Act 115
    Dematerialized Share 115
    Form of Shares 115
    GmbH 133
    Share Certificates 115
    Share Register 115
Allocation of Powers between Shareholders and Directors
    Administrative Bodies 68
    Administrative Council 68
    AG 128
    Allocation of Powers in Takeover Process. 100
    Amendment of Articles 97
    Appointment of Mandatory Auditions 97
    Appointment of Special Auditions 97
    "Block Holder" Model 95
    Board of Directors 69
    Companies Act 95–97
    Dissolution of Company 97
    Distribution of Profits 97
    Election and Revocation of Membership 97
    Give Approval of Business Decisions 97
    GmbH 128
    Increase and Reduction of Share 97
    Issuance of Clearance 97
    Listing and Delisting of Company's Shares 97
    One-tier Board System 95–96
    Shareholders Right to Make Business Proposals. 97
    Takeover Process 100
    Two-tier Board System 95

B

Basic Corporate Structure
    Closely-held Corporation 212
    Colorado 212
    Corporate Purpose 213–214
    Delaware 212

Hierarchical Entity 214
Pass-through Tax Entity 213
Privately-held Corporations 212
Privately-held Entities 211
Publically-held Corporations 212
Shareholders' Equity Value 214
Single Person Corporations 212
Texas 212
The Delaware Code 213
The Model Business Corporation Act 212, 213
Unintended Liability 212
Voting Power 214

C

Claims of Company against Its Shareholders
    Commercial Register 138
Classes of Shareholders
    Capital Market Act 102
    Common Shares 70
    Founder Shares 71
    Preferred Shares 70
    Statutes 69–70
    Stock Exchange 70
Classes of Shares
    AG 129
    GmbH 128
Companies and Partnerships
    General Law of Commercial Companies 166
    General Partnership 165
    Legal Personality 162
    Limited-liability Company 164
    Partnerships 164
    Promotion of Investment Stock Company 164
    Public Registry of Commerce 162, 169
    Shares and Equity Quotes 165
    Simplified Stock Company 163
    Special Partnership with Shares 164
    Stock Company 163
    Types of Companies 163
    Types of Partnerships 163
Corporate Formalities
    Adopting Bylaws 216
    Annual Meetings 216

Board Meetings 216
Corporate Veil of Protection 216
Drafting Bylaws 216
Organizational Meetings 216
Proper Financial Records 217
Signing Documents 217

D

Derivative Suits
   AG 136
   Bankruptcy Proceedings 116
   Corporate Governance Rules 82
   Executive Directors 116
   GmbH 136
   Liability Suits 83
   Litigation by Management Board 116
   Management Board 116
   Violation 82
Distributions
   AG 137
   Dividends 89
   GmbH 136
   Income 87
   Reserves 88
Distribution of Profits
   Companies Act 117–118

I

Inspection of Shareholder Lists
   AG 134
   GmbH 134

L

Labor Law
   Labor Contract Law 34–35
Liability at Early Stages of Company
   Companies Code 46
   Corporate Veil 46
   Cooperative Limited-liability Company 46
   Insufficient Initial Share Capital 47

Irregularities Committed at Incorporation 46
Liability of Founders 46
Private Limited-liability Company 46
Liability During Lifetime of Company
    Acquisition of Shares Not Fully Paid Up 51
    Acquisition of Shares of Listed Companies: Takeover Bid 49
    Acquisition of Shares of Non-Listed Companies 48
    Belgian Regulatory Framework 49
    Companies Code 52–53
    Distribution of Dividends 53
    Irregularities Committed at Incorporation 51
    Liability 54
    Mandatory Takeover Bid 50
    Sole Shareholder Liability 48
    Takeover Bid 49
    Takeover Decree 49, 51
    Takeover Law 49
    Transfer of Shares 52
Liability in Shareholder Disputes
    Abuse of Power under General Tort Law 54
    Civil Code 55
    Companies Code 55–57
    Dispute Procedure 56
Liability of Shareholders in Listed Companies
    Administrative 57
    Civil 57
    Criminal 57
Liability upon Exit
    Contractual Transfer Restrictions 61
    Legal Transfer Restrictions. 60
    Mandatory Acceptance of Shares 65
    Mandatory Transfer 64
    Public Takeover Bid 65
    Squeeze Out 64
    Takeover Decree 65
    Transfer of Restrictions 60
Liability of Shareholders
    Affiliated Companies 207
    Checks and Balances 3
    Commercial Companies Code 201, 203–210
    Controlling Shareholders 11
    European Commission 16
    European Union Approach to Shareholder Liability 15
    General Liability 203
    Joint Liability of Shareholders 204

Liability for Abusive Resolutions 203
Liability of Directors 201
Liability of Shareholders 202
Liability of Supervisory Board 201
Limitation Period 210
Piercing Company's Protective Veil 9
Piercing Corporate Veil 209
Private Limited Companies 200
Public Limited Companies 200
Sole Shareholder Liability 205
Specific Liabilities 206

M

Market Abuse
Belgium Corporate Law 57
Notification of Participations 59
Treaty on the Functioning of the European Union 58

O

Officer Duties
Conflict of Interest 84
Duty of Diligence 83
Duty of Loyalty 83
Duty to Inform 84
Liability Actions 86
Securities and Exchange Commission 85
Technical and Consultative Bodies 87

P

Private Limited Companies and Public Limited Companies
Access to Corporate Information 197
Accounting 193
Allocation of Powers 193
Annual Report 197
Default 193
Dissolution 200
Dividend Distribution 199
Financial Statements 197
Inspection of Shareholder Lists 197
Legal Requirements for Repayment 192
Loss Distribution 199

    Minimum Capital 190
    Number of Shareholders 190
    Object 192
    Private Limited Companies 190, 192, 194
    Profit Distribution 199
    Public Limited Companies 191, 193
    Rights in Proxy Voting 197
    Share Transfer Restrictions 198
    Shareholder Meetings 194
    Shareholder Voting 194
    Supplementary Capital Contributions 192
Piercing Corporate Veil
    Kentucky Statute 229
    The Model Business Corporation Act 229

R

Right to Make Business Proposals
    AG 135
    GmbH 135
Rights in Proxy Voting
    AG 132
    Companies Act 112
    GmbH 132
    Voting by Credit 110

S

Shareholder and Tender Offers
    AG 137
    Brokerage House 91
    By-laws Provisions 90
    Companies Act 123–125
    Control Agreement 125
    Controlling Shareholders 89–90
    Entrepreneurial Contracts and Reorganization Measures 125
    GmbH 137
    Investment Portfolio 91
    Non-controlling Shareholders 90
    Profit Transfer Agreement 125
    Publicely-held Companies 90
    Securities and Exchange Commission 90–91
    Sell-Out Rights 123
    Squeeze-Out Rights 123

Index

Takeover Act 121, 123–124
Takeover Regulation 121
Shareholder General Status
    Classes of Stock 217
    Corporate Records 223
    Delaware Code 217–218, 220
    Distribution to Shareholders 226
    Financial Records 225
    Internal Revenue Code 226
    Model Business Corporation Act 217–229
    Restriction of Share Transfer 228
    Share Certificates 218
    Shareholder Access 223
    Shareholder Control of Board of Directors 219
    Shareholder Meetings 220
    Shareholder Records 225–226
    Voting Block 219
    Voting Group 219
Shareholders' Liability
    Abuse of Privileged Information 32
    Capital Market Law 27, 33, 34
    Companies Law 23, 26, 28–38
    Company Actions Pursuant to Extra-Corporate Goals 29
    Competent Jurisdiction 34
    Conflict of Interest with Corporation 33
    Frustrations of Third-Party Rights 31
    Good Faith 30
    Indirect Disregard 32
    Liability of Controlling Shareholder 27
    National Securities Commission 33
    Null or Invalid Shareholder Meetings 25
    Piercing Corporate Veil 27
    Public Policy 30
    Public Registry of Commerce 23–25
    Registration of Corporation 24
    Resolution 25
Shareholder Meetings
    AG 130
    Companies Act 104–105
    Convocation of Shareholder Meetings 104
    GmbH 130
    Right to Include Items of Agenda 105
    Table Draft Resolutions 105
Shareholders' Duty
    AG 138

GmbH 138
Shareholder Suits and Derivative Actions
   Derivative Proceedings 235
   Oregon 236
   Standing 235
   The Model Business Corporation Act 230, 237, 240
   Written Demand 237
Shareholder Veil of Protection
   Delaware Code 215
   Limited Shareholder Liability 216
   Non-Voting Shares 215
   Subchapter-c 215
   Subchapter-s 215
   The Model Business Corporation Act 215
   The Supreme Court of Hawaii 215
Shareholder Voting
   Access to Company Information 79
   Administrative Council 80–81
   AG 131
   Annual Meetings 75–76
   Approval of Business Decisions 82
   Arbitration 75
   Brasilian Securities and Exchange Commission 73
   Closed-held Company 75
   Controlling Shareholder 73
   Exchange Market 73
   Extraordinary Meetings 75–76
   General Meetings 75
   GmbH 131
   Inspection of Shareholder Lists 81
   Publicly-held Company 75
   Right to Make Business Proposals 82
   Rights in Proxy Voting 78
   Share Transfer Restrictions 77
   Shareholder Agreement 72
   Shareholder Meetings 74
   Shareholder Rights Directive 106
Shareholder and Partner Liability
   Acts of Domain 187
   Administration Acts in Customs Matters 186
   Administration Acts in Labor Matters 186
   Administration Acts in Social Security 186
   Administration Acts in Tax 186
   Allocation of Powers of Attorney 185
   Director and Officers 177

Index

   Distribution 170
   General Partnership 168, 175
   Liability Among Shareholders and Partners 169
   Limited-liability Company 167, 174
   Partner Liability to Third Parties 166
   Partnerships 167
   Power of Attorney for Administration Acts 186
   Power of Attorney for Collections 186
   Power of Attorney for Lawsuits 186
   Shareholder and Partner Meetings 172
   Shareholder Liability to Third Parties 166
   Shares and Equity Quotas Transfer Restrictions 175
   Simplified Stock Company 167, 173
   Special Partnership with Shares 167
   Special Partnership 168, 174
   Stock Company 166, 172
Shares and Shareholders
   Access to Corporate Information 158
   Acquisition and Tender Offers 154
   Agenda 152
   Business Plan 157
   Classification of Shares 145
   Company Law 142–144
   Derivative Suits 156
   Distributions 155
   Inspection of Shareholder Lists 153
   Media 153
   Notice 152
   Piercing the Corporate Veil 143
   Quorum and Voting in Conflict-of-Interest Transactions 149
   Rights in Proxy Voting 151
   Shareholder Meetings 151
   Shareholder Voting Rights and Quorum 148
   Shareholders' Liability 143
   Transfer of Shares 145
Share Transfer Restriction
   AG 132
   Companies Act 112–113
   GmbH 132